Martha Stewart's
CAKES

Martha Stewart's
CAKES

our first-ever book of bundts, loaves,
layers, coffee cakes, and more

From the editors of
Martha Stewart Living

Clarkson Potter/Publishers
New York

Copyright © 2013 by Martha Stewart
Living Omnimedia, Inc.

All rights reserved.
Published in the United States by
Clarkson Potter/Publishers, an
imprint of the Crown Publishing
Group, a division of Random House
LLC, a Penguin Random House
Company, New York.

www.crownpublishing.com
www.clarksonpotter.com

CLARKSON POTTER is a trademark
and POTTER with colophon is a
registered trademark of Random
House LLC.

Selected photographs and recipes
appeared in Martha Stewart Living
publications.

Library of Congress Cataloging-in-
Publication Data
Martha Stewart's cakes / The editors
of Martha Stewart Living.
     pages cm
Includes index.
   1. Cake.   I. Martha Stewart Living.
TX771.M314824 2013
641.86'53—dc23
2013004803

ISBN 978-0-307-95434-3
eISBN 978-0-307-95435-0

Printed in the
United States of America

Book design by Michele Outland
Cover design by Gillian MacLeod
and Jennifer Wagner
Cover photographs by
Jonathan Lovekin (cake) and
Miller Mobley (portrait)

10 9 8 7 6 5 4 3 2 1

First Edition

Acknowledgments

Many talented people worked together to create this book, in particular
Jennifer Aaronson, editorial director of food, and Ellen Morrissey,
editorial director of the Special Projects Group at Martha Stewart
Living Omnimedia. Executive editor Evelyn Battaglia, managing
editor Susanne Ruppert, and editor at large Amy Conway also worked
diligently on the recipes and supporting text throughout the book.
We are grateful to contributing art director Michele Outland for
the book's beautiful design and for the art direction of the photography,
particularly the new work by photographers Jonathan Lovekin and
Con Poulos, who lent their considerable talents to this project (a complete
list of contributing photographers appears on page 346). Miller Mobley
photographed the lovely portrait of Martha that graces the cover. Thank
you to design director Jennifer Wagner and deputy art director Gillian
MacLeod for their work as well, particularly on the book's cover design.
We are grateful, as always, to editorial and brand director Eric A. Pike
for his guidance, to design production associate John Myers for his
assistance with the voluminous photography, and to photo assistant
Anna Ross for her valuable contributions. Others who provided ideas
and support include:

The team at Martha Stewart Living Omnimedia

Kate Bittman
Jessi Blackham
Jana Branson
Denise Clappi
Nicole Coppola
Janine Desiderio
Alison Vanek Devine
Beth Eakin
Stephanie Fletcher
Tanya Graff
Aida Ibarra
Kiyomi Marsh
Kelsey Mirando
Ryan Monaghan
Ayesha Patel
Gertrude Porter
Lucinda Scala Quinn
Michelle Wong

Our partners at Clarkson Potter

Angelin Borsics
Doris Cooper
Carly Gorga
Derek Gullino
Linnea Knollmueller
Pam Krauss
Maya Mavjee
Mark McCauslin
Marysarah Quinn
Patricia Shaw
Jane Treuhaft
Kate Tyler

This book is dedicated to everyone who desires to create the perfect cake for any special occasion.

CONTENTS

Introduction
by Martha Stewart 11

Cake Recipes 15
The Basics 313
Sources 345
Photo Credits 346
Index 347

Loaves

Basic Pound Cake with
Variations 17
Lemon Pound Cakes 21
Blood Orange–Olive Oil Cake 22
Cream-Cheese Pound Cake 25
Gingerbread 26
Two-Colored-Squash
Loaf Cake 29
Clementine–Vanilla Bean
Loaf Cake 30
Rhubarb Tea Cakes 33
Pistachio Pound Cake 34
Fruitcake 37
Pumpkin, Sage, and
Browned-Butter Cakes 38
Cornmeal-Buttermilk
Loaf Cake 41
Rosemary Pound Cakes 42
Chocolate-Ginger
Marble Cakes 45
Cranberry-Orange-
Walnut Tea Cakes 46
Carrot Tea Cake 49

Bundts & Tubes

Lemon-Ginger Bundt Cake 53
Peaches-and-Cream
Bundt Cake 54
Mini Rum Bundt Cakes 57
Chocolate Bundt Cake 58
Angel-Food Cake
with Variations 61
Blueberry-Lemon Bundt Cake 64
Allspice Angel-Food Cakes 67
Spiced Prune Cake 68
Lemon Chiffon Cake 71
Cannelés 72
Banana Chiffon Cake 75
Coconut–Rum Raisin Cake 76
Fresh Ginger-Molasses Cake 79
Sour Cherry Savarins 80
Glazed Pecan-Raisin Cake 83
Olive Oil–Anise
Mini Bundt Cakes 84
Tangerine Cake 87
Zucchini Bundt Cake 88
Golden Cakes with Ginger–
Poached Fruit 91

Pictured, left to right:
Marble Pound Cake,
Tangerine Cake, New
York–Style Crumb Cake,
and Breton Butter Cake

Coffee Cakes

New York–Style Crumb Cake 95
Ultimate Streusel Cake 96
Mini Almond Coffee Cakes 99
Cinnamon Streusel
Coffee Cake 100
Applesauce Coffee Cake 103
Plum-Nectarine Buckle 104
Wild-Blueberry Buckle 107
Meyer-Lemon Coffee Cake 108
Mini Cherry-Pecan
Streusel Loaves 111
Sticky Buckwheat Cake 112
Almond-Berry Coffee Cake 115

Single Layers

Rich Chocolate Cake 119
Maple Cake 120
Vanilla Sheet Cake with Malted-
Chocolate Frosting 123
Breton Butter Cake 124
Lighter Chocolate Cake 127
Walnut–Olive Oil Cake 128
Honey Cake with Pears 131
Chocolate and Hazelnut
Meringue Cake 132
Applesauce Cake 135
Flourless Chocolate-Espresso
Cake 136
Orange-Yogurt Cake 139

Flourless Pecan Torte 140
Poppy-Seed Torte 143
Coconut Cake with
Tropical Fruit 144
Molten Chocolate Cakes 147
Molasses-Spice Cake 148
Chocolate-Coconut
Sheet Cake 151
Almond Semolina Cake 152
Chocolate-Cherry-Stout Cake 155
Almond Torte with Pears 156
Citrus Cake 159
Banana Pecan Cake 160
Pumpkin Spice Cake 163

Cheesecakes

New York–Style Cheesecake **167**

Cheesecake with
Poached Apricots **168**

Strawberries-and-Cream
Cheesecake **171**

Lemon-Swirl Cheesecake
with Variations **172**

Blood-Orange No-Bake
Cheesecake **177**

Ricotta Cheesecake **178**

Margarita Cheesecake **181**

No-Bake Spiderweb
Cheesecake **182**

Maple Cheesecake with
Roasted Pears **185**

Chocolate Cheesecake **186**

Gingerbread Cheesecake **189**

No-Bake Cheesecakes
with Pomegranate **190**

Pictured, left to right: Raspberry-
Swirl Cheesecake, Chocolate
Icebox Cake, Pineapple Upside-
Down Cake, and Buttermilk Cake
with Chocolate Frosting

Icebox

Striped Ice-Cream Cake **195**

Chocolate–Peanut Butter
Icebox Cake **196**

Mint Chocolate-Chip Cake **199**

Chocolate-Chestnut
Mousse Cake **200**

Chocolate, Banana, and
Graham Cracker Icebox Cake **203**

Lemon-Blackberry
Semifreddo Roll **204**

Chocolate Baked Alaskas **207**

Raspberry Ice-Cream Cake **209**

Chocolate-Chip-Cookie
Icebox Cake **211**

Chocolate-Berry
Ice-Cream Cake **212**

Frozen Espresso Cheesecake **215**

Chocolate-Hazelnut
Ice-Cream Cake **216**

Gingerbread Icebox Cake **219**

Cakes with Fruit

Cranberry Upside-Down Cake **223**

Pineapple Upside-Down Cake **224**

Stone Fruit Upside-Down Cakes **227**

Coconut-Lime-Berry Cake **228**

Mandarin Orange and Vanilla
Upside-Down Cake **231**

Lemon-Fig Cake **232**

Apple Pie Upside-Down Cake **235**

Rhubarb Upside-Down Cake **236**

Strawberry Cake **239**

Pear Pavlova **240**

Olive-Oil Cake with Red Grapes **243**

Plum Skillet Cake **245**

Strawberry-Basil Shortcake **246**

Peach and Cornmeal
Upside-Down Cake **249**

Blackberry Cornmeal Cake **250**

Gingerbread-Pear
Upside-Down Cake **253**

Chocolate-Cherry
Upside-Down Cakes **254**

Layer Cakes

Buttermilk Cake with
Chocolate Frosting **259**

Chiffon Cake with
Strawberries and Cream **260**

Coconut-Pecan Cake with
Milk Chocolate Ganache **263**

Candied-Pecan Cake with
Browned-Butter Pears **264**

Tender Lemon Cake **267**

Red Velvet Cake **268**

Chocolate Truffle Cake **271**

Citrus–Poppy Seed Cake **272**

One-Bowl Chocolate Cake
with Mocha Buttercream **275**

Lemon Meringue Cake **276**

Pumpkin Layer Cake **279**

Sugar-and-Spice Cake **280**

Vanilla Layer Cake **283**

Apple-Ginger Stack Cake **284**

Hummingbird Cake **287**

Devil's Food Cake **288**

Rum Rose Cake **291**

German Chocolate Cake **292**

Raspberry White Cake **295**

Double-Chocolate Cake **296**

1–2–3–4 Lemon Cake **299**

Carrot Cake **300**

Chestnut-Chocolate
Layer Cake **303**

Almond-Orange Layer Cake **304**

Coconut Layer Cake **307**

Gluten-Free Chocolate
Layer Cake **308**

Black Forest Cake **311**

Introduction

In one's lifetime, there are so many occasions that call for celebration, so many rites of passage that require "something special"—birthdays, anniversaries, graduations, engagements, weddings, showers, new jobs, retirements, and more. A homemade, home-baked, and handcrafted cake somehow makes these events feel even more joyful. But you don't need to wait for a special occasion to bake a cake. A loaf or Bundt or coffee cake is just right for serving with afternoon tea, for bringing to a friend's for brunch, or simply for snacking on. These "any day" cakes are just as memorable as those we bake and decorate to say "congratulations" or "happy birthday" or "bon voyage."

Following in the tradition of *Cookies, Cupcakes,* and *Pies and Tarts, Martha Stewart's Cakes* covers the gamut of cake-making with more than 150 foolproof recipes and techniques that will keep you baking and embellishing all sorts of desserts—traditional and modern—for many years to come. These cakes are flavorful and unforgettable, made from the very best ingredients, well filled or frosted (or both), tender with a perfect crumb or delicate texture, and understated, elegant, or knock-em-dead gorgeous!

Try some, try all. Your family and friends will adore you, and you will maintain that "hero in the kitchen" status we all strive so hard to attain.

Martha Stewart

GOLDEN RULES FOR CAKES

1 **Read the recipe all the way through before you begin,** and have everything you need measured and at the ready. Plan ahead, so you can have ingredients at the proper temperatures and allow for cooling and chilling as needed.

2 **Choose your ingredients wisely.** It makes all the difference to use the freshest, best-quality butter, eggs, chocolate, vanilla (and other extracts), nuts, and spices.

3 **Be mindful of recipe details.** If the ingredients list calls for "1 cup sifted flour," then sift it first before you measure. If it calls for "1 cup flour, sifted," then measure before sifting.

4 **Don't rush the mixing process** for batter or frosting. Scrape down the sides of the bowl often to avoid lumps and to ensure a smooth batter or creamy frosting. Take care not to overbeat once the mixture is combined.

5 **Prepare your pans properly.** Unless otherwise specified, brush with softened (never melted) butter, line with parchment paper, brush with more butter, and finally, dust with flour, shaking out any excess. (Use cocoa powder to dust pans for chocolate cakes.)

6 **A good oven thermometer is key.** Oven temperatures may vary by as much as 50 degrees; rely on a stand-alone thermometer for accuracy instead.

7 **Rotate cake pans** halfway through the baking time, to ensure even baking.

8 **Watch out for clues** when gauging whether a cake is done (instead of relying solely on the suggested baking time). When a cake begins to pull away from the side of the pan and a cake tester comes out clean, you know it is done.

9 **Let cakes cool completely** before you frost them; a good-quality wire cooling rack will allow air to circulate beneath pans as they cool. Make sure the frosting itself is at room temperature in order to get the desired swoop, swirl, or smooth finish.

10 **Serve your cake at the right temperature** as well. Some, like cheesecakes and icebox cakes, are best chilled; others, especially those covered in buttercream frostings and ganache glazes, should come to room temperature for the best consistency and texture contrast between cake and topping.

Loaves

These are anytime cakes, easy ones you will want to whip up and keep on the kitchen counter to enjoy for breakfast, slice for snacks, or serve with pots of tea. Pound cakes may be the most well-known, but plenty of other batters can be baked in the familiar rectangular pans, too. The loaves are also a cinch to dress up with fresh fruit, sauces, curds, compotes, or whipped cream for a plated dessert.

BASIC POUND CAKE, PAGE 17

Basic Pound Cake

Light on effort, heavy on satisfaction, pound cake owes its name to the traditional ingredients—one pound each of flour, butter, sugar, and eggs—which remain essentially the same today. This batter makes a delicious classic pound cake, and it's also the base for the variations on the following pages. A couple of tips for success: Leave the butter and eggs out at room temperature for an hour before mixing; if they're cold, the batter will not be properly smooth. Creaming the butter and sugar thoroughly is crucial, because it gives the batter the necessary volume.

MAKES TWO 9-BY-5-INCH LOAVES

2 cups (1 pound) unsalted butter, room temperature, plus more for pans

1 pound (about 3 cups) all-purpose flour

1 teaspoon coarse salt

2¼ cups sugar (1 pound)

1 teaspoon vanilla extract

9 large eggs, room temperature, lightly beaten

Whipped Cream, for serving (optional; page 333)

Macerated Berries, for serving (optional; page 333)

1. Preheat oven to 325°F. Butter two 9-by-5-inch loaf pans. In a medium bowl, whisk together flour and salt.

2. With an electric mixer on high speed, beat butter and sugar until pale and fluffy, about 8 minutes. Scrape down sides of bowl. Reduce speed to medium; beat in vanilla. Add eggs in 4 batches, beating thoroughly after each and scraping down sides of bowl. Reduce speed to low; add flour mixture in 4 batches, beating until just incorporated.

3. Divide batter evenly between prepared pans. Tap pans on counter; smooth tops with an offset spatula. Bake until a cake tester comes out clean, about 65 minutes. Transfer pans to a wire rack to cool 30 minutes. Turn out cakes onto rack to cool completely. Serve with whipped cream and macerated berries, if desired.

Five More Pound Cakes

VANILLA BEAN–GINGER POUND CAKE

Follow Pound Cake recipe (page 17), substituting seeds of 1 vanilla bean (split lengthwise and scraped) for the extract. Bake and cool as directed. For the ginger glaze: Heat $\frac{1}{4}$ cup plus 2 tablespoons milk and $\frac{1}{4}$ cup sliced fresh ginger in a saucepan over medium heat until milk begins to simmer. Let cool; discard ginger. Stir in 2 cups confectioners' sugar. Drizzle over cooled cakes. Sprinkle some chopped candied ginger on top.

CHOCOLATE-CHIP POUND CAKE

Follow Pound Cake recipe (page 17), folding 2 cups semisweet or bittersweet chocolate chips or chunks into batter. Bake and cool as directed. Serve cake with Chocolate–Coffee Liqueur Sauce (page 333) and vanilla ice cream.

BLUEBERRY–SOUR CREAM POUND CAKE

Follow Pound Cake recipe (page 17), substituting ½ cup sour cream for ½ cup butter. Toss 2 cups fresh blueberries with 2 tablespoons flour; fold into batter. Before baking, sprinkle 2 tablespoons sanding sugar over each cake. Bake and cool as directed. Serve with Whipped Cream (lemon variation; page 333).

TOASTED COCONUT POUND CAKE

Follow Pound Cake recipe (page 17), folding 2 cups sweetened shredded coconut into batter. Before baking, sprinkle ⅓ cup additional coconut over each cake; bake, tented with foil, and cool as directed. Serve with mango-lime sauce: Purée 1 chopped pitted mango, 2 tablespoons fresh lime juice, 1 teaspoon sugar, and a pinch of salt in a food processor until smooth. Stir in ¾ cup diced mango and 1 teaspoon finely grated lime zest.

MARBLE POUND CAKE

Follow Pound Cake recipe (page 17), omitting flour and salt, and dividing batter in half after the eggs are mixed into the batter in step 2. Mix 1½ cups plus 2 table-spoons flour and 1½ teaspoons salt into half the batter; mix 1 cup plus 2 tablespoons flour, ½ cup unsweetened cocoa powder, and 1½ teaspoons salt into the other half. Scoop batters into prepared pan, ½ cup at a time, alternating plain and chocolate. Swirl with a knife. Bake and cool as directed.

Lemon Pound Cakes

Lemon-flavored desserts always top the list of favorites among *Martha Stewart Living* staffers—and readers, too. This one is guaranteed to be a crowd-pleaser, with lemon zest mixed in the batter, syrup soaked into the warm cakes, and glaze poured over the top—not to mention the beautiful garnish of candied lemon slices. **MAKES TWO 9-BY-5-INCH LOAVES**

FOR THE CAKES

- 1 cup (2 sticks) unsalted butter, room temperature, plus more for pans
- 3 cups all-purpose flour, plus more for pans
- ³⁄₄ teaspoon salt
- ¹⁄₂ teaspoon baking soda
- 2 tablespoons finely grated lemon zest (from 2 lemons)
- 2¹⁄₂ cups granulated sugar
- 6 large eggs
- 1 teaspoon vanilla extract
- 1 cup sour cream

FOR THE CANDIED LEMON SLICES AND SYRUP

- 1 cup granulated sugar
- 1 cup water
- 2 lemons, sliced ¹⁄₈ inch thick or thinner, seeds removed
- ¹⁄₃ to ¹⁄₂ cup fresh lemon juice (from 3 to 4 lemons)

FOR THE GLAZE

- 2 cups confectioners' sugar
- 4 to 6 tablespoons fresh lemon juice (from about 2 lemons)

1. Make the cakes: Preheat oven to 350°F. Butter two 9-by-5-inch loaf pans; dust with flour, tapping out excess. In a medium bowl, whisk together flour, salt, baking soda, and lemon zest.

2. With an electric mixer on high speed, beat butter and granulated sugar until pale and fluffy, about 5 minutes. Add eggs, 1 at a time, beating well after each addition; mix in vanilla. Reduce speed to low; beat in flour mixture in 3 batches, alternating with 2 batches of sour cream.

3. Divide batter evenly between prepared pans; smooth tops with an offset spatula. Bake until a cake tester comes out clean, 55 to 65 minutes (tent loosely with foil if tops begin to brown too quickly).

4. Meanwhile, make candied lemon slices and syrup: In a medium saucepan, combine granulated sugar and the water; bring to a boil, stirring to dissolve sugar. Add lemon slices; simmer very gently over medium-low heat, swirling pan occasionally, until slices are opaque throughout, about 35 minutes. Remove from heat; with a slotted spoon, transfer slices to a sheet of waxed paper. Stir lemon juice into syrup to taste.

5. Remove cakes from oven. While still in pans, use a wooden skewer or toothpick to poke several holes in tops. Set aside ¹⁄₄ cup lemon syrup; pour remainder over cakes. Transfer pans to a wire rack to cool completely, about 2 hours. Turn out cakes onto rack; set rack over a parchment-lined rimmed baking sheet. Brush tops and sides of cakes all over with reserved syrup.

6. Make the glaze: In a small bowl, whisk together confectioners' sugar and 4 tablespoons lemon juice; add up to 2 more tablespoons juice until glaze is pourable but thick. Pour over cakes (still on rack), letting it drip down sides. Let set, about 30 minutes. Garnish with candied lemon slices.

Blood Orange-Olive Oil Cake

The winning combination of chocolate and orange gets a twist: Blood-orange zest and juice flavor an olive-oil cake that is generously drizzled with a deep, dark chocolate glaze. Each slice of cake is topped with a honey-sweetened blood-orange compote. **MAKES ONE 9-BY-5-INCH LOAF**

Unsalted butter, room temperature, for pan

1¾ cups all-purpose flour, plus more for pan

6 blood oranges

1 cup sugar

½ cup buttermilk

3 large eggs

⅔ cup extra-virgin olive oil

1½ teaspoons baking powder

¼ teaspoon baking soda

¼ teaspoon salt

¼ cup honey

2 ounces bittersweet chocolate (preferably 70 percent cacao), finely chopped (⅓ cup)

¼ cup heavy cream

1. Preheat oven to 350°F. Butter a 9-by-5-inch loaf pan; dust with flour, tapping out excess. With a vegetable peeler, remove colorful peel from 1 orange, leaving white pith behind. With a paring knife, cut rind into enough matchsticks to yield 2 tablespoons. Finely grate enough rind of remaining oranges to yield 1 packed tablespoon zest.

2. Peel 6 oranges, and then working over a bowl, cut segments free of membranes. Squeeze orange juice from membranes into a bowl (you will need ¼ cup juice). Cut segments in half, and place in bowl with orange-peel matchsticks.

3. Combine sugar and zest in another bowl; using your fingers, rub together well. Add juice and the buttermilk; whisk to combine. Add eggs and oil; whisk to combine. Sift together flour, baking powder, baking soda, and salt into a small bowl; add to buttermilk mixture, whisking until smooth.

4. Transfer batter to prepared pan. Bake until golden and a cake tester comes out clean, 40 to 45 minutes. Transfer pan to a wire rack to cool 15 minutes. Turn out cake onto rack to cool completely. (Cake can be stored at room temperature, wrapped in plastic, up to 2 days.)

5. Stir honey into bowl with orange segments. Place chocolate in a heatproof bowl. Bring cream to a gentle simmer in a small saucepan. Pour over chocolate, let stand 5 minutes, and then whisk until smooth. Drizzle ganache over cooled cake and let set, about 1 hour. Serve with orange compote.

Cream-Cheese Pound Cake

The addition of cream cheese to the classic recipe results in an irresistibly moist and flavorful pound cake. Instead of making two loaves, you can make a single cake by baking the batter in a four-quart tube or Bundt pan; increase the cooking time by about five minutes. These cakes taste better the next day, and they store beautifully in the freezer (up to three months), wrapped well in plastic and foil. **MAKES TWO 9-BY-5-INCH LOAVES**

3 cups all-purpose flour

2 teaspoons salt

1½ cups (3 sticks) unsalted butter, room temperature

8 ounces (1 bar) cream cheese, room temperature

3 cups sugar

6 large eggs

1 teaspoon vanilla extract

Vegetable oil cooking spray

1. Preheat oven to 350°F. Generously coat two 9-by-5-inch loaf pans with cooking spray. In a medium bowl, whisk together flour and salt.

2. With an electric mixer on high speed, beat butter and cream cheese until smooth. Add sugar slowly; beat until pale and fluffy, about 5 minutes. Add eggs, 1 at a time, beating well after each addition. Mix in vanilla. Reduce speed to low; add flour mixture in 2 batches, beating until just combined.

3. Divide batter between prepared pans (pans will seem full). Tap pans on counter; smooth tops with an offset spatula. Bake until golden and a cake tester comes out with a few crumbs attached, 70 to 85 minutes (tent with foil if tops brown too quickly). Transfer pans to a wire rack to cool 10 minutes. Turn out cakes onto rack to cool completely.

Gingerbread

Gingerbread has somehow been relegated to the holiday season, but this loaf is so easy and delicious that it merits being made throughout the year. Dust the cake with confectioners' sugar before serving, and top slices with Whipped Cream (page 333) sprinkled with the same spices used in the cake, if desired. **MAKES ONE 9-BY-5-INCH LOAF**

1 cup (2 sticks) unsalted butter, room temperature, plus more for pan

1¼ cups all-purpose flour

1 teaspoon salt

½ teaspoon baking soda

½ teaspoon baking powder

1 teaspoon ground cinnamon

¾ teaspoon ground ginger

¾ teaspoon freshly grated nutmeg

¼ teaspoon ground cloves

½ cup packed dark brown sugar

½ cup granulated sugar

4 large eggs

1 teaspoon vanilla extract

Confectioners' sugar, for dusting

1. Preheat oven to 350°F. Butter a 9-by-5-inch loaf pan. Sift together flour, salt, baking soda, baking powder, cinnamon, ginger, nutmeg, and cloves into a large bowl.

2. With an electric mixer on medium speed, beat butter, brown sugar, and granulated sugar until pale and fluffy, 2 to 3 minutes. Add eggs, 1 at a time, mixing well after each addition. Beat in vanilla. Reduce speed to low; gradually add flour mixture and beat until just incorporated.

3. Transfer batter to prepared pan; smooth top with an offset spatula. Bake until a cake tester comes out clean, 50 to 55 minutes. Transfer pan to a wire rack to cool completely. Run a thin knife around edge of cake to loosen. Turn out cake onto a serving platter; dust generously with confectioners' sugar.

Two-Colored-Squash Loaf Cake

Once August rolls around and farm stands are overflowing with summer squash, this snacking cake is just the thing to bake. Here, two varieties—zucchini and yellow squash—are combined with nuts in a flavorful loaf.

MAKES ONE 9-BY-5-INCH LOAF

½ cup plus 2 tablespoons (1¼ sticks) unsalted butter, room temperature, plus more for pan

2 cups all-purpose flour, plus more for pan

4 summer squash (combination of zucchini and yellow squash)

1 cup shelled unsalted pistachios, coarsely chopped

1 teaspoon salt

1½ teaspoons baking powder

1¼ cups sugar

4 large eggs

1 teaspoon vanilla extract

2 teaspoons fennel seeds

1. Preheat oven to 425°F. Generously butter a 9-by-5-inch loaf pan; dust with flour, tapping out excess. Using a box grater, coarsely grate both types of squash. Place grated squash in a piece of cheesecloth (or clean thin dish towel); squeeze out as much liquid as possible.

2. Spread pistachios on a rimmed baking sheet; toast in oven 5 minutes. Transfer sheet to a wire rack to cool. Sift together flour, salt, and baking powder into a medium bowl.

3. With an electric mixer on medium-high speed, beat butter and sugar until pale and fluffy, 3 to 5 minutes. Add eggs, 1 at a time, beating well after each addition. Beat in vanilla. Add flour mixture; beat until just combined. Fold in squash, pistachios, and fennel seeds.

4. Transfer batter to prepared pan. Bake 10 minutes. Reduce heat to 350°F. Continue to bake until cake is golden brown and a cake tester comes out clean, about 1 hour. Transfer pan to a wire rack to cool 10 minutes. Turn out cake onto rack to cool completely. (Cake can be stored at room temperature, wrapped in plastic, up to 2 days.)

Clementine-Vanilla Bean Loaf Cake

This fragrant cake makes the most of a plentiful supply of candy-sweet clementines—zest, juice, and segments. Vanilla beans contribute to the flavor in a big way. Save the split pods for making vanilla sugar: Place them in a jar of sugar, seal lid, and leave for at least a week; the sugar should keep for several months. **MAKES ONE 9-BY-5-INCH LOAF**

1/2 cup (1 stick) unsalted butter, plus more for pan

2 cups all-purpose flour, plus more for pan

10 clementines or tangerines

3/4 cup heavy cream

1 tablespoon vanilla extract

1/4 teaspoon baking powder

1/4 teaspoon baking soda

1/4 teaspoon salt

1 1/4 cups sugar

2 vanilla beans, split lengthwise and scraped, pods reserved for another use

2 large eggs

1. Preheat oven to 350°F. Butter a 9-by-5-inch loaf pan; dust with flour, tapping out excess. Finely grate the zest of 4 clementines to yield 1 tablespoon zest. Peel 2 zested clementines, then slice fruit along membranes to release segments into a bowl; discard membranes and any seeds. Juice remaining 8 clementines (including zested ones) to yield 3/4 cup juice.

2. Combine 1/4 cup clementine juice, the cream, and vanilla extract in a medium bowl. In another bowl, whisk together flour, baking powder, baking soda, and salt.

3. With an electric mixer on medium speed, beat butter, zest, 1 cup sugar, and the vanilla seeds until pale and fluffy, about 4 minutes. Add eggs, 1 at a time, beating well after each addition. Reduce speed to low; beat in flour mixture in 3 batches, alternating with 2 batches of cream mixture. Fold clementine segments into the batter.

4. Transfer to prepared pan; smooth top with an offset spatula. Place pan on a rimmed baking sheet. Bake until a cake tester comes out clean, 55 to 65 minutes. Meanwhile, bring remaining 1/2 cup clementine juice and 1/4 cup sugar to a boil in a small saucepan. Reduce heat; simmer 3 minutes.

5. Remove cake from oven. With a wooden skewer, poke holes all over top; brush with half the clementine syrup. Transfer pan to a wire rack to cool 15 minutes. Turn out cake onto rack to cool completely.

6. Brush remaining clementine syrup onto sides and top of cake. (Cake can be wrapped in plastic and stored at room temperature overnight, refrigerated up to 5 days, or frozen up to 2 weeks; let thaw at room temperature before serving.)

Rhubarb Tea Cakes

Although once commonly known as "pie plant," rhubarb is versatile enough to be baked into other sweets, including these charming little cakes. Diced fruit is not only stirred into the batter, it is also simmered with water and sugar, then spooned over the whipped cream on top.

MAKES 8

FOR THE CAKES

- 1/2 cup (1 stick) unsalted butter, room temperature, plus more for pans
- 1 1/2 cups all-purpose flour
- 1/2 teaspoon coarse salt
- 1/4 teaspoon baking powder
- 1/4 teaspoon baking soda
- 1 cup sugar
- 2 large eggs
- 1 teaspoon vanilla extract
- 1/2 cup sour cream
- 2 cups diced (1/4 inch) rhubarb (about 8 ounces)

FOR THE TOPPINGS

- 1 vanilla bean, split lengthwise
- 1 cup water
- 1 cup sugar
- 1 cup diced (1/4 inch) rhubarb (about 4 ounces)
- Whipped Cream, for serving (page 333)

1. Make the cakes: Preheat oven to 350°F. Butter eight 4-by-2½-inch mini loaf pans, line with parchment, and butter parchment. In a bowl, whisk together flour, salt, baking powder, and baking soda.

2. With an electric mixer on medium-high speed, beat butter and sugar until pale and fluffy, about 3 minutes. Add eggs, 1 at a time, beating well after each addition. Beat in vanilla. Reduce speed to low; add flour mixture in 2 batches, alternating with the sour cream and beginning and ending with the flour; beat until just combined. Stir in rhubarb.

3. Divide batter evenly among prepared pans. Place on a rimmed baking sheet. Bake until a cake tester comes out clean, about 40 minutes. Transfer pans to a wire rack to cool completely. (Cakes can be stored at room temperature in airtight containers up to 3 days.)

4. Make the toppings: Using the tip of a sharp paring knife, scrape vanilla seeds into a saucepan, reserving pod for another use (see note, page 30). Add the water and sugar; bring to a simmer, stirring until sugar is dissolved. Remove from heat; stir in rhubarb. Let cool. Remove rhubarb with a slotted spoon, and reserve. Return liquid to a simmer; cook until reduced by half, 5 to 8 minutes. Let cool slightly; return rhubarb to syrup and let cool to room temperature. (Rhubarb and syrup can be refrigerated in an airtight container up to 1 week. Bring to room temperature before serving.)

5. To serve, spoon a generous amount of whipped cream over each cake, and top with rhubarb and syrup.

Pistachio Pound Cake

To give this cake a pronounced nuttiness, pistachios are ground to a paste in a food processor before being mixed into the batter. Buy best-quality pistachios, and pick through the nuts for the greenest ones (snack on the rest!). Finish the cake with creamy white icing and slivered nuts. **MAKES TWO 9-BY-5-INCH LOAVES**

FOR THE CAKES

- 1¼ cups (2½ sticks) unsalted butter, room temperature, plus more for pan
- 3 cups all-purpose flour, plus more for pans
- 6 ounces (¾ cup) cream cheese, room temperature
- 1 cup shelled salted pistachios, ground to a paste in a food processor, plus ¾ cup coarsely chopped shelled salted pistachios
- 3 cups granulated sugar
- 6 large eggs, room temperature
- 2 teaspoons vanilla extract
- 1 tablespoon coarse salt

FOR THE ICING

- 1 cup plus 3 tablespoons confectioners' sugar
- ¾ cup heavy cream
- 1 teaspoon fresh lemon juice

- 1½ cups unsalted slivered pistachios

1. Make the cakes: Preheat oven to 325°F. Butter two 9-by-5-inch loaf pans; line with parchment. Butter parchment; dust with flour, tapping out excess.

2. With an electric mixer on medium speed, beat butter, cream cheese, and pistachio paste until fluffy, about 3 minutes. Reduce speed to medium-low. Gradually add granulated sugar; beat until smooth. Scrape down sides of bowl. Add eggs, 1 at a time, beating well after each addition; mix in vanilla. Reduce speed to low. Add flour and salt; beat until just combined. Fold in chopped pistachios.

3. Divide batter evenly between prepared pans; smooth tops with an offset spatula. Bake until a cake tester comes out clean, about 1 hour 35 minutes. Transfer pans to a wire rack to cool 20 minutes. Turn out cakes onto rack to cool completely. (Cakes can be stored at room temperature, wrapped well in plastic, up to 1 day.)

4. Make the icing: Whisk confectioners' sugar, heavy cream, and lemon juice in a small bowl until smooth. Pour mixture through a sieve into another bowl. Immediately drizzle cakes with icing, and sprinkle with pistachio slivers.

Fruitcake

Since the early eighteenth century, fruitcake has been served at celebrations—especially Christmas. It's also become something of a punch line, but it shouldn't be. This recipe doesn't require soaking the cake in liquor for weeks like old-fashioned versions, and it makes good use of best-quality dried fruit, not the supermarket mixes that have given fruitcake its bad name. **MAKES TWO 9-BY-5-INCH LOAVES**

1 cup golden raisins

1 cup dried Calimyrna figs, chopped

1 cup dried apricots, chopped

1 cup dried pears, chopped

1/3 cup candied ginger, chopped

1/4 cup candied orange peel, chopped

3/4 cup Cointreau, plus more (optional) for brushing

1 cup (2 sticks) unsalted butter, melted, plus more for pans

3 cups all-purpose flour, plus more for pans

1 1/2 teaspoons baking powder

1 teaspoon ground cinnamon

1/2 teaspoon ground ginger

1/2 teaspoon ground cloves

1/2 teaspoon salt

1 1/2 cups granulated sugar

3/4 cup packed dark brown sugar

4 large eggs

2 tablespoons dark unsulfured molasses (not blackstrap)

1 tablespoon vanilla extract

1 cup chopped toasted walnuts (see page 344)

1 cup sweetened flaked coconut

1/2 cup apricot jam

5 tablespoons water

1. Stir together dried fruit, candied ginger, candied orange peel, and 3/4 cup liqueur. Let stand at room temperature 3 hours or overnight.

2. Preheat oven to 325°F. Butter two 9-by-5-inch loaf pans; line with parchment. Butter parchment; dust pans with flour, tapping out excess. In a medium bowl, whisk together flour, baking powder, spices, and salt.

3. With an electric mixer on medium speed, beat butter and both sugars until smooth, about 2 minutes. Mix in eggs, 1 at a time, followed by molasses and vanilla. Gradually add flour mixture; mix until smooth. Mix in fruit mixture, walnuts, and coconut.

4. Divide batter evenly between prepared pans. Bake until a cake tester comes out clean, about 1 hour 35 minutes. Transfer pans to a wire rack. If desired, brush tops with up to 1/2 cup liqueur; let cool 15 minutes. Turn out cakes onto rack. (Cooled, unglazed cakes can be stored, wrapped in plastic, at room temperature up to 3 days or in the refrigerator up to 1 month.)

5. Heat jam and the water in a small saucepan until loose. Brush half the glaze over warm cakes. Let cakes cool completely; brush again with remaining glaze.

Pumpkin, Sage, and Browned-Butter Cakes

Pumpkin and warm spices, sage and browned butter: Fall's flavor combinations come together to good effect in these miniature loaves. Browned butter strikes a nice balance between sweet and savory. To make a large loaf instead of several smaller ones, use a 9-by-5-inch loaf pan, and bake for 40 minutes. **MAKES 8**

3/4 cup (1½ sticks) unsalted butter, plus more for pans

1⅔ cups all-purpose flour, plus more for pans

1/4 cup fresh sage, cut into thin strips, plus whole leaves for garnish (optional)

2 teaspoons baking powder

1/2 teaspoon ground cinnamon

1/4 teaspoon freshly grated nutmeg

1/8 teaspoon ground cloves

1 teaspoon salt

1 cup solid-pack pumpkin (not pumpkin pie filling)

1 cup packed light brown sugar

2 large eggs

1. Preheat oven to 350°F. Butter eight 4-by-2½-inch loaf pans; dust with flour, tapping out excess. Melt butter in a saucepan over medium-low heat. Add sage strips; cook until butter turns golden brown, 5 to 8 minutes. Transfer mixture to a bowl; let cool slightly.

2. Meanwhile, whisk together flour, baking powder, cinnamon, nutmeg, cloves, and salt. In a another bowl, whisk together pumpkin, brown sugar, eggs, and sage-butter mixture. Add flour mixture; whisk until incorporated.

3. Divide batter evenly among prepared pans; smooth tops with an offset spatula. Place pans on a rimmed baking sheet; bake until a cake tester comes out clean, about 30 minutes. Transfer pans to a wire rack to cool 15 minutes. Turn out cakes onto rack to cool completely. (Cakes can be wrapped in plastic and stored at room temperature overnight or refrigerated up to 5 days.) Garnish with whole sage leaves before serving, if desired.

Cornmeal-Buttermilk Loaf Cake

This tender loaf makes a great base for nectarines or other summer fruits. Substitute apricots or peaches, or whatever berries look plumpest and juiciest at your market. Depending on the sweetness of the fruit, adjust the sugar in step 5 as needed. **MAKES ONE 9-BY-5-INCH LOAF**

3/4 cup (1 1/2 sticks) unsalted butter, room temperature, plus more for pan

1 cup plus 2 tablespoons sugar, plus more for pan

1 1/4 cups plus 2 tablespoons all-purpose flour, plus more for pan

1/2 cup plus 2 tablespoons yellow cornmeal

1 tablespoon grated lemon zest, plus 2 tablespoons fresh lemon juice

1 1/2 teaspoons baking powder

1 teaspoon baking soda

1/2 teaspoon salt

3 large eggs

3/4 cup buttermilk

4 medium nectarines, halved, pitted, and cut into 1/4-inch-thick wedges

2 tablespoons water

1. Preheat oven to 350°F. Generously butter a 9-by-5-inch loaf pan. Dust with sugar and flour, tapping out excess. In a bowl, whisk together flour, cornmeal, lemon zest, baking powder, baking soda, and salt.

2. With an electric mixer on medium-high speed, beat butter until smooth, about 2 minutes. Add 1 cup sugar; beat until pale and fluffy, about 3 minutes. In a separate bowl, whisk together eggs, buttermilk, and lemon juice.

3. Reduce mixer speed to low. Add flour mixture to butter mixture in 2 batches, alternating with the buttermilk mixture and beginning and ending with the flour. Beat until just combined, scraping down sides of bowl as needed.

4. Transfer batter to prepared pan; tap pan on counter. Bake until center is springy to the touch, about 55 minutes (tent with foil if top begins to brown too quickly). Transfer pan to a wire rack to cool 10 minutes. Turn out cake onto rack to cool completely. (Cake can be stored at room temperature, wrapped in plastic, up to 2 days.)

5. In a skillet, stir together nectarines and remaining 2 tablespoons sugar; add the water. Cook, stirring, until fruit is soft and liquid is syrupy, about 5 minutes. Let cool before serving with the cake.

Rosemary Pound Cakes

These cakes are excellent served warm, when the delicate flavors of honey and rosemary are most pronounced. Drizzle any leftover herb-infused honey over ricotta and other soft cheeses, or stir it into a hot cup of tea. MAKES TWO 9-BY-5-INCH LOAVES

FOR THE ROSEMARY HONEY

- 1 cup light-flavored honey, such as clover
- 5 rosemary sprigs (3 inches each)

FOR THE CAKES

- 1 cup (2 sticks) unsalted butter, room temperature, plus more for pans
- 2¾ cups all-purpose flour, plus more for pans
- 1 cup cake flour (not self-rising)
- 1 tablespoon baking powder
- 1 teaspoon salt
- 2¼ cups sugar
- 3 tablespoons finely chopped fresh rosemary
- 1½ teaspoons vanilla extract
- 3 large whole eggs plus 1 large egg white
- 1 cup milk

1. Make the rosemary honey: Bring honey and rosemary to a simmer in a small saucepan; cook 5 minutes. Remove from heat; let steep until cool, about 45 minutes. Remove rosemary, or leave in for a stronger flavor. (Honey can be stored in an airtight container at room temperature up to 1 week.)

2. Make the cakes: Preheat oven to 350°F. Butter two 9-by-5-inch loaf pans; line with parchment, leaving a 1-inch overhang on each long side. Butter parchment; dust with flour, tapping out excess. In a medium bowl, whisk together both flours, baking powder, and salt.

3. With an electric mixer on medium speed, beat butter, sugar, chopped rosemary, and vanilla until pale and fluffy, about 4 minutes. Add whole eggs and the egg white, 1 at a time, beating well after each addition. Reduce speed to low; add flour mixture in 2 batches, alternating with the milk and beginning and ending with the flour; beat until just combined.

4. Divide batter evenly between prepared pans. Bake, rotating halfway through, until deep golden and a cake tester comes out with only a few moist crumbs attached, 50 to 60 minutes. Remove from oven; brush tops of cakes with ¾ cup rosemary honey. Transfer pans to a wire rack to cool 10 minutes. Using parchment, lift cakes from pans; cool on rack 15 minutes more. Serve warm with more honey drizzled over slices. (Cooled cakes can be stored at room temperature, wrapped in plastic, up to 3 days.)

Chocolate-Ginger Marble Cakes

Chocolate and ginger join forces in these holiday-worthy loaves. A full tablespoon of ground ginger flavors the cakes, and candied ginger is used as a garnish atop the chocolate ganache glaze. MAKES TWO 9-BY-5-INCH LOAVES

FOR THE CAKES

- 1 cup (2 sticks) unsalted butter, room temperature, plus more for pans
- 3 cups all-purpose flour, plus more for pans
- 1 teaspoon salt
- 1 teaspoon baking soda
- 1 tablespoon ground ginger
- 4 ounces semisweet or bittersweet chocolate, chopped
- 2 cups sugar
- 6 large eggs, room temperature
- 1 teaspoon vanilla extract
- 1 cup sour cream

FOR THE GLAZE

- 8 ounces semisweet chocolate, chopped
- 3/4 cup heavy cream

  Candied ginger, for garnish

1. Make the cakes: Preheat oven to 350°F. Butter two 9-by-5-inch loaf pans; dust with flour, tapping out excess. In a medium bowl, whisk together flour, salt, baking soda, and ginger.

2. Place chocolate in a medium heatproof bowl set over (not in) a pan of simmering water. Stir occasionally just until melted, 4 to 5 minutes; remove from heat to cool slightly.

3. With an electric mixer on medium-high speed, beat butter and sugar until pale and fluffy, 4 to 5 minutes. Add eggs, 1 at a time, beating well after each addition; mix in vanilla. Reduce mixer speed to low. Add flour mixture in 3 batches, alternating with 2 batches of sour cream; beat just until incorporated (do not overmix). Add half the batter to melted chocolate; fold to combine.

4. Drop alternating dollops of plain and chocolate batters into each pan. Drag a paring knife back and forth through them several times to swirl. Bake until a cake tester comes out clean, 60 to 65 minutes (tent loosely with foil if tops begin to brown too quickly). Transfer pans to a wire rack to cool 30 minutes. Turn out cakes onto racks to cool completely.

5. Make the glaze: Place chocolate in a heatproof bowl. Bring cream to a simmer in a small saucepan. Pour over chocolate, let stand 2 minutes, and then whisk until smooth. Let cool until slightly thickened but pourable. Set cakes, still on rack, over a rimmed baking sheet. Pour glaze over tops, allowing it to drip down sides; let set about 30 minutes. Garnish with strips of candied ginger.

SWIRLING THE BATTER

Cranberry-Orange-Walnut Tea Cakes

Wrapped in pink glassine paper and tied with waxed twine, these mini loaves make terrific hostess gifts, at holiday time or any time of year. To make a large loaf instead of several smaller ones, use a 9-by-5-inch loaf pan, and bake for 55 minutes. **MAKES 9**

½ cup (1 stick) unsalted butter, room temperature, plus more for pans

2 cups all-purpose flour, plus more for pans

¾ cup heavy cream

Finely grated zest of 1 orange, plus 2 tablespoons fresh orange juice

1 teaspoon vanilla extract

¼ teaspoon baking powder

¼ teaspoon baking soda

¼ teaspoon salt

1 cup sugar

2 large eggs

¾ cup fresh or frozen (thawed) cranberries

½ cup walnuts, toasted (see page 344) and coarsely chopped

1. Preheat oven to 350°F. Butter nine 4-by-2½-inch loaf pans; dust with flour, tapping out excess. Combine cream, orange juice, and vanilla in a small bowl. In a medium bowl, whisk together flour, baking powder, baking soda, and salt.

2. With an electric mixer on medium speed, beat butter, orange zest, and sugar until pale and fluffy, 3 to 5 minutes. Reduce speed to low; add eggs, 1 at a time, beating well after each addition. Add flour mixture in 3 batches, alternating with 2 batches of cream mixture; beat until combined. Gently fold in cranberries and walnuts.

3. Divide batter evenly among prepared pans; smooth tops with an offset spatula. Place pans on a rimmed baking sheet; bake until cakes are golden and a cake tester comes out clean, about 30 minutes. Transfer pans to wire racks to cool 15 minutes. Turn out cakes onto racks to cool completely. (Cakes can be stored in an airtight container at room temperature up to 2 days.)

Carrot Tea Cake

This loaf-pan version of the beloved layer cake has the same signature flavors but is simpler to prepare. Serve the frosted cake with tea for an afternoon pick-me-up; unfrosted, it makes a welcome option on the breakfast table. **MAKES ONE 9-BY-5-INCH LOAF**

FOR THE CAKE

- ½ cup (1 stick) unsalted butter, room temperature, plus more for pan
- 1¼ cups all-purpose flour, plus more for pan
- 1 teaspoon baking powder
- ½ teaspoon baking soda
- ½ teaspoon salt
- ½ teaspoon ground cinnamon
- ½ teaspoon freshly grated nutmeg
- ½ cup packed dark brown sugar
- 2 large eggs
- 1 teaspoon vanilla extract
- 1 cup packed grated carrots (from about 2 carrots)

FOR THE FROSTING

- 8 ounces (1 bar) cream cheese, room temperature
- 1 cup confectioners' sugar
- ½ teaspoon vanilla extract

1. Make the cake: Preheat oven to 350°F. Butter a 9-by-5-inch loaf pan; dust with flour, tapping out excess. In a bowl, whisk together flour, baking powder, baking soda, salt, cinnamon, and nutmeg.

2. With an electric mixer on medium-high speed, beat butter and brown sugar until pale and fluffy, 3 to 5 minutes. Beat in eggs and vanilla until incorporated, scraping down sides of bowl as necessary. Beat in carrots. Reduce speed to low. Gradually add flour mixture; beat just until combined.

3. Transfer batter to prepared pan; smooth top with an offset spatula. Bake until a cake tester comes out clean, 40 to 45 minutes. Transfer pan to a wire rack to cool 15 minutes. Turn out cake onto rack to cool completely. (Cake can be stored at room temperature, wrapped well in plastic, up to 2 days.)

4. Make the frosting: With an electric mixer on medium-high speed, beat cream cheese, confectioners' sugar, and vanilla until fluffy. Spread frosting over top of cake.

Bundts & Tubes

It may have been based on European cake molds, but the Bundt pan is an American classic—so American, in fact, that one of the first ones ever made, in 1950, now resides in the Smithsonian Institution. Ring-shaped cakes with fluted sides have graced tables across the country ever since. But the Bundt is not the only ring-shaped cake: In this category, too, reside chiffon, angel-food, and other molded cakes, such as the French cannelés. Thanks to their distinctive forms, a sprinkling of sugar or a drizzle of glaze is the only embellishment necessary, making these desserts among the simplest to create.

CHOCOLATE BUNDT CAKE, PAGE 58

Lemon-Ginger Bundt Cake

A generous amount of minced crystallized ginger sets this cake apart from the rest. Instead of reaching for your knife to mince the ginger, grab your kitchen shears; they make quick work of the task. **SERVES 12**

1 cup (2 sticks) unsalted butter, room temperature, plus more for pan

3 cups all-purpose flour, plus more for pan

2 tablespoons finely grated lemon zest plus 1/3 cup fresh lemon juice (from 2 lemons)

1/3 cup minced candied ginger

1 teaspoon baking soda

1 teaspoon salt

2 1/2 cups granulated sugar

6 large eggs

1 cup sour cream

Confectioners' sugar, for dusting

1. Preheat oven to 350°F. Butter a 12-cup Bundt pan; dust with flour, tapping out excess. In a medium bowl, whisk together flour, zest, ginger, baking soda, and salt.

2. With an electric mixer on medium-high speed, beat butter and granulated sugar until pale and fluffy, 3 to 5 minutes. Add eggs, 1 at a time, beating well after each addition. Beat in lemon juice. Reduce speed to low. Add flour mixture in 3 batches, alternating with 2 batches of sour cream; beat just until incorporated (do not overmix).

3. Transfer batter to prepared pan; tap pan on counter, and smooth top with an offset spatula. Bake until light golden and a cake tester comes out clean, 55 to 60 minutes (tent with foil if top begins to brown too quickly). Transfer pan to a wire rack to cool 30 minutes. Turn out cake onto rack to cool completely. (Cake can be stored at room temperature, wrapped in plastic, up to 3 days.) Dust with confectioners' sugar before serving.

Peaches-and-Cream Bundt Cake

Try a new take on a beloved flavor combination, peaches and cream. Fresh fruit and sour cream make a cake that's wonderfully moist. Instead of icing, the cake gets brushed with melted butter and then generously dusted with cinnamon-sugar. Whipped cream makes a fitting finish, though vanilla ice cream (or, better yet, peach) would be welcome, too.

SERVES 14

1½ cups (3 sticks) unsalted butter, room temperature, plus more for pan

3 cups plus 2 tablespoons all-purpose flour, plus more for pan

1 teaspoon baking soda

1 teaspoon salt

4 peaches, peeled, pitted, and diced small

2¼ cups sugar

6 large eggs, room temperature

1¼ cups sour cream

1¼ teaspoons vanilla extract

1¼ teaspoons ground cinnamon

Whipped Cream, for serving (optional; page 333)

1. Preheat oven to 350°F. Butter a 14-cup Bundt pan; dust with flour, tapping out excess. In a medium bowl, whisk together 3 cups flour, the baking soda, and salt. In another bowl, toss peaches with remaining 2 tablespoons flour to coat.

2. With an electric mixer on medium-high speed, beat 1 cup butter and 2 cups sugar until pale and fluffy, 3 to 5 minutes. Add eggs, 1 at a time, beating well after each addition. Reduce speed to low; add flour mixture in 2 additions, alternating with sour cream and beginning and ending with the flour; beat until combined. Fold in peaches and vanilla.

3. Transfer batter to prepared pan; tap pan firmly on counter several times. Bake until a cake tester comes out clean, about 60 minutes. Transfer pan to a wire rack set over a rimmed baking sheet to cool 15 minutes.

4. Meanwhile, melt remaining ½ cup butter. Combine remaining ¼ cup sugar and the cinnamon. Run an offset spatula or small knife around edge of cake to loosen; turn out onto rack. Working in sections, brush cake with butter and sprinkle liberally with cinnamon-sugar. Serve warm or at room temperature, with whipped cream, if desired. (Cake can be stored at room temperature, covered, up to 3 days.)

Mini Rum Bundt Cakes

It's about time that once-popular rum cake came back into fashion, and these petite versions are enticing reasons to make it so. Dark rum, aged in wood casks, is the most complex and the best for baking. To neatly fill the mini Bundt pans with batter, use a pastry bag fitted with just a coupler, or a large resealable plastic bag with one corner cut off. If you don't have nine pans, you may bake the cakes in multiple batches.

MAKES 9

FOR THE CAKES

- 1 cup (2 sticks) butter, room temperature, plus more for pans
- 2 cups all-purpose flour, plus more for pans
- 2 teaspoons baking powder
- ½ teaspoon coarse salt
- ½ cup buttermilk
- 2 tablespoons dark rum
- 1 cup packed light brown sugar
- ½ cup granulated sugar
- 5 large eggs

FOR THE GLAZE

- 2 cups confectioners' sugar
- 1 tablespoon rum, plus up to 1½ teaspoons more, if needed
- 1 tablespoon plus 1½ teaspoons milk

1. Make the cakes: Preheat oven to 325°F. Generously butter nine 1-cup mini Bundt pans; dust with flour, tapping out excess. Sift together flour, baking powder, and salt into a medium bowl. Combine buttermilk and rum in a glass measuring cup.

2. With an electric mixer on high speed, beat butter, brown sugar, and granulated sugar until pale and fluffy, about 3 minutes. Reduce speed to medium. Add eggs, 1 at a time, beating well after each addition. Reduce speed to low. Add flour mixture in 2 batches, alternating with the buttermilk mixture and beginning and ending with the flour; beat until just combined.

3. Fill each pan with about ½ cup batter; tap pan on counter. Bake until tops spring back when lightly touched, edges begin to pull away from pan, and a cake tester comes out clean, 18 to 25 minutes. Transfer pans to a wire rack to cool 10 minutes; turn out cakes onto rack to cool completely. (Cakes can be stored at room temperature, wrapped in plastic, up to 3 days.)

4. Make the glaze: Whisk together confectioners' sugar, 1 tablespoon rum, and milk until smooth, adding more rum if needed to reach desired consistency. Set cakes on a wire rack over a rimmed baking sheet. Drizzle 1½ tablespoons glaze over each cake.

Chocolate Bundt Cake

Guaranteed to satisfy any chocolate craving, this is an excellent cake to keep in mind when you have a houseful of guests. The ganache glaze makes it dressy enough for dessert after a special dinner. **SERVES 14**

FOR THE CAKE

- 1 cup (2 sticks) unsalted butter, plus more for pan
- 2¼ cups all-purpose flour
- ¾ cup unsweetened cocoa powder
- 1 teaspoon baking soda
- 1 teaspoon salt
- ½ cup milk
- ½ cup sour cream
- 1½ cups sugar
- 4 large eggs
- 1 teaspoon vanilla extract

FOR THE GLAZE

- 3 ounces bittersweet chocolate, chopped
- ½ cup heavy cream
- 2 tablespoons unsalted butter

1. Make the cake: Preheat oven to 325°F. Butter a 14-cup Bundt pan. In a large bowl, whisk together flour, cocoa, baking soda, and salt. Mix milk and sour cream in a glass measuring cup.

2. With an electric mixer on medium-high speed, beat butter and sugar until pale and fluffy, 3 to 5 minutes. Add eggs, 1 at a time, beating well after each addition; add vanilla. Reduce speed to low; add flour mixture in 2 batches, alternating with the milk mixture and beginning and ending with the flour; beat until just combined.

3. Transfer batter to prepared pan; smooth top with an offset spatula. Bake until a cake tester comes out clean, about 55 minutes. Transfer pan to a wire rack to cool completely. (Cake can be stored at room temperature, wrapped in plastic, up to 1 day.)

4. Make the glaze: Place chocolate in a heatproof bowl. Bring cream to a simmer in a small saucepan; pour over chocolate. Let stand 2 minutes. Add butter, and mix until smooth. Let stand, stirring occasionally, until slightly thickened. Pour glaze over cake.

Angel-Food Cake

Angel-food cakes are airy and light (no butter or oil in the batter), and very versatile; the classic recipe here is a good place to start before trying your hand at the variations that follow. Because angel-food cakes do not contain any leaveners, whisking up the perfect meringue is crucial; overbeating will cause the whites to deflate, while underbeating won't incorporate enough air. It's also important to cool the cake upside down, either on the pan's legs or over a glass bottle; otherwise the top will sink. Serve alone or topped with whipped cream, chocolate sauce, or fresh fruit; slices are excellent toasted the next day. **SERVES 10 TO 12**

1 cup sifted cake flour
(not self-rising)

1½ cups granulated sugar

12 large egg whites,
room temperature

1 teaspoon cream of tartar

1 tablespoon fresh lemon juice

2 teaspoons vanilla extract

¼ teaspoon salt

Confectioners' sugar,
for dusting

1. Preheat oven to 325°F, with rack in lower third (but not on bottom shelf). Using a sieve, sift flour and ½ cup granulated sugar onto a piece of parchment. Set sieve over a bowl, and sift again.

2. With an electric mixer on medium speed, beat egg whites until frothy, about 1 minute. Add cream of tartar, lemon juice, vanilla, and salt; beat until soft peaks form, about 2½ minutes. With mixer running, add remaining 1 cup sugar, a little at a time, beating no longer than 1 minute.

3. Raise speed to medium-high; continue beating until firm, but not stiff, peaks form (when beater is lifted, only the tip of the peak should fall over slightly). Gently transfer egg-white mixture to a large, wide bowl. Sprinkle a third of reserved flour mixture over the whites. Using a whisk, gently combine in a folding motion, allowing batter to fall through the whisk as you fold. Sprinkle remaining flour mixture over whites in 2 more batches; fold in with a flexible spatula until just combined. Be careful not to overmix or the egg whites will deflate.

4. Gently spoon batter into a 10-inch tube pan. Run an offset spatula gently through the center of the batter to remove any large air bubbles. Bake until a cake tester comes out clean, and cake is springy to the touch, 45 to 50 minutes.

5. Remove cake from oven; invert pan onto its legs or over a glass bottle and let cool completely. Turn pan right side up. Run a knife around edge of cake to loosen; turn out cake onto serving plate. (Cake can be stored at room temperature, wrapped in plastic, up to 2 days.) Dust with confectioners' sugar. To serve, slice with a serrated knife.

REMOVING AIR BUBBLES FROM BATTER

Five More Angel-Food Cakes

MOCHA-CHIP ANGEL-FOOD CAKE
Mix 2 tablespoons instant espresso powder with 1 tablespoon water. Follow Angel-Food Cake recipe (page 61), but in step 3, after folding flour mixture into egg whites, gently fold in espresso mixture and 1 cup miniature chocolate chips. Bake about 55 minutes. Finish cake with mocha glaze: Heat 1/4 cup milk, 3 ounces chopped semisweet chocolate, and 1 teaspoon espresso powder in a saucepan, stirring, until chocolate is melted; drizzle glaze over cooled cake.

RASPBERRY-SWIRL ANGEL-FOOD CAKE
Mash 3/4 cup fresh raspberries, and pass through a sieve, discarding solids; you should have 1/4 cup purée. Follow Angel-Food Cake recipe (page 61), transferring only one third of batter to prepared pan. Spoon 2 tablespoons raspberry purée over batter. Add another one third of batter, remaining 2 tablespoons purée, and remaining batter. Run a knife through batter to swirl. Bake cake at 350°F; serve with additional fresh raspberries.

CHOCOLATE ANGEL-FOOD CAKE

Follow Angel-Food Cake recipe (page 61), substituting ¼ cup sifted unsweetened cocoa powder for ¼ cup of the cake flour; sift flour and cocoa together in step 1. Bake about 55 minutes. Dust cooled cake with cocoa powder before serving.

LEMON ANGEL-FOOD CAKE

Follow Angel-Food Cake recipe (page 61), adding 1 tablespoon plus 1 teaspoon fresh lemon juice (from 2 lemons) and decreasing vanilla to 1 teaspoon. Add 2 tablespoons finely grated lemon zest to the egg-white mixture in step 2. Bake 40 to 45 minutes. If desired, make a glaze by combining 2 cups confectioners' sugar with 2 teaspoons grated lemon zest and ¼ cup lemon juice (from 3 to 4 lemons); drizzle over cooled cake before serving.

BROWN SUGAR ANGEL-FOOD CAKE

Follow Angel-Food Cake recipe (page 61), replacing granulated sugar with an equal amount of packed light brown sugar. Serve with Whipped Cream (page 333), if desired.

Blueberry-Lemon Bundt Cake

This cake is dotted with tart-sweet blueberries and laced with lemon, and, best of all, it's a breeze to put together. Here's a trick for preventing the berries from sinking to the bottom while baking: Just toss them and the zest with a teaspoon of flour before mixing them into the batter.

SERVES 12

- 1 cup (2 sticks) unsalted butter, room temperature, plus more for pan
- 2½ cups all-purpose flour, plus 1 teaspoon for blueberries and zest, plus more for pan
- 2 teaspoons baking powder
- ½ teaspoon salt
- 1 cup packed light brown sugar
- 1 cup granulated sugar
- 4 large eggs
- 1 teaspoon vanilla extract
- 1 cup sour cream
- 2 cups fresh blueberries
- 2 tablespoons finely grated lemon zest
- Confectioners' sugar, for dusting (optional)

1. Preheat oven to 350°F, with rack on bottom shelf. Butter a 12-cup Bundt pan; dust with flour, tapping out excess. In a medium bowl, whisk together 2½ cups flour, the baking powder, and salt.

2. With an electric mixer on high speed, beat butter, brown sugar, and granulated sugar until pale and fluffy, 3 to 5 minutes. Add eggs, 1 at a time, beating well after each addition. Beat in vanilla. Reduce speed to low; add flour mixture in 3 batches, alternating with 2 batches of sour cream and beating until just combined. Toss blueberries and zest with remaining 1 teaspoon flour; gently fold into batter.

3. Transfer batter to prepared pan; smooth top with an offset spatula. Bake until a cake tester comes out clean, 60 to 70 minutes. Transfer pan to a wire rack to cool 20 minutes. Turn out cake onto rack to cool completely. (Cake can be stored at room temperature, wrapped in plastic, up to 3 days.) Dust with confectioners' sugar before serving, if desired.

Allspice Angel-Food Cakes

This tropical take on angel-food cake features allspice in the batter. Pineapple, a refreshing change of pace from citrus, is added to the curd that is drizzled over each cake; it also makes a lovely garnish when thinly cut and dried in the oven. For best results, use an adjustable-blade slicer.

MAKES 6 MINI 4-INCH CAKES (OR ONE 10-INCH CAKE)

FOR THE CAKES

- ½ cup plus 2 tablespoons sifted cake flour (not self-rising)
- ¼ teaspoon ground allspice
- Pinch of salt
- 7 large egg whites, room temperature
- ¾ cup sugar
- ¾ teaspoon cream of tartar

FOR THE PINEAPPLE SLICES

- ½ fresh pineapple (about 2¼ pounds), peeled, thinly sliced into rounds, and cored

FOR THE CURD

- 7 large egg yolks
- ¾ cup sugar
- ¼ teaspoon coarse salt
- ½ cup fresh pineapple juice
- 1 tablespoon fresh lemon juice
- ½ cup (1 stick) unsalted butter, cut into small pieces

1. Make the cakes: Preheat oven to 350°F. In a medium bowl, whisk together flour, allspice, and a pinch of salt.

2. With an electric mixer on medium speed, whisk egg whites and sugar until foamy, about 1 minute. Beat in cream of tartar. Raise speed to high; beat until mixture is stiff and glossy and has tripled in volume, about 3 minutes. Gently fold in flour mixture in 3 batches.

3. Spoon batter into a resealable plastic bag; snip off a corner of the bag. Squeeze batter into 6 mini tube pans (about 4 inches in diameter and 2¼ inches high), dividing evenly. (Alternatively, spoon batter into a 10-inch tube pan.) Bake until golden and cakes spring back when touched, about 30 minutes (or about 40 minutes for a 10-inch cake). Transfer pans to a wire rack to cool 30 minutes. Run a thin knife around edges of cakes to loosen; turn out onto rack to cool completely. (Cakes can be stored at room temperature in an airtight container up to 1 day.)

4. Make the pineapple slices: Preheat oven to 200°F. Spread pineapple rounds in a single layer on a rimmed baking sheet lined with a nonstick baking mat. Cook, flipping once, until dried, about 2 hours. Transfer to a wire rack to cool completely. (Dried pineapple slices can be stored in an airtight container up to 3 days.)

5. Make the curd: Whisk together egg yolks, sugar, and salt in a large heatproof bowl until smooth. Gradually whisk in pineapple and lemon juices. Set bowl over (not in) a pan of simmering water; whisk until thickened, about 8 minutes. Remove from heat; whisk in butter, 1 piece at a time, until smooth. Cover with plastic, pressing wrap directly on surface to prevent a skin from forming; refrigerate curd at least 1 hour or up to overnight.

6. To serve, drizzle curd over each cake, and top with a dried pineapple slice. Serve remaining curd on the side.

Spiced Prune Cake

Prune cakes enjoy a long tradition as holiday desserts, especially in England and Australia. This updated version scales back the sweetness factor with a mix of spices and buttermilk. Be sure to bake this cake for as long as the recipe specifies; any shorter and it might not be easy to remove it from the pan. **SERVES 12**

Unsalted butter, for pan

2 cups all-purpose flour, plus more for pan

1 cup pitted prunes (dried plums)

2 cups granulated sugar

1 teaspoon ground cinnamon

1 teaspoon ground cloves

1/2 teaspoon freshly grated nutmeg

1 teaspoon salt

1 teaspoon baking soda

1 cup canola or safflower oil

1 cup low-fat buttermilk

3 large eggs

1 cup coarsely chopped walnuts, toasted (see page 344)

Confectioners' sugar, for dusting (optional)

1. Preheat oven to 325°F. Butter a 12-cup Bundt pan; dust with flour, tapping out excess.

2. Bring a small saucepan of water to a boil; remove from heat, and add prunes. Cover; let soak 10 minutes. Drain prunes and finely chop.

3. Meanwhile, in a large bowl, whisk together flour, granulated sugar, cinnamon, cloves, nutmeg, salt, and baking soda. In a medium bowl, whisk together oil, buttermilk, and eggs. Add oil mixture to flour mixture; mix just until combined. Stir in prunes and walnuts.

4. Transfer batter to prepared pan. Bake until a cake tester comes out clean and cake has pulled away completely from sides of pan, 1 hour 45 minutes to 2 hours. Immediately turn out cake onto a wire rack to cool completely. (Cake can be stored at room temperature, wrapped in plastic, up to 2 days.) Dust with confectioners' sugar before serving, if desired.

Lemon Chiffon Cake

Chiffon cake is a true American classic, and for good reason: It's light and airy and tender all at once. Whipped egg whites are folded into the batter for loft; using oil instead of butter makes for a softer texture—and helps the cake keep well. **SERVES 8**

¾ cup cake flour
(not self-rising)

¼ teaspoon baking soda

¼ teaspoon salt

¾ cup plus 1 tablespoon
granulated sugar

3 large eggs, separated,
room temperature

¼ cup canola or safflower oil

⅓ cup water

2 tablespoons grated lemon
zest plus 1 tablespoon fresh
lemon juice (about 2 lemons)

½ teaspoon vanilla extract

¼ teaspoon cream of tartar

Confectioners' sugar,
for dusting

Lemon Curd, for serving
(optional; page 332)

1. Preheat oven to 325°F. In a medium bowl, sift together flour, baking soda, salt, and ¾ cup granulated sugar.

2. In a large bowl, whisk together egg yolks, oil, the water, lemon zest and juice, and vanilla. Add flour mixture; beat until smooth.

3. With an electric mixer on medium speed, beat egg whites until foamy. Add cream of tartar; beat on high speed until soft peaks form, about 1 minute. Gradually add remaining 1 tablespoon granulated sugar; beat on high speed until stiff peaks form, about 2 minutes.

4. Fold one third of egg-white mixture into batter, then fold in remaining two thirds. Transfer batter to an ungreased 7-inch tube pan; smooth top with an offset spatula. Bake until a cake tester comes out clean and the cake is golden, about 45 minutes.

5. Remove cake from oven; invert pan onto its legs or over a glass bottle and let cool completely. Turn pan right side up. Run a knife around edges of cake to loosen; turn out cake onto serving plate. Dust cake with confectioners' sugar before serving with lemon curd, if desired.

Cannelés

The crisp, crunchy shells don't begin to hint at the richness of these little cakes—and their ultra-moist interiors. To make cannelés, a mixture of milk, butter, egg, sugar, and pastry flour—which has less protein than all-purpose, but more than cake flour—is whisked into a thin batter similar to that of Yorkshire pudding. When baked in their namesake molds, the outside hardens into a fluted shell (*cannelé* is French for "fluted") while the inside remains custardy. The molds are available at baking-supply stores and from online retailers. Be sure to use extra-large (rather than large) eggs; they are essential to achieving the proper result.

MAKES ABOUT 20

4¼ cups milk

3 tablespoons unsalted butter

1 extra-large whole egg plus 5 extra-large egg yolks

2¼ cups plus 3 tablespoons sugar

2 teaspoons vanilla extract

2 cups plus 2 tablespoons unbleached pastry flour

Vegetable oil cooking spray

1. In a medium saucepan, bring 2½ cups milk and the butter to a boil. Remove from heat; let cool slightly.

2. In a large bowl, whisk together whole egg, yolks, sugar, vanilla, and remaining 1¾ cups milk. Whisk in flour to combine. Add milk-butter mixture in a slow, steady stream, whisking until combined. Pass batter through a fine sieve into a medium bowl. Cover; refrigerate 24 to 48 hours.

3. Preheat oven to 400°F. Coat 20 cannelé molds with cooking spray; freeze molds 20 minutes. Place molds 1½ inches apart on a rimmed baking sheet. Gently whisk batter. Fill each mold to ⅛ inch from the top.

4. Bake, rotating halfway through, until cannelés slip easily from molds with a gentle tap and are evenly browned, 1 hour 30 minutes to 1 hour 45 minutes. Transfer baking sheet to a wire rack to cool 15 minutes. Turn out cannelés onto rack to cool completely. Cannelés are best eaten the day they are made.

Banana Chiffon Cake

Bananas may be common in baked goods, but we're betting you've never tasted a cake quite like this one. Unlike the familiar hearty, spiced quick breads and muffins, this chiffon cake has subtle flavor from just one mashed banana and gets its height from whipped egg whites.

SERVES 12

2 cups all-purpose flour

1½ cups granulated sugar

1 tablespoon baking powder

1 teaspoon salt

1 ripe banana

½ cup canola or safflower oil

7 large eggs, separated

1 teaspoon vanilla extract

¾ cup cold water

½ teaspoon cream of tartar

Confectioners' sugar, for dusting

1. Preheat oven to 350°F. In a large bowl, whisk together flour, granulated sugar, baking powder, and salt. In a medium bowl, mash banana. Add oil, egg yolks, vanilla, and the water; mix to combine. Add to flour mixture; whisk batter until smooth.

2. With an electric mixer on medium-high speed, beat egg whites and cream of tartar until stiff peaks form, about 3 minutes. Gently fold into batter just until combined (do not overmix).

3. Transfer batter to an ungreased 10-inch tube pan. Bake until a cake tester comes out clean, about 55 minutes. Remove cake from oven; invert pan onto its legs or over a glass bottle and let cool completely. Turn pan right side up. Run a knife around edges of cake to loosen; turn out cake onto serving plate. Dust with confectioners' sugar before serving.

Coconut-Rum Raisin Cake

Take a favorite ice-cream flavor combination—rum raisin—and add coconut and caramel sauce, and you have a winner of a cake. Soaking the raisins in the rum makes them plump *and* flavorful. **SERVES 12**

FOR THE CAKE

- 1¼ cups (2½ sticks) unsalted butter, room temperature, plus more for pan
- 3 cups all-purpose flour, plus more for pan
- 1 cup raisins
- ½ cup dark rum
- 1 teaspoon salt
- ½ teaspoon baking powder
- 2¾ cups plus 2 tablespoons packed light brown sugar
- 6 large eggs
- 2 teaspoons vanilla extract
- ¾ cup heavy cream
- 1 cup sweetened flaked coconut

FOR THE GLAZE

- 1 cup granulated sugar
- ¼ cup water
- ¼ cup dark rum
- 2 tablespoons heavy cream

1. Make the cake: Preheat oven to 325°F. Butter a 12-cup Bundt or kugelhopf pan; dust with flour, tapping out excess. Place raisins and rum in a bowl, and let soak.

2. Whisk together flour, salt, and baking powder. With an electric mixer on medium speed, beat butter and brown sugar until smooth, about 3 minutes. Add eggs, 1 at a time, beating well after each addition. Add vanilla. Reduce speed to low. Add flour mixture in 3 batches, alternating with 2 batches of cream; beat until just combined. Mix in raisin mixture and coconut.

3. Transfer batter to prepared pan; smooth top with an offset spatula. Bake, rotating halfway through, until a cake tester comes out clean, about 1 hour 55 minutes. Transfer pan to a wire rack to cool 20 minutes. Run a thin knife around edge of cake to loosen; turn out onto rack to cool completely. (Cake can be stored at room temperature, wrapped in plastic, up to 2 days.)

4. Make the glaze: Heat granulated sugar and the water in a small saucepan over medium-high heat, gently stirring, until sugar is dissolved and syrup is clear. Cook, without stirring, until syrup comes to a boil, washing down sides of pan with a wet pastry brush to prevent crystals from forming. Let boil, gently swirling, until mixture turns medium amber. Remove from heat. Carefully pour in rum and cream. Let cool, stirring, until thickened. Drizzle over cake.

Fresh Ginger-Molasses Cake

This Bundt cake is so easy and versatile, you'll want to make it all year long. It's equally delicious with fresh berry compote in spring, sautéed stone fruits (plums and peaches) in summer, apples and pears in fall, and lemon curd and whipped cream in winter. **SERVES 12**

8 ounces (about two 6-inch pieces) fresh ginger, peeled and coarsely chopped

3 cups all-purpose flour, plus more for pan

2 teaspoons baking soda

1 teaspoon salt

1½ cups granulated sugar

⅔ cup unsulfured molasses

2 large eggs

1 cup (2 sticks) unsalted butter, melted, room temperature, plus more for pan

⅓ cup hot water

Confectioners' sugar, for dusting

1. Preheat oven to 350°F. Brush a 12-cup Bundt pan with butter; dust with flour, tapping out excess. In a food processor, pulse ginger until finely chopped (or chop by hand). You should have 1 cup.

2. In a large bowl, whisk together flour, baking soda, and salt. In another bowl, whisk together granulated sugar, molasses, and eggs until smooth. Whisk in butter and the hot water. Stir in flour mixture just until incorporated; stir in ginger.

3. Transfer batter to prepared pan. Bake until a cake tester comes out clean, about 45 minutes. Transfer pan to a wire rack to cool completely, about 1 hour. Run a knife around edge of cake to loosen; turn out cake onto rack. Dust with confectioners' sugar before serving.

Sour Cherry Savarins

Juicy, wine-simmered sour cherries capture the essence of early summer. Savarins are classic French yeasted cakes traditionally baked in large ring molds (of the same name), but miniature versions are also common. You can use either size savarin mold or substitute an 8-inch Bundt pan. It will take about 15 minutes to bake a large cake. **MAKES 6**

FOR THE SAVARINS

1⅛ teaspoons active dry yeast

¼ cup warm water (110°F to 115°F)

1 tablespoon sugar

1¼ cups all-purpose flour

½ teaspoon salt

2 large eggs, room temperature, lightly beaten

5 tablespoons unsalted butter, room temperature, plus more for molds

FOR THE CHERRIES AND GLAZE

2½ cups fresh sour cherries, pitted (or 2 cups thawed frozen sour cherries)

½ cup sugar

½ cup Muscat de Beaumes-de-Venise or Sauternes

Pinch of salt

1. Make the savarins: Sprinkle yeast over the warm water in a small bowl; stir in ½ teaspoon sugar. Let stand until foamy, about 5 minutes.

2. Mix together flour, salt, and remaining 2½ teaspoons sugar in a large bowl. Make a well in the center; add yeast mixture and eggs. With an electric mixer on medium speed, beat until a sticky, elastic dough forms, 2 to 3 minutes. Scrape down sides of bowl. Cover with plastic wrap; let stand in a warm place until doubled in volume, about 1 hour.

3. Preheat oven to 400°F. Butter six 3½-inch savarin molds; place on a rimmed baking sheet. Add butter to dough; beat on medium-high speed until incorporated, about 1 minute.

4. Using a pastry bag fitted only with a plain round tip, pipe dough into molds, filling halfway. Let stand, uncovered, in a warm place until dough rises and almost fills the molds, 25 to 30 minutes.

5. Bake savarins until golden brown and beginning to pull away from sides of molds, 10 to 12 minutes. Transfer molds to a wire rack to cool slightly, about 5 minutes. Turn out cakes onto rack to cool completely.

6. Make the cherries and glaze: Bring cherries, sugar, wine, and salt to a boil in a small saucepan. Reduce heat; simmer gently 2 minutes. Remove cherries with a slotted spoon. Simmer remaining liquid until reduced to a glaze, about 5 minutes (you should have about ¾ cup). Spoon glaze over warm cakes; top with cherries. Serve immediately.

PIPING THE BATTER

Glazed Pecan-Raisin Cake

Chock-full of raisins and nuts and laced with brandy and nutmeg, this is an easy alternative to fruitcake. It will last for several days after baking, so it's a great make-ahead dessert option. **SERVES 10 TO 12**

FOR THE CAKE

- 2 cups (4 sticks) unsalted butter, room temperature, plus more for pan
- 4 cups all-purpose flour, plus more for pan
- 2 tablespoons freshly grated nutmeg
- 1 teaspoon baking powder
- 2¼ cups packed light brown sugar (1 pound)
- 6 large eggs
- ½ cup brandy
- 3 cups pecans (about 12 ounces), chopped
- 3 cups raisins (1 pound)

FOR THE GLAZE

- 1 cup confectioners' sugar
- 1 tablespoon plus 1 teaspoon fresh orange juice

1. Make the cake: Preheat oven to 350°F. Butter a 12-cup Bundt pan; dust with flour, tapping out excess. In a large bowl, whisk together flour, nutmeg, and baking powder.

2. With an electric mixer on medium-high speed, beat butter and brown sugar until pale and fluffy, 3 to 5 minutes. Add eggs, 1 at a time, beating well after each addition. Add brandy; beat until combined. Reduce speed to low. Gradually add flour mixture; beat just until combined (do not overmix). Fold in pecans and raisins.

3. Transfer batter to prepared pan; smooth top with an offset spatula. Bake until cake has pulled away from sides of pan and a cake tester comes out clean, about 1 hour 30 minutes. Immediately turn out cake onto a wire rack to cool completely. (Cake can be stored at room temperature, wrapped in plastic, up to 3 days.)

4. Make the glaze: In a small bowl, whisk together confectioners' sugar and orange juice until smooth. Drizzle over cake.

Olive Oil–Anise Mini Bundt Cakes

The combination of anise and olive oil is typical in Italian baking; here it works wonders in a batch of moderately sweet miniature cakes. Toasting the anise seeds helps release their flavor: Heat the seeds in a dry skillet over medium heat, gently shaking the pan, just until they are fragrant and begin to pop, about three minutes, then let cool slightly. This recipe doubles easily. **MAKES 4**

Unsalted butter, for pan

2/3 cup cake flour (not self-rising), plus more for pans

2 large whole eggs plus 1 large egg yolk

1/2 cup granulated sugar

1 packed teaspoon finely grated orange zest

1 1/2 teaspoons toasted anise seeds

1/2 cup extra-virgin olive oil

1/2 teaspoon coarse salt

1/2 teaspoon baking powder

Confectioners' sugar, for dusting

1. Preheat oven to 325°F. Butter four 1-cup mini Bundt pans; dust with flour, tapping out excess. Whisk whole eggs, yolk, granulated sugar, zest, and anise seeds until foamy. Add oil in a slow, steady stream, whisking constantly until combined.

2. Whisk together flour, salt, and baking powder in a small bowl. Fold flour mixture into egg mixture in 3 batches.

3. Divide batter evenly among prepared pans; smooth tops with an offset spatula. Bake until light golden and a cake tester comes out clean, about 20 minutes. Transfer pans to a wire rack to cool 10 minutes. Turn out cakes, and serve warm, dusted with confectioners' sugar.

Tangerine Cake

Chase away the winter doldrums with a slice of this bright, sunny cake. Tangerines are a refreshing change of pace from other types of citrus, and their thin skins make it easy to juice them by hand. (If you can't find tangerines, this cake is equally delicious made with oranges.) The two-ingredient glaze makes a foolproof finish. For a smooth glaze, strain the juice through a fine-mesh sieve before mixing with the sugar. **SERVES 12**

FOR THE CAKE

- 1 cup (2 sticks) unsalted butter, room temperature, plus more for pan
- 3 cups all-purpose flour, plus more for pan
- 1 teaspoon baking soda
- 1 teaspoon salt
- 2 cups granulated sugar
- 6 large eggs
- 2 tablespoons finely grated tangerine zest plus 1/2 cup fresh tangerine juice (from 6 tangerines)
- 2 tablespoons orange-flavored liqueur, such as Grand Marnier
- 1 teaspoon vanilla extract
- 3/4 cup plain yogurt

FOR THE GLAZE AND GARNISH

- 1 1/2 cups confectioners' sugar
- 3 tablespoons fresh tangerine juice (from 2 tangerines)
- Sugared currants (optional; see Sugared Garnishes, page 327)

1. Make the cake: Preheat oven to 350°F. Butter a 12-cup Bundt pan; dust with flour, tapping out excess. In a medium bowl, whisk together flour, baking soda, and salt.

2. With an electric mixer on medium-high speed, beat butter and granulated sugar until pale and fluffy, 3 to 5 minutes. Add eggs, 1 at a time, beating well after each addition. Beat in tangerine zest and juice, liqueur, and vanilla. Reduce speed to low. Add flour mixture in 3 batches, alternating with 2 batches of yogurt and beating to combine.

3. Transfer batter to prepared pan; smooth top with an offset spatula, and firmly tap pan on counter. Bake until a cake tester comes out clean, 50 to 55 minutes. Transfer pan to a wire rack to cool 30 minutes. Turn out cake onto rack to cool completely. (Cake can be stored at room temperature, wrapped in plastic, up to 2 days.)

4. Make the glaze: Whisk together confectioners' sugar and tangerine juice until smooth. With a serrated knife, trim cake to sit flat, if necessary. Set cake on rack over a rimmed baking sheet. Spoon glaze evenly over cake; let set before serving, garnished with sugared currants, if desired.

Zucchini Bundt Cake

Here's another way to use a bumper crop of zucchini (besides making muffins and quick breads): Bake it into a Bundt cake. This one is flavored with orange and a lovely combination of spices—cinnamon, anise, and cardamom. Zucchini is naturally high in water, so be sure to squeeze out as much moisture as possible in step 2. You can use this recipe to make either one large or two smaller Bundt cakes as directed below. **SERVES 10**

FOR THE CAKE

- ¾ cup (1½ sticks) unsalted butter, melted, plus more for pan
- 2½ cups all-purpose flour, plus more for pan
- 2½ teaspoons baking powder
- ¼ teaspoon ground cinnamon
- ¼ teaspoon anise seeds
- ⅛ teaspoon ground cardamom (optional)
- 1 teaspoon coarse salt
- 1 pound zucchini (about 2 medium)
- 3 large eggs
- 1½ cups granulated sugar
- ½ teaspoon grated orange zest plus 1 tablespoon fresh orange juice

FOR THE GLAZE

- 1¼ cups confectioners' sugar, sifted
- 2 pinches of ground cardamom (optional)
- ¼ teaspoon finely grated orange zest plus 3 tablespoons fresh orange juice
- Whole milk, as needed, for thinning

1. Make the cake: Preheat oven to 325°F. Brush a 14-cup Bundt pan or two 4-cup Bundt pans with butter. Dust with flour, tapping out excess. Whisk together flour, baking powder, spices, and salt.

2. Grate zucchini on the large holes of a box grater; squeeze dry in a clean kitchen towel (you will need 2½ cups). In a large bowl, stir together eggs and granulated sugar; stir in melted butter, zucchini, and orange zest and juice. Stir in flour mixture.

3. Transfer batter to prepared pan. Bake until a cake tester comes out clean, about 60 minutes for 14-cup cake or about 48 minutes for 4-cup cakes (cake will rise quite a bit over the top of the pan but should not run over). Transfer to a wire rack to cool 10 minutes. Run a knife around edges of cake to loosen, and turn out onto rack to cool completely. (Cake can be wrapped in plastic and stored at room temperature up to 1 day or frozen up to 1 month.)

4. Make the glaze: Whisk together confectioners' sugar and cardamom, if using. Add orange zest and juice, whisking until mixture reaches the consistency of thick honey. If mixture is too thick, whisk in milk, 1 teaspoon at a time. (If not using immediately, refrigerate glaze, with plastic wrap on the surface to prevent a skin from forming, up to 1 day. Stir before using.) Brush several layers of orange glaze evenly over cake, then drizzle more glaze on top.

Golden Cakes with Ginger-Poached Fruit

These little cakes are baked in a pan made up of six individual angel-food cake molds. They get their singular golden color and rich taste from the addition of four egg yolks (and no whites) in the batter. **MAKES 6**

FOR THE GINGER-POACHED FRUIT

- ³/₄ cup sugar
- 4 slices (¹/₈ inch each) fresh ginger (unpeeled)
- 4 whole allspice berries
- ³/₄ cup water
- 1 cup diced pineapple
- 1 cup diced mango (from 2 small pitted mangoes)
- 1 tablespoon golden rum

FOR THE CAKES

- ¹/₂ cup (1 stick) unsalted butter, room temperature, plus more for pan
- 2 cups sifted all-purpose flour, plus more for pan
- 1³/₄ teaspoons baking powder
- ¹/₄ teaspoon baking soda
- ¹/₂ teaspoon salt
- ¹/₈ teaspoon freshly grated nutmeg
- 1 cup sugar
- 4 large egg yolks
- 1¹/₂ teaspoons vanilla extract
- ²/₃ cup buttermilk

FOR SERVING

- 2 pints coconut sorbet

1. Make the ginger-poached fruit: Bring sugar, ginger, allspice, and the water to a boil in a medium saucepan, stirring; cook 1 minute. Add pineapple, mango, and rum; return to a boil. Remove from heat; let cool 1 hour. Discard ginger and allspice. (Fruit in syrup can be refrigerated in an airtight container up to 1 week.)

2. Make the cakes: Preheat oven to 350°F. Butter cups of a 6-cake mini angel-food mold; dust with flour, tapping out excess. Whisk together flour, baking powder, baking soda, salt, and nutmeg until combined.

3. With an electric mixer on medium-high speed, beat butter and sugar until pale and fluffy, about 3 minutes. Beat in egg yolks, 1 at a time. Beat in vanilla. Add flour mixture in 3 batches, alternating with 2 batches of buttermilk; beat until just combined.

4. Using a pastry bag fitted only with a coupler, pipe dough into molds, filling halfway. Bake until cakes are golden and spring back when touched, about 25 minutes. Transfer pan to a wire rack to cool 10 minutes. Run a knife around edges of cakes to loosen; turn out onto rack to cool completely.

5. To serve, cut out a bit from the top of each cake to make a hollow for sorbet. Place a scoop of sorbet on each plate. Flip cakes; place hollow over sorbet. Top each with another scoop of sorbet, spoon fruit and syrup on top, and serve immediately.

Coffee Cakes

These treats, with their crumbly toppings, are named for the drink they pair with so well. European immigrants are to thank for the tradition of enjoying sweet baked goods with coffee and conversation ("klatsch," as in "kaffeeklatsch," means "gossip"). Bake one of these cakes and linger over breakfast, brunch, or any afternoon get-together with friends or family—and a cup (or two) of freshly brewed coffee.

WILD-BLUEBERRY BUCKLE, PAGE 107

New York–Style Crumb Cake

Make crumb cake from scratch just once, and chances are slim that you'll even think of buying a boxed version again. This one hits all the right notes—rich buttermilk cake topped with a thick layer of sugary, buttery, cinnamon-spiked crumbs. To mix things up just a bit, try sandwiching a cup of fruit jam between the batter and the topping before baking.

SERVES 10 TO 12

FOR THE CRUMB TOPPING

- 3½ cups cake flour (not self-rising)
- ⅔ cup granulated sugar
- ⅔ cup packed dark brown sugar
- 1½ teaspoons ground cinnamon
- ½ teaspoon coarse salt
- 1¼ cups (2½ sticks) unsalted butter, melted

FOR THE CAKE

- ¾ cup (1½ sticks) unsalted butter, room temperature, plus more for pan
- 2½ cups cake flour (not self-rising)
- ½ teaspoon baking soda
- ½ teaspoon coarse salt
- 1 cup granulated sugar
- 2 large whole eggs plus 2 large egg yolks
- 1 teaspoon vanilla extract
- ⅔ cup buttermilk
- Confectioners' sugar, for dusting

1. Make the crumb topping: Mix together flour, granulated sugar, brown sugar, cinnamon, and salt in a medium bowl. Pour warm melted butter over mixture; using your hands, mix until medium to large clumps form.

2. Make the cake: Preheat oven to 325°F. Butter a 9-by-13-inch baking pan, line with parchment with overhang on both long sides, and butter parchment. Whisk together flour, baking soda, and salt in a medium bowl.

3. With an electric mixer on medium speed, beat butter and granulated sugar until pale and fluffy, about 2 minutes. Add eggs and yolks, 1 at a time, beating well after each addition; mix in vanilla. Add flour mixture in 3 additions, alternating with 2 additions of buttermilk; beat until well combined.

4. Transfer batter to prepared pan; spread evenly with an offset spatula. Sprinkle crumb-topping mixture evenly over batter. Bake until golden brown and a cake tester comes out clean, about 1 hour. Transfer pan to a wire rack to cool slightly, about 15 minutes. Dust with confectioners' sugar. Transfer cake, with parchment, to wire rack. Serve warm or at room temperature. (Cake can be stored at room temperature, covered, up to 5 days.)

Ultimate Streusel Cake

One generous-size coffee cake is easier to make for brunch than a bunch of muffins or scones. Here, a ring of pecan streusel is concealed inside the golden-brown exterior of a sour cream cake. Keep the streusel mixture in the freezer until ready to top the loaves; this will prevent it from melting too quickly in the hot oven. **SERVES 10 TO 12**

FOR THE STREUSEL

1½ cups lightly packed light brown sugar

½ cup granulated sugar

1½ cups chopped pecans

½ cup all-purpose flour

1 tablespoon ground cinnamon

Pinch of ground cloves

½ cup (1 stick) butter, room temperature

FOR THE CAKE

½ cup plus 2 tablespoons (1¼ sticks) unsalted butter, room temperature, plus more for pan

2½ cups all-purpose flour

1 teaspoon baking soda

1 teaspoon baking powder

¼ teaspoon coarse salt

1 cup granulated sugar

3 large eggs

1 teaspoon vanilla extract

1¼ cups sour cream (or 1 cup buttermilk)

FOR THE GLAZE

2½ cups sifted confectioners' sugar

¼ cup milk

1. Make the streusel: Combine brown sugar, granulated sugar, pecans, flour, cinnamon, and cloves in a medium bowl. Cut in butter with a pastry blender or rub in with your fingers until mixture is well combined and crumbly. Cover and refrigerate until ready to use (up to 3 days).

2. Make the cake: Preheat oven to 350°F. Butter a 10-inch Bundt pan. Sift together flour, baking soda, baking powder, and salt into a bowl.

3. With an electric mixer on medium speed, beat butter and granulated sugar until pale and fluffy, about 4 minutes. Add eggs, 1 at a time, beating well after each addition. Add vanilla; beat until combined. Add the flour mixture in 2 batches, alternating with the sour cream and beginning and ending with the flour; beat just until well combined.

4. Transfer half the batter to prepared pan. Make a well in the batter; crumble two thirds of the streusel mixture into the well. Top with remaining batter, smoothing top with an offset spatula. Sprinkle remaining streusel evenly over top. Bake until golden brown and a cake tester comes out clean, about 60 minutes. Transfer to a wire rack to cool 10 minutes; turn out cake onto rack to cool.

5. Meanwhile, make the glaze: In a medium bowl, whisk together confectioners' sugar and milk until well combined. Drizzle icing over slightly warm cake before serving.

Mini Almond Coffee Cakes

Each of these little treats is like the very best coffee cake, rendered in miniature. Toasted almonds are added to the brown-sugar streusel layered in the middle; browned butter flavors the glaze on top. Bake a couple of batches for a bake sale, or serve them as part of a brunch buffet. To make one large cake, double the recipe, and bake the batter in a ten-inch Bundt pan for forty-five to fifty minutes. **MAKES 6**

½ cup plus 2 tablespoons (1¼ sticks) unsalted butter, room temperature, plus more for pans

1½ cups all-purpose flour, plus more for pans

⅓ cup whole almonds

¼ cup plus 2 tablespoons sliced almonds

5 tablespoons packed light brown sugar

1 teaspoon ground cinnamon

⅛ teaspoon freshly grated nutmeg

1 teaspoon baking powder

½ teaspoon baking soda

¼ teaspoon salt

¾ cup granulated sugar

1 large egg

3 teaspoons vanilla extract

¾ cup sour cream or plain yogurt

2 cups sifted confectioners' sugar

3 to 4 tablespoons milk

1. Preheat oven to 350°F. Generously butter six 1-cup mini Bundt pans; dust with flour, tapping out excess. Spread whole almonds on a rimmed baking sheet; toast until fragrant, about 10 minutes. Meanwhile, spread sliced almonds in a single layer on another baking sheet; toast until golden brown, 5 to 7 minutes. Let cool; chop whole almonds.

2. In a medium bowl, combine chopped almonds, brown sugar, cinnamon, and nutmeg. Into another bowl, sift together flour, baking powder, baking soda, and salt.

3. With an electric mixer on medium speed, beat 6 tablespoons butter and the granulated sugar until light and fluffy, about 3 minutes. Add egg; beat until combined. Add 1 teaspoon vanilla; beat until smooth. Add flour mixture in 3 batches, alternating with 2 batches of sour cream; beat to combine.

4. Fill each Bundt pan with 3 tablespoons batter; spread evenly with an offset spatula. Sprinkle each with 2 tablespoons almond-spice mixture. Divide remaining batter among pans.

5. Bake until cakes are golden brown and a cake tester comes out clean, 20 to 25 minutes. Transfer pans to a wire rack to cool 10 minutes. Turn out cakes onto rack to cool completely.

6. Set rack over a rimmed baking sheet. Heat remaining 4 tablespoons butter over medium-high until color turns nut-brown, about 5 minutes. Pour butter into a medium bowl, leaving behind any dark sediment. Stir in confectioners' sugar, remaining 2 teaspoons vanilla, and 3 tablespoons milk until smooth; add an additional tablespoon milk, if necessary, so glaze is pourable. Drizzle glaze over cakes, and sprinkle with toasted sliced almonds before serving.

Cinnamon Streusel Coffee Cake

With streusel on top and layered within, plus a basic milk glaze drizzled on top, this is about as close to a classic example of a Swedish coffee cake as you are likely to find. To make a banana-coconut variation, substitute walnuts for the pecans, and add about three mashed ripe bananas and ¾ cup unsweetened shredded coconut to the batter at the end of step 3. Bake and glaze as directed. **SERVES 12**

FOR THE STREUSEL

- 1¾ cups all-purpose flour
- 1 cup packed light brown sugar
- 1¼ teaspoons ground cinnamon
- 1 teaspoon coarse salt
- ¾ cup (1½ sticks) cold unsalted butter, cut into small pieces
- 1½ cups coarsely chopped toasted walnuts (see page 344)

FOR THE CAKE

- ½ cup (1 stick) unsalted butter, room temperature, plus more for pan
- 2 cups all-purpose flour
- 1¼ teaspoons baking powder
- ½ teaspoon baking soda
- ½ teaspoon coarse salt
- 1 cup granulated sugar
- 2 large eggs
- 1½ teaspoons vanilla extract
- 1 cup sour cream

FOR THE GLAZE

- 1 cup confectioners' sugar
- 2 tablespoons whole milk

1. Make the streusel: Mix together flour, ¾ cup brown sugar, 1 teaspoon cinnamon, and the salt. Cut in butter with a pastry blender or rub in with your fingers until small to medium clumps form. Mix in ½ cup nuts. Refrigerate topping until ready to use. Make the streusel center: Mix together remaining ¼ cup brown sugar, ¼ teaspoon cinnamon, and 1 cup nuts; reserve for layering in center of batter.

2. Make the cake: Preheat oven to 350°F. Butter a 9-inch tube pan with a removable bottom. Sift flour, baking powder, baking soda, and salt into a medium bowl.

3. With an electric mixer on medium, beat butter and granulated sugar until pale and fluffy, about 2 minutes. Add eggs, 1 at a time, beating well after each addition. Beat in vanilla. Add flour mixture in 3 batches, alternating with 2 batches of sour cream; beat until well combined.

4. Transfer half the batter to prepared pan. Sprinkle streusel evenly over batter. Top with remaining batter; spread evenly with an offset spatula. Sprinkle streusel topping evenly over batter.

5. Bake until cake is golden brown and a cake tester comes out clean, about 55 minutes. Transfer pan to a wire rack to cool completely. Remove cake from pan; transfer to a parchment-lined work surface or serving platter.

6. Make the glaze: Mix together confectioners' sugar and milk. Drizzle over cake, allowing glaze to drip down sides. Let set 5 minutes before serving. (Cake can be stored at room temperature, covered, up to 5 days.)

Applesauce Coffee Cake

Making this rustic coffee cake is a great way to use up an abundance of apples (especially any bruised or otherwise imperfect ones) after a trip to the orchard. Some are used to make an applesauce that is mixed into the batter; others are sliced and layered atop the cake before baking, along with a delicious oat-cinnamon crumb topping. You can use store-bought unsweetened applesauce in a pinch. **SERVES 10 TO 12**

FOR THE CRUMB TOPPING

- 4 tablespoons unsalted butter, room temperature
- ½ cup packed dark brown sugar
- ¼ cup old-fashioned rolled oats
- ¾ teaspoon ground cinnamon
- ¼ teaspoon salt
- ½ cup chopped toasted pecans (see page 344)

FOR THE CAKE

- ½ cup (1 stick) unsalted butter, room temperature, plus more for pan
- 2 cups all-purpose flour, plus more for pan
- 1 teaspoon baking soda
- ½ teaspoon freshly grated nutmeg
- ⅛ teaspoon ground cloves
- 2 teaspoons ground cinnamon
- ¾ teaspoon salt
- 1 cup granulated sugar
- ½ cup packed light brown sugar
- 4 large eggs
- Apple-Cider Applesauce (page 341) or 1½ cups store-bought applesauce
- 1½ cups chopped toasted pecans (see page 344)
- 2 small, juicy apples, such as McIntosh, peeled, cored, and cut into ¼-inch-thick wedges

1. Preheat oven to 350°F. Make the crumb topping: Mix together butter, dark brown sugar, oats, cinnamon, and salt in a medium bowl until crumbly. Stir in pecans.

2. Make the cake: Butter a 10-inch tube pan with a removable bottom; dust with flour, tapping out excess. Sift together flour, baking soda, nutmeg, cloves, cinnamon, and salt into a medium bowl. With an electric mixer on medium speed, beat butter and both sugars until smooth, about 3 minutes. Add eggs, 1 at a time, beating well after each addition. Reduce speed to low; mix in applesauce and then flour mixture. Stir in pecans.

3. Transfer batter to prepared pan; sprinkle crumb topping over batter. Arrange apples on top, tucking some into batter. Bake until a cake tester comes out clean, about 70 minutes. Transfer to a wire rack to cool completely. (Cake can be stored at room temperature, covered with plastic wrap, up to 3 days.)

Plum-Nectarine Buckle

Of all the old-fashioned desserts with odd names—think grunts, slumps, betties, and cobblers—a buckle is the closest thing to a cake, with its fruit-heavy batter and streusel topping. As this dessert bakes, cracks and crevices form, "buckling" the batter as it rises (hence the name). Here the batter, lightly scented with vanilla and allspice, is covered with wedges of plums and nectarines, but you could substitute other stone fruits or berries, or try a combination of the two. **SERVES 8 TO 10**

FOR THE STREUSEL

6	tablespoons unsalted butter, room temperature
1/4	cup packed light brown sugar
1	cup all-purpose flour
	Pinch of salt

FOR THE CAKE

6	tablespoons unsalted butter, melted
1 1/2	cups all-purpose flour
1	cup plus 2 tablespoons granulated sugar
1 1/2	teaspoons baking powder
1/8	teaspoon ground allspice
3/4	teaspoon plus a pinch of salt
1	large egg
2/3	cup milk
1	teaspoon vanilla extract
3/4	pound plums, halved, pitted, and cut into 1/2-inch-thick wedges (2 cups)
3/4	pound nectarines, halved, pitted, and cut into 1/2-inch-thick wedges (2 cups)
1	tablespoon fresh lemon juice

1. Make the streusel: With an electric mixer on medium speed, beat butter and brown sugar until creamy, about 3 minutes. Stir in flour and salt. Work mixture through fingers until it forms coarse crumbs ranging in size from peas to gum balls.

2. Make the cake: Preheat oven to 350°F. Brush a 9-inch square cake pan or 10-inch cast-iron skillet with 2 tablespoons butter. Whisk together flour, 3/4 cup granulated sugar, the baking powder, allspice, and 3/4 teaspoon salt in a medium bowl.

3. Whisk together egg, milk, vanilla, and remaining 4 tablespoons butter in another medium bowl. Add to flour mixture; stir to combine. Transfer batter to prepared pan, spreading with an offset spatula.

4. Toss plums, nectarines, lemon juice, remaining 1/4 cup plus 2 table-spoons sugar, and pinch of salt in a large bowl. Scatter fruit mixture evenly over batter. Sprinkle with crumble topping. Bake until a cake tester comes out with moist crumbs attached, about 1 hour 15 minutes. Transfer to a wire rack to cool 1 hour before serving.

Wild-Blueberry Buckle

Because this recipe was developed at Martha's home in Maine, it makes good use of wild blueberries, which are smaller and have a more concentrated flavor than more widely available cultivated varieties. If you can't find fresh wild berries, use thawed frozen blueberries or cultivated ones from the supermarket or farmers' market. **SERVES 8 TO 10**

FOR THE STREUSEL

- 1 teaspoon ground cinnamon
- ¼ teaspoon salt
- ¼ cup packed light brown sugar
- 1 cup all-purpose flour
- 6 tablespoons unsalted butter, room temperature

FOR THE CAKE

- 4 tablespoons butter, room temperature, plus more for pan
- 1½ cups all-purpose flour, plus more for pan
- 1½ teaspoons baking powder
- ¼ teaspoon coarse salt
- ¾ cup granulated sugar
- 1 egg
- 1 teaspoon vanilla extract
- ⅔ cup milk
- 5 cups wild or cultivated fresh blueberries

1. Make the streusel: In a medium bowl, mix cinnamon, salt, brown sugar, and flour together. Mix in butter until mixture forms fine crumbs. Using your hands, squeeze together most of mixture to form large clumps. Refrigerate in an airtight container until ready to use (up to 3 days).

2. Make the cake: Preheat oven to 350°F. Butter a 10-inch springform pan; dust with flour, tapping out excess. In a medium bowl, whisk together flour, baking powder, and salt.

3. With an electric mixer on medium speed, beat butter and granulated sugar until pale and fluffy, about 3 minutes. Reduce speed to low; add egg and vanilla. Add flour mixture in 2 batches, alternating with the milk and beginning and ending with the flour; beat until just combined. Stir in berries.

4. Transfer batter to prepared pan; sprinkle topping over batter. Bake until a cake tester comes out clean, about 60 minutes. Transfer to a wire rack to cool 10 minutes. Run a knife around edge of pan to loosen. Remove side of pan. Let cool 15 minutes before serving.

Meyer-Lemon Coffee Cake

If you've never baked with Meyer lemons, this cake is an excellent place to start (you'll need about ten). Thought to be a cross between a lemon and a mandarin orange, the fruit is slightly sweeter and more floral than regular lemons. Here, they are sliced extremely thin (near-transparent) and blanched before being layered in the batter. A mandoline (or other adjustable blade slicer) slices the lemons paper thin, but a well-sharpened chef's knife will also work. **SERVES 10 TO 12**

FOR THE STREUSEL

- 1¾ cups all-purpose flour
- ¾ cup packed light brown sugar
- 1 teaspoon coarse salt
- ¾ cup (1½ sticks) cold unsalted butter

FOR THE CAKE

- 5 Meyer lemons, cut into paper-thin slices, ends discarded
- ½ cup (1 stick) unsalted butter, room temperature, plus more for pan
- 2 cups all-purpose flour
- 1 teaspoon baking powder
- 1 teaspoon baking soda
- 1½ teaspoons coarse salt
- 1 cup granulated sugar
- 3 tablespoons finely grated Meyer-lemon zest (from 4 to 5 lemons)
- 2 large eggs
- 1 teaspoon vanilla extract
- 1 cup sour cream

FOR THE GLAZE

- 1 cup confectioners' sugar
- 3 to 4 tablespoons Meyer-lemon juice

1. Make the streusel: Mix together flour, brown sugar, and salt. Cut in butter with a pastry blender or rub in with your fingers until mixture forms clumps. Cover and refrigerate until ready to use (up to 3 days).

2. Make the cake: Cook lemon slices in a medium saucepan of simmering water for 1 minute. Drain; repeat. Arrange lemon slices in a single layer on a parchment-lined baking sheet.

3. Preheat oven to 350°F. Butter a 9-inch tube pan with a removable bottom. Sift together flour, baking powder, baking soda, and salt into a medium bowl. With an electric mixer on medium speed, beat butter, granulated sugar, and zest until pale and fluffy, about 2 minutes. Add eggs, 1 at a time, beating well after each addition; then add vanilla. Reduce speed to low. Add flour mixture in 3 batches, alternating with 2 batches of sour cream; beat until just combined.

4. Transfer half the batter to prepared pan. Arrange half the lemon slices in a single layer over the batter. Add remaining batter; spread evenly with an offset spatula. Cover with remaining lemon slices in a single layer. Sprinkle chilled streusel evenly over top.

5. Bake until cake is golden brown and a cake tester comes out clean, about 55 minutes. Transfer pan to a wire rack set over a parchment-lined baking sheet to cool 15 minutes. Run a knife around the edges of cake to loosen. Let cool on rack 15 minutes more. Run a knife around the center tube. Slide 2 wide spatulas between the bottom of the cake and the pan, and lift cake to remove from the center tube. Let cool completely on rack.

6. Make the glaze: Just before serving, stir together confectioners' sugar and lemon juice in a medium bowl. Drizzle over cooled cake, letting excess drip down the sides. Let glaze set before slicing, about 5 minutes. Cake can be stored at room temperature, covered, up to 3 days. (The lemon flavor will intensify with time.)

Mini Cherry-Pecan Streusel Loaves

Coffee cakes can come in all shapes and sizes, including these miniature loaves. Try swapping in equal amounts of other dried fruits and nuts for the cherries and pecans. **MAKES 6**

FOR THE STREUSEL

- 1/2 cup all-purpose flour
- 1/2 cup packed light brown sugar
- 1/2 cup coarsely chopped pecans
- 4 tablespoons cold unsalted butter, cut into small pieces

FOR THE CAKE

- 1/2 cup (1 stick) unsalted butter, melted, plus more for pans
- 2 1/2 cups all-purpose flour, plus more for pans
- 1 1/2 teaspoons baking powder
- 3/4 teaspoon coarse salt
- 1/2 teaspoon baking soda
- 1 1/2 cups granulated sugar
- 1 cup sour cream
- 2 large eggs
- 1/2 teaspoon vanilla extract
- 1 1/2 cups dried cherries
- 1 cup coarsely chopped pecans

1. Make the streusel: In a bowl, mix together flour, brown sugar, pecans, and butter with fingertips until moist clumps form. Cover and freeze until ready to use.

2. Make the cake: Preheat oven to 350°F. Butter six 5¾-by-3-inch mini loaf pans; dust with flour, tapping out excess. In a medium bowl, whisk together flour, baking powder, salt, and baking soda. In a large bowl, whisk together butter, granulated sugar, sour cream, eggs, and vanilla until smooth. Mix in dry ingredients until moistened. Fold in dried cherries and pecans.

3. Divide batter evenly among prepared pans; spread to fill corners and smooth tops with an offset spatula. Place pans on a rimmed baking sheet. Bake 15 minutes, then remove from oven; quickly sprinkle loaves with streusel topping, dividing evenly.

4. Return loaves to oven, and bake until golden and a cake tester comes out with only a few moist crumbs attached, 25 to 30 minutes. Transfer pans to a wire rack to cool 10 minutes, and turn out cakes onto rack to cool completely.

Sticky Buckwheat Cake

Famously compatible baking ingredients—apples, raisins, pecans, cinnamon, and brown sugar—are combined to create a topping for this rustic ginger cake made heartier with buckwheat flour. It's best when baked in a well-seasoned cast-iron skillet, inverted, and served while the cake is still warm, so you can get every last drop of the syrupy glaze.

SERVES 8 TO 10

FOR THE TOPPING

- ½ cup raisins
- ½ cup brandy
- 1 tablespoon unsalted butter
- ½ cup packed dark brown sugar
- 1½ teaspoons ground cinnamon
- ⅔ cup light corn syrup
- ½ cup coarsely chopped pecans (1¾ ounces)
- 1 apple, peeled, cored, and cut into ½-inch cubes

FOR THE CAKE

- ¾ cup (1½ sticks) unsalted butter, room temperature
- 1¼ cups packed light brown sugar
- 3 large eggs
- 1¾ cups all-purpose flour
- 1 cup buckwheat flour
- 1½ teaspoons ground ginger
- 1 tablespoon baking powder
- ½ teaspoon salt
- 1 cup milk
- 1 tablespoon peeled and grated fresh ginger

1. Make the topping: In a bowl, combine raisins and brandy; let stand until raisins are plump, about 20 minutes. Drain raisins; discard liquid.

2. In a 10-inch seasoned cast-iron skillet, melt butter over medium heat. Sprinkle with brown sugar and cinnamon; remove from heat. Drizzle with corn syrup. Strew pecans, apple, and raisins over syrup.

3. Make the cake: Preheat oven to 350°F. With an electric mixer on medium speed, beat butter until smooth, about 2 minutes. Add brown sugar; beat until pale and fluffy. Add eggs, 1 at a time, beating well after each addition.

4. Into a large bowl, sift together both flours, the ground ginger, baking powder, and salt. In another bowl, combine milk and fresh ginger. Add flour mixture to butter mixture in 3 batches, alternating with 2 batches of milk mixture, and beating well after each addition.

5. Pour batter over topping in prepared skillet; smooth top with an offset spatula. Bake until golden brown and a cake tester comes out clean, about 50 minutes. Transfer to a wire rack to cool 5 minutes before inverting onto serving platter. Serve warm or at room temperature.

Almond-Berry Coffee Cake

One way to change up coffee cake is to incorporate seasonal fruit into the mix. Here, fresh raspberries are folded into blackberry jam and then layered with the batter in the pan, so the berry mixture forms a ring in the middle. Other fruit and jam combinations would also work, such as diced peaches and apricot jam, or diced plums and Concord grape jam.

SERVES 10 TO 12

FOR THE STREUSEL

- 1 cup all-purpose flour
- 2/3 cup packed light brown sugar
- 1/4 teaspoon ground cinnamon
- 1/2 teaspoon salt
- 3/4 cup sliced almonds, toasted (see page 344)
- 1/2 cup (1 stick) unsalted butter, room temperature
- 1/4 teaspoon almond extract

FOR THE CAKE

- 2 1/2 cups all-purpose flour
- 1 teaspoon baking powder
- 1/2 teaspoon baking soda
- 1/2 teaspoon salt
- 6 ounces fresh raspberries (about 1 1/2 cups)
- 2/3 cup blackberry jam
- 3/4 cup (1 1/2 sticks) unsalted butter, room temperature
- 1 1/4 cups granulated sugar
- 1 1/4 teaspoons finely grated lemon zest
- 3 large eggs
- 2 teaspoons vanilla extract
- 1 1/4 cups sour cream

1. Make the streusel: Whisk together flour, brown sugar, cinnamon, salt, and almonds in a medium bowl. Mix in butter with your fingers until mixture forms coarse crumbs. Sprinkle with almond extract; toss to combine.

2. Make the cake: Preheat oven to 350°F. Butter a 10-inch tube pan with a removable bottom; dust with flour, tapping out excess. Place pan on a baking sheet. Sift together flour, baking powder, baking soda, and salt into a bowl. Fold raspberries into jam in another bowl.

3. With an electric mixer on medium-high speed, beat butter, granulated sugar, and zest until pale and fluffy, 3 to 4 minutes. Reduce speed to medium. Add eggs, 1 at a time, beating well after each addition and scraping down sides of bowl as needed. Mix in vanilla. Reduce speed to low. Add flour mixture in 2 batches, alternating with the sour cream and beginning and ending with the flour; beat until just combined.

4. Transfer half the batter to prepared pan. Mound berry mixture in a ring in center of batter. Top with remaining batter. Smooth top with an offset spatula. Sprinkle streusel over batter.

5. Bake until golden brown and a cake tester comes out clean, 65 to 70 minutes. Transfer pan to a wire rack to cool slightly, 10 to 15 minutes. Run a knife around edges of cake to loosen. Pull up on tube to lift cake from outer ring. Let cool on rack 15 minutes (with tube still attached to cake). Remove cake from tube, and cool completely on rack. (Cake can be stored at room temperature, covered, up to 3 days.)

Single Layers

Although these desserts keep a low profile, their flavors, charm, and versatility really stand out. Whatever you feel like, you'll find it here: lemon, chocolate, coconut, or apple; homespun or elegant; crunchy or gooey. None of these cakes takes much time or any special supplies to put together, so when you have a craving, just start baking.

MAPLE CAKE, PAGE 120

Rich Chocolate Cake

This dense, one-layer cake is great for beginners: It's supposed to look imperfect, and it is simply dusted with confectioners' sugar rather than frosted. It's heavenly served with coffee or caramel ice cream. **SERVES 8 TO 10**

1¾ cups (3½ sticks) unsalted butter, room temperature, cut into tablespoons, plus more for pan

12 ounces bittersweet chocolate, finely chopped

3 tablespoons water

12 large eggs, separated, room temperature

2 cups granulated sugar

2 teaspoons vanilla extract

1 tablespoon dark rum

¼ cup all-purpose flour

½ cup unsweetened cocoa powder

½ teaspoon salt

Confectioners' sugar, for dusting

1. Preheat oven to 325°F. Butter a 10-inch springform pan. Place chocolate and the water in a heatproof bowl set over (not in) a pan of simmering water. Stir until melted and smooth; let cool slightly.

2. With an electric mixer on high speed, beat egg yolks and sugar until pale and thick, about 3 minutes. Reduce speed to medium-low; add vanilla and rum. Raise speed to medium. Gradually add chocolate mixture and butter; mix until smooth. Transfer mixture to a large bowl. Sift flour, cocoa, and salt over top of mixture; gently but thoroughly fold into batter with a flexible spatula.

3. In the clean bowl of an electric mixer, beat egg whites until almost-stiff peaks form. Fold into chocolate mixture in 2 batches (do not overmix).

4. Carefully transfer batter to prepared pan and bake until puffed, cracked, and set, about 1 hour 20 minutes. Transfer pan to wire rack to cool completely. Just before serving, run a knife around edge, remove cake from pan, and dust with confectioners' sugar.

Maple Cake

The incomparable flavor of pure maple syrup is reason enough to make this sweet treat; that it is also quick to prepare is an added bonus. Maple syrup is marked and graded by its color, ranging from light to dark—the darker the color, the more intense the flavor. If you can find grade B, use it here for both the batter and the icing. **SERVES 16**

FOR THE CAKE

- 1 cup (2 sticks) unsalted butter, room temperature, plus more for pan
- 2½ cups all-purpose flour, plus more for pan
- 2 teaspoons baking powder
- ½ teaspoon baking soda
- ½ teaspoon coarse salt
- ¾ cup pure maple syrup
- ½ cup granulated sugar
- 2 large eggs
- 1 teaspoon vanilla extract
- ¾ cup sour cream

FOR THE ICING

- ⅓ cup pure maple syrup, plus more if needed
- 3 tablespoons unsalted butter, melted
- 2½ cups confectioners' sugar, plus more if needed

1. Make the cake: Preheat oven to 350°F. Butter a 9-inch square baking pan; line with parchment, and butter parchment. Dust with flour, tapping out excess. In a medium bowl, whisk together flour, baking powder, baking soda, and salt.

2. With an electric mixer on medium speed, beat butter, maple syrup, and granulated sugar until pale and fluffy, 3 to 5 minutes. Add eggs, 1 at a time, beating well after each addition; mix in vanilla.

3. Reduce mixer speed to low. Add flour mixture in 3 batches, alternating with 2 batches of sour cream; beat until just combined. Transfer batter to prepared pan; smooth top with an offset spatula. Bake until a cake tester comes out clean, about 40 minutes. Transfer pan to a wire rack to cool 10 minutes. Turn out cake onto rack to cool completely.

4. Make the icing: Combine maple syrup and butter in a bowl. Sift in confectioners' sugar, and whisk until combined. Adjust consistency with more syrup or sugar, if necessary. Spread maple icing over top of cake. Let set, at least 15 minutes, before serving.

Vanilla Sheet Cake with Malted-Chocolate Frosting

Sheet cakes, long a staple of bake sales and potlucks, are easy to make and even easier to transport. Be sure to let the cake cool completely before you frost it. Once frosted, the cake can be covered with plastic wrap and kept at room temperature up to three days. **SERVES 12**

FOR THE CAKE

- ½ cup (1 stick) plus 1 tablespoon unsalted butter, room temperature, plus more for pan
- 2¼ cups all-purpose flour, plus more for pan
- 2¼ teaspoons baking powder
- ¾ teaspoon baking soda
- ½ teaspoon salt
- 1 cup plus 2 tablespoons sugar
- 3 large eggs
- 1 cup buttermilk
- 1⅛ teaspoons vanilla extract

FOR THE FROSTING

- 3 tablespoons unsweetened cocoa powder
- 1¾ cups plus 2 tablespoons malted milk powder
- ¼ cup plus 2 tablespoons boiling water
- ¾ cup (1½ sticks) plus 1½ tablespoons unsalted butter, room temperature
- 10½ ounces milk chocolate, melted and cooled
- Pinch of salt
- Chopped malted milk balls (optional), for decorating

1. Make the cake: Preheat oven to 350°F. Lightly butter a 9-by-13-inch baking pan. Dust with flour, tapping out excess. In a large bowl, whisk together flour, baking powder, baking soda, and salt.

2. With an electric mixer on high speed, beat butter and sugar until pale and fluffy, about 5 minutes. Beat in eggs, 1 at a time, until combined. Reduce mixer speed to low. Add flour mixture in 3 batches, alternating with 2 batches of buttermilk; beat to combine, scraping down sides of bowl as needed. Beat in vanilla.

3. Transfer batter to prepared pan; smooth top with an offset spatula. Bake, rotating halfway through, until cake is golden and puffed and a cake tester comes out clean, about 30 minutes. Transfer pan to a wire rack to cool completely.

4. Meanwhile, make the frosting: In a medium bowl, whisk together cocoa and malted milk powders. Add the boiling water, whisk until smooth, and let cool. With mixer on high speed, beat butter until smooth. Add cocoa mixture; beat until combined. Add chocolate and salt. Raise mixer speed to medium-high; beat until frosting is smooth and peaks form, about 3 minutes. Spread frosting over cake; sprinkle with malted milk balls, if desired.

Breton Butter Cake

Made with little more than butter, flour, sugar, and eggs, this dessert hails from Brittany (the westernmost region in France). Baking the batter in a fluted tart pan creates an attractive profile; the signature crosshatch pattern on top is marked with the tines of a fork. We served ours with fresh strawberry compote spiked with Grand Marnier, but it's perfect all on its own. SERVES 8 TO 10

FOR THE CAKE

- 1 cup (2 sticks) unsalted butter, room temperature, plus more for pan
- 1 cup sugar
- 1 tablespoon vanilla extract
- 1 large whole egg, lightly beaten, plus 6 large egg yolks
- 2¾ cups all-purpose flour
- ¼ teaspoon salt

FOR THE COMPOTE

- 1½ pounds fresh strawberries, stemmed and cut lengthwise into slices
- 2 tablespoons Grand Marnier
- 1 tablespoon finely grated orange zest plus 1½ cups fresh orange juice, strained

1. Make the cake: Preheat oven to 350°F. With an electric mixer on medium speed, beat butter and sugar until pale and fluffy, about 6 minutes. Beat in vanilla and yolks, 1 at a time, beating well after each addition. Add flour and salt; beat just until combined (do not overmix).

2. Transfer batter to a 9-inch tart pan with a removable bottom; spread batter and smooth top with a small offset spatula. (If necessary, chill batter 10 minutes before smoothing.) Refrigerate 15 minutes.

3. Brush top with beaten egg, and mark a criss-cross pattern with a fork. Brush again with egg. Bake until cake is deep golden brown and edges pull away from sides of pan, about 50 minutes. Transfer pan to a wire rack to cool slightly.

4. While cake is baking, make the compote: Toss berries, Grand Marnier, and zest in a medium bowl; let stand 30 minutes. Bring juice to a boil in a small saucepan. Reduce heat; simmer until liquid is reduced to ¼ cup, about 20 minutes. Remove from heat; let cool. Pour over strawberries, and toss to combine.

5. Remove cake from pan and serve warm with strawberry compote.

MARKING THE CRISS-CROSS PATTERN

Lighter Chocolate Cake

Take heart: You can swap out the butter and eggs with oil and water to make a lightened—and vegan—version of devil's food cake that still feels sinful. It's finished with a thin layer of dark chocolate glaze; if you prefer, simply dust it with cocoa powder or confectioners' sugar, for a study in restrained extravagance. **SERVES 8 TO 10**

FOR THE CAKE

- 1 cup warm water
- $\frac{1}{2}$ cup unsweetened cocoa powder
- 1$\frac{1}{2}$ cups all-purpose flour
- 1 cup granulated sugar
- $\frac{3}{4}$ teaspoon baking soda
- $\frac{1}{2}$ teaspoon salt
- $\frac{1}{2}$ cup canola or safflower oil
- 1 tablespoon vanilla extract
- 2 teaspoons distilled white vinegar
- Vegetable oil cooking spray

FOR THE GLAZE

- 2 ounces dark chocolate (preferably at least 70 percent cacao), finely chopped
- $\frac{1}{2}$ cup confectioners' sugar, sifted
- 2 tablespoons water

1. Make the cake: Preheat oven to 375°F. Coat an 8-inch round cake pan with cooking spray. Whisk water and cocoa in a small bowl until smooth. Combine flour, sugar, baking soda, and salt in a large bowl; make a well in center. Add cocoa mixture, oil, and vanilla. Whisk until smooth. Whisk in vinegar.

2. Transfer batter to prepared pan. Bake until a cake tester comes out clean, 30 to 35 minutes. Transfer pan to a wire rack to cool 20 minutes. Run a knife around edge of cake to loosen; turn out onto rack to cool completely. Transfer cake to a serving plate or cake stand.

3. Make the glaze: Melt chocolate in a heatproof bowl set over (not in) a pan of simmering water, stirring until smooth. Let cool slightly.

4. Whisk together confectioners' sugar and water until smooth. Add melted chocolate in a slow, steady stream, whisking until thickened and spreadable. Immediately pour glaze onto center of cooled cake. Using an offset spatula, gently spread glaze over top and sides. Cake can be stored at room temperature, covered, up to 2 days.

Walnut-Olive Oil Cake

This recipe was originally developed for a lunch in a California olive grove. Nocello, a nut-flavored liqueur from Italy, complements the finely chopped walnuts in the batter. The other accompaniments—apple compote and crème fraîche—are entirely optional but highly recommended. **SERVES 8 TO 10**

FOR THE APPLE COMPOTE

- 3 pounds mixed apples, such as Granny Smith, Pink Lady, and Rome Beauty, peeled, cored, and cut into 1-inch chunks
- 2 tablespoons fresh lemon juice
- 1 tablespoon Calvados, apple brandy, or Cognac (optional)
- ¼ cup granulated sugar
- ¼ teaspoon ground cinnamon

FOR THE CAKE

- Unsalted butter, for pan
- 1½ cups unbleached all-purpose flour
- 2 teaspoons baking powder
- ¼ teaspoon coarse salt
- 3 large eggs, room temperature
- ¾ cup plus 2 tablespoons granulated sugar
- ⅓ cup extra-virgin olive oil
- ⅓ cup Italian walnut-and-hazelnut liqueur, such as Nocello
- ¾ cup walnut halves, toasted and finely chopped (see page 344)

FOR SERVING

- Confectioners' sugar, for dusting
- Crème fraîche (optional)

1. Make the apple compote: Combine apples, lemon juice, Calvados, granulated sugar, and cinnamon in a large pot. Cover; cook over low heat, stirring occasionally, until apples are tender, about 30 minutes. Remove from heat; let cool completely. Apple compote can be refrigerated in an airtight container up to 1 week.

2. Make the cake: Preheat oven to 350°F. Generously butter a 9-inch round cake pan. Sift flour, baking powder, and salt into a bowl. With an electric mixer on high speed, whisk eggs until light in color, about 2 minutes. Reduce speed to medium. Add granulated sugar; mix until mixture is pale and thick, about 4 minutes. Reduce speed to low; mix in oil and liqueur. Using a flexible spatula, gently fold in flour mixture in 3 batches, then fold in toasted walnuts.

3. Transfer batter to prepared pan. Bake until a cake tester comes out clean, about 20 minutes. Transfer pan to a wire rack to cool 10 minutes. Turn out cake onto rack to cool completely.

4. Serve cake dusted with confectioners' sugar, with apple compote and crème fraîche, if desired.

Honey Cake with Pears

This moist honey-infused cake, and its luscious topping of warm pears in honey syrup, is inspired by the Rosh Hashanah tradition of eating honey-dipped fruit to represent hope for a sweet year ahead. A generous dollop of cold whipped cream makes the perfect complement. For either a kosher or dairy-free version, substitute margarine for the butter and soy milk for the regular milk. **SERVES 8 TO 10**

FOR THE CAKE

Unsalted butter, for pan

1¾ cups all-purpose flour, plus more for dusting

¾ teaspoon baking powder

½ teaspoon baking soda

1 teaspoon coarse salt

½ teaspoon ground cinnamon

2 large eggs

½ cup granulated sugar

¼ cup packed light brown sugar

½ cup plus 2 tablespoons honey

½ cup milk

½ cup canola or safflower oil

½ teaspoon grated lemon zest

FOR THE CARAMELIZED PEARS

1 tablespoon unsalted butter

¼ cup granulated sugar

1¾ pounds red Anjou pears, cut into ½-inch-thick slices (or ¼-inch-thick slices if pears are firm)

¼ cup honey

FOR SERVING

Whipped Cream (page 333) or nondairy whipped topping (optional)

1. Make the cake: Preheat oven to 325°F. Butter a 10-inch springform pan; dust with flour, tapping out excess. Whisk together flour, baking powder, baking soda, salt, and cinnamon in a bowl. With an electric mixer on high speed, mix eggs and both sugars until pale and thick, about 3 minutes.

2. Whisk together honey, milk, oil, and zest. With mixer on low speed, add honey mixture to egg mixture; mix until combined, about 1 minute. Add half the flour mixture; mix until smooth. Mix in remaining flour mixture.

3. Transfer batter to prepared pan. Bake until dark golden brown and a cake tester comes out clean, about 50 minutes. Transfer pan to a wire rack to cool 15 minutes. Run a knife around edge of cake to loosen; carefully remove side of pan. Transfer cake to a serving platter.

4. Make the caramelized pears: Heat butter in a large skillet over medium. Add granulated sugar; cook, stirring, until almost dissolved, 1 to 2 minutes. Add pears; cook, stirring occasionally, until soft and just golden, 12 to 20 minutes. Pour in honey; cook, stirring, until pears are coated and very soft, 3 to 5 minutes.

5. Top cake with pears. Serve with whipped cream or topping, if desired.

Chocolate and Hazelnut Meringue Cake

A two-step baking process results in a meringue topping studded with nuts and chocolate chunks atop a rich chocolate cake. The cake is also delicious without the topping; bake it until crackling and slightly firm, 40 to 45 minutes. **SERVES 8 TO 10**

10 tablespoons unsalted butter, plus more for pan

All-purpose flour, for pan

3/4 cup packed light brown sugar

6 large whole eggs, separated, plus 4 large egg whites, room temperature

12 ounces bittersweet chocolate, melted and cooled, plus 4 ounces coarsely chopped (1 cup)

1 tablespoon vanilla extract

1 tablespoon dark rum

Pinch of salt

1 cup hazelnuts, toasted (see page 344), skinned, and coarsely chopped

1 tablespoon cornstarch

1/4 teaspoon cream of tartar

1 cup superfine sugar

1. Preheat oven to 350°F. Butter a 9-inch round springform pan; line with a parchment round, and butter parchment. Dust with flour, tapping out excess.

2. With an electric mixer on medium-high speed, beat butter and brown sugar until pale and smooth. Add egg yolks, 1 at a time, beating well after each addition, until mixture is fluffy. Add melted chocolate, vanilla, and rum; beat until combined.

3. In a clean mixer bowl, with mixer on high speed, whisk 6 egg whites and the salt until soft peaks form, about 2 minutes. Stir one third of egg whites into chocolate mixture. Using a flexible spatula, fold in remaining beaten egg whites just until combined. Transfer batter to prepared pan; bake 25 minutes.

4. Meanwhile, combine hazelnuts, chopped chocolate, and cornstarch in a small bowl. In a clean mixer bowl, with mixer on high speed, whisk remaining 4 egg whites and the cream of tartar until frothy. With mixer running, slowly add superfine sugar; continue beating until stiff peaks form, about 8 minutes. Fold in hazelnut mixture.

5. Using an offset spatula, spread meringue mixture over top of cake. Bake until meringue is lightly browned and crisp, 25 to 30 minutes. Transfer pan to a wire rack to cool 10 minutes. Run a knife around edge of cake to loosen; release sides of pan. Let cool about 30 minutes more before slicing and serving warm.

SPREADING MERINGUE OVER THE CAKE

Applesauce Cake

Preparing your own applesauce may seem like a needless step, but it makes all the difference in the flavor of this one-layer cake, and it's not at all difficult to do. Using a combination of apples produces a sauce with more complexity. The recipe used here yields just a bit more applesauce than you will need for the cake; use the extra as a topping for pancakes or as a side dish for savory chops and roasts. **SERVES 8**

FOR THE CAKE

- ½ cup (1 stick) unsalted butter, room temperature, plus more for pan
- 1½ cups all-purpose flour, plus more for pan
- 1 teaspoon baking soda
- ½ teaspoon salt
- ¾ teaspoon ground cinnamon
- ½ plus ⅛ teaspoon ground cardamom
- 1 cup packed light brown sugar
- 2 tablespoons honey
- 1 large egg
- 1 cup Apple-Cider Applesauce (page 341) or store-bought chunky applesauce

FOR THE GLAZE

- 3 tablespoons apple cider
- 1¾ cups confectioners' sugar
- Dried Apple Slices, for garnish (see page 327)

1. Make the cake: Preheat oven to 350°F. Butter an 8-inch round cake pan; line with a parchment round. Butter parchment; dust with flour, tapping out excess. In a large bowl, whisk together flour, baking soda, salt, cinnamon, and cardamom.

2. With an electric mixer on medium-high speed, beat butter, brown sugar, and honey until pale and fluffy, 3 to 5 minutes. Add egg; beat until combined. Reduce mixer speed to low; gradually add flour mixture and beat just until combined. Beat in applesauce.

3. Transfer batter to prepared pan; smooth top with an offset spatula. Bake until a cake tester comes out clean, but slightly wet, about 50 minutes. Transfer pan to a wire rack to cool 10 minutes. Turn out cake onto rack to cool completely.

4. Make the glaze: Whisk together apple cider and confectioners' sugar until smooth and pourable. Place cake, still on rack, over a rimmed baking sheet. Pour glaze over cake. Garnish with dried apple slices.

Flourless Chocolate-Espresso Cake

These days, everyone needs a good gluten-free cake recipe. This one is bound to be kept in heavy rotation. **SERVES 8**

FOR THE CAKE

- 3 tablespoons unsalted butter, plus more for pan
- 6 ounces bittersweet chocolate (preferably 70 percent cacao), chopped
- 6 large eggs, separated, room temperature
- 1 cup sugar
- 3 tablespoons instant espresso powder
- ¼ teaspoon coarse salt
- 1 tablespoon vanilla extract

FOR THE GLAZE

- 3 ounces bittersweet chocolate, chopped
- 1½ tablespoons unsalted butter
- 2 teaspoons vanilla extract
- ⅓ cup heavy cream
- ⅓ cup sugar
- 1 tablespoon instant espresso powder
- ¼ teaspoon coarse salt

FOR SERVING

- Ice cream (optional)

1. Make the cake: Preheat oven to 350°F. Butter bottom of a 9-inch springform pan; line with a parchment round. Melt butter and chocolate in a heatproof bowl set over (not in) a pan of simmering water.

2. With an electric mixer on medium-high speed, whisk egg yolks with ½ cup sugar until thick and pale, about 3 minutes. Add espresso powder and salt; whisk about 1 minute. Add vanilla and the chocolate mixture; whisk about 1 minute more.

3. In the clean bowl of an electric mixer, whisk egg whites on medium-high speed until foamy. Raise mixer speed to high. Slowly add remaining ½ cup sugar, whisking until stiff peaks form, about 5 minutes. Using a flexible spatula, fold whites into chocolate mixture in 3 batches.

4. Transfer batter to prepared pan. Bake until set, 40 to 45 minutes. Transfer pan to a wire rack to cool completely. Remove side of pan. Carefully transfer cake to a serving plate.

5. Make the glaze: Place chocolate, butter, and vanilla in a heatproof bowl. Bring remaining ingredients to a boil in a small saucepan, stirring to dissolve sugar and espresso powder; pour over chocolate mixture. Whisk until smooth. Serve cake with warm glaze and scoops of ice cream, if desired.

Orange-Yogurt Cake

Yogurt cake deserves to be as well known in the United States as it is in France. It's easy to prepare—two steps and you're done—and lighter than American pound cakes (but just as tasty). This one is flavored with orange and a touch of vanilla extract. **SERVES 8**

Unsalted butter, for pan

2 large oranges

1 cup all-purpose flour

½ cup plus 3 tablespoons granulated sugar

½ teaspoon baking powder

⅛ teaspoon baking soda

Pinch of salt

½ cup plain whole-milk yogurt

¼ cup canola or safflower oil

1 large egg

½ teaspoon vanilla extract

Confectioners' sugar, for dusting

1. Preheat oven to 350°F. Butter an 8-inch round cake pan. Finely grate zest of 1 orange to yield 1 teaspoon, then remove remaining zest in long strips and reserve for garnish. Peel both oranges; working over a bowl to catch the juices, use a paring knife to release whole segments from membranes. Squeeze membranes into bowl to extract juice; reserve 1 tablespoon.

2. Into a large bowl, sift together flour, ½ cup plus 2 tablespoons granulated sugar, the baking powder, baking soda, and salt. In a separate bowl, whisk together yogurt, oil, grated orange zest and juice, egg, and vanilla. Stir yogurt mixture into flour mixture until just combined. Transfer batter to prepared pan. Bake until a cake tester comes out clean, about 25 minutes. Transfer pan to a wire rack to cool completely.

3. Place reserved orange zest strips in a bowl and stir in orange segments and remaining 1 tablespoon granulated sugar. Remove cake from pan, dust with confectioners' sugar, and garnish with some of the orange mixture. Serve remaining citrus alongside.

Flourless Pecan Torte

Whipped egg whites and ground pecans stand in for flour and leavening in this cake. To make it kosher for Passover, use margarine instead of butter in the lemon curd, and omit the confectioners' sugar on top. Or, make your own confectioners' sugar by pulsing a cup of granulated sugar with a tablespoon of potato starch in a food processor until powdery.

SERVES 8 TO 10

9 large eggs, separated, room temperature

1½ cups granulated sugar

1 tablespoon finely grated lemon zest, plus more for garnish

1 teaspoon vanilla extract

1 teaspoon salt

12 ounces pecans, toasted (see page 344) and finely ground (3 cups)

Confectioners' sugar, for dusting (see note, above)

Lemon Curd, for serving (page 332)

Mixed berries, for serving

1. Preheat oven to 350°F. With an electric mixer on medium-high speed, whisk egg yolks, granulated sugar, zest, vanilla, and salt until pale and thickened, about 4 minutes. Gently fold in pecans with a flexible spatula.

2. In a clean mixer bowl, with mixer on high speed, whisk egg whites until stiff but not dry peaks form, then fold whites into yolk mixture.

3. Transfer batter to a 10-inch springform pan. Bake until golden brown, about 60 minutes (if top browns too quickly, tent with foil). Transfer pan to a wire rack to cool 30 minutes. Run a knife around edge of pan to loosen. Remove side of pan. Let cool completely. Dust with confectioners' sugar, garnish with zest, and serve with curd and berries.

Poppy-Seed Torte

The word *torte* can refer to any number of Austrian cakes. There are single-layer tortes and multilayer tortes, flourless tortes, tortes glazed with chocolate ganache, and tortes dusted with confectioners' sugar. The poppy-seed torte, or *Mohntorte*, is among the best-known examples. It needs little adornment, but for an authentic Viennese experience, serve a slice *mit schlag* (with unsweetened whipped cream)—and the essential strong cup of coffee. **SERVES 6 TO 8**

Unsalted butter, for pan

3 tablespoons all-purpose flour, plus more for pan

½ cup poppy seeds

3 tablespoons finely ground toasted walnuts (see page 344)

½ teaspoon almond extract

¼ teaspoon salt

2 large eggs, separated, room temperature

½ cup granulated sugar

Confectioners' sugar, for dusting

1. Preheat oven to 350°F. Butter a 7-inch springform pan; line with a parchment round, and butter parchment. Dust with flour, tapping out excess. In a small bowl, combine poppy seeds, walnuts, flour, almond extract, and salt.

2. With an electric mixer on medium-high speed, whisk egg yolks and ¼ cup granulated sugar until pale and thick, about 3 minutes. Transfer to a large mixing bowl. Add poppy-seed mixture, but do not stir in.

3. Place egg whites in a clean heatproof bowl set over (not in) a pan of simmering water; whisk until warm to the touch. Remove bowl from heat; with an electric mixer on high speed, whisk until soft peaks form. Add remaining ¼ cup granulated sugar; beat until stiff, glossy peaks form. Using a flexible spatula, fold egg whites into yolk mixture in 3 batches, gently incorporating the poppy-seed mixture.

4. Transfer batter to the prepared pan. Bake until lightly golden and firm on top, about 30 minutes. Transfer pan to a wire rack to cool completely. Run a knife around edge of pan to loosen. Carefully remove sides of pan, and transfer torte to a serving plate. Dust with confectioners' sugar before serving.

Coconut Cake with Tropical Fruit

Think of this as a take on Tres Leches Cake, a Mexican favorite. The sponge cake itself is relatively light; the richness comes only after it's baked, when it is soaked in a heady combination of milk in three forms: in this case, heavy cream, sweetened condensed milk, and coconut milk. Serve it with fresh fruit and whipped cream. **SERVES 12 TO 14**

½ cup (1 stick) unsalted butter, melted and cooled, plus more for baking dish

6 large eggs, separated, room temperature

¼ teaspoon baking soda

¼ teaspoon salt

1 cup sugar

⅓ cup unsweetened flaked coconut, toasted and finely ground (see page 344); plus large-flake coconut, toasted, for serving

1 cup all-purpose flour

2 cups heavy cream

1 can (14 ounces) unsweetened coconut milk

1 can (14 ounces) sweetened condensed milk

Sliced tropical fruit, such as pineapple and star fruit, for serving

1. Preheat oven to 350°F. Generously butter a 9-by-13-inch glass baking dish. With an electric mixer on medium speed, whisk together egg whites, baking soda, and salt until soft peaks form, 4 to 5 minutes.

2. Add egg yolks to egg-white mixture; whisk until completely combined. Gradually add sugar; whisk until combined. Fold in butter and finely ground coconut with a flexible spatula.

3. Sift ¼ cup flour onto mixture; fold to combine. Repeat with remaining flour, folding in ¼ cup at a time. Transfer batter to prepared pan. Bake until golden and a cake tester comes out clean, 20 to 25 minutes.

4. Meanwhile, whisk together 1 cup heavy cream, the coconut milk, and condensed milk. As soon as cake is removed from oven, pour cream mixture over cake. Transfer pan to a wire rack to cool completely. Cover cake with plastic wrap; refrigerate at least 5 hours and up to 8 hours.

5. Just before serving, whisk remaining 1 cup heavy cream until soft peaks form. Serve cake with whipped cream, sliced fruit, and toasted flaked coconut.

Molten Chocolate Cakes

Who would have guessed that this restaurant favorite happens to be extremely easy to re-create at home? The cakes are not entirely flourless, since a little flour helps the formation of a delicate crust on the outside, leaving the inside soft and molten. Because these desserts are all about the flavor of chocolate, use a good-quality bittersweet chocolate that is at least 70 percent cacao. **MAKES 6**

½ cup (1 stick) plus 3 tablespoons unsalted butter, cut into small pieces, plus more for ramekins

Unsweetened cocoa powder, for dusting

½ cup all-purpose flour

6 ounces bittersweet chocolate (preferably 70 percent cacao), chopped (1¼ cups)

5 large eggs, room temperature

¾ cup sugar

Pinch of salt

1. Butter six 6-ounce (2-inch-deep) ramekins. Dust with cocoa, tapping out excess.

2. Melt butter and chocolate in a heatproof bowl set over (not in) a pan of simmering water. Meanwhile, whisk together eggs and sugar until pale and thick, about 4 minutes. Sift flour and salt together into another bowl.

3. Using a flexible spatula, fold egg mixture into chocolate mixture, then immediately fold in flour mixture. Divide batter among ramekins, filling each three-quarters full. Transfer to a rimmed baking sheet. Refrigerate at least 1 hour.

4. Preheat oven to 400°F. Bake cakes until just set, 14 to 16 minutes. Transfer baking sheet to a wire rack to cool 3 minutes. Turn out cakes onto plates and serve immediately, dusted with cocoa, if desired.

Molasses-Spice Cake

Warming spices, hearty molasses, and a hefty amount of fresh ginger bring to mind the flavor of a favorite old-fashioned drop cookie. Consider offering this crowd-pleasing cake as an alternative to more familiar apple and pumpkin pies on the Thanksgiving table. **SERVES 8 TO 10**

1 cup (2 sticks) unsalted butter, room temperature, plus more for pan

2 cups all-purpose flour

1 teaspoon baking powder

1/2 teaspoon salt

1/2 teaspoon ground cinnamon

1/4 teaspoon ground mace

1/4 teaspoon freshly ground black pepper

Pinch of ground cloves

4 large eggs, room temperature, lightly beaten

1/3 cup sour cream, room temperature

1/3 cup unsulfured molasses

3 tablespoons finely grated peeled fresh ginger

1 tablespoon finely grated lemon zest (from 1 to 2 lemons)

1 teaspoon vanilla extract

1 1/3 cups packed light brown sugar

Cream Cheese–Sour Cream Frosting (page 335)

Brown-Sugar Glaze (page 330)

1. Preheat oven to 350°F. Butter a 9-inch round cake pan, line with a parchment round, and butter parchment. Whisk together flour, baking powder, salt, and spices in a large bowl. In another bowl, whisk together eggs, sour cream, molasses, ginger, lemon zest, and vanilla.

2. With an electric mixer on medium-high speed, beat butter and brown sugar until pale and fluffy, about 3 minutes. Reduce speed to low. Add flour mixture in 3 batches, alternating with 2 batches of egg mixture; beat until just combined.

3. Transfer batter to prepared pan. Bake until golden brown and a cake tester comes out clean, 40 to 45 minutes. Transfer pan to a wire rack to cool 15 minutes. Turn out cake onto rack to cool completely.

4. To serve, spread frosting over top of cake, and drizzle with glaze.

Chocolate-Coconut Sheet Cake

Here's an unintimidating, foolproof cake anyone can make. A generous amount of coconut topping, spread over the moist cake while it's still warm, provides richness and a deliciously gooey texture. **SERVES 10 TO 12**

FOR THE CAKE

Unsalted butter, for baking dish

¾ cup unsweetened cocoa powder, plus more for baking dish

1½ cups all-purpose flour

1½ cups granulated sugar

1½ teaspoons baking soda

¾ teaspoon baking powder

¾ teaspoon coarse salt

2 large eggs, lightly beaten

¾ cup buttermilk

¾ cup warm strong brewed coffee

3 tablespoons canola or safflower oil

1 teaspoon vanilla extract

FOR THE TOPPING

½ cup plus 2 tablespoons (1¼ sticks) unsalted butter

2 cups confectioners' sugar

¼ cup plus 2 tablespoons unsweetened cocoa powder

3 cups finely shredded dried unsweetened coconut

⅔ cup warm strong brewed coffee

1 teaspoon vanilla extract

FOR SERVING

Whipped Cream (page 333)

Toasted large-flake coconut (see page 344)

1. Make the cake: Preheat oven to 350°F. Butter a 9-by-13-inch baking dish; line with parchment, leaving an overhang on both long sides. Butter parchment; dust with cocoa, tapping out excess. Whisk together cocoa, flour, granulated sugar, baking soda, baking powder, and salt in a large bowl.

2. Gather flour mixture into a mound, and create a well in center. Pour eggs, buttermilk, coffee, oil, and vanilla into well, and whisk until thoroughly combined and smooth. Transfer batter to prepared baking dish, and spread evenly with an offset spatula. Bake until set and a cake tester comes out clean, about 25 minutes. Transfer dish to a wire rack.

3. Make the topping: Melt butter in a small saucepan. Combine confectioners' sugar, cocoa, and coconut in a large bowl. Stir coffee and vanilla into butter, and then pour over coconut mixture. Stir to combine, and immediately spread evenly over warm cake. Let cool completely on rack. Cake can be refrigerated in dish, covered with plastic wrap (do not let plastic touch cake), up to 3 days.

4. To serve, use parchment to transfer cake to a cutting board. Cut into pieces; serve each piece with whipped cream and toasted coconut.

Almond Semolina Cake

Recipes for semolina cake come from all over the Mediterranean region—Italy, Greece, Turkey, the Middle East, and parts of France. This one features almond paste in the batter and sliced almonds (coated in a brown-sugar egg-white mixture to make them extra-crisp) in the topping. You can substitute yellow cornmeal for the semolina if you wish; the cake will still be delicious, but a tad bit crumblier. **SERVES 8 TO 10**

½ cup (1 stick) unsalted butter, room temperature, plus more for pan

1 cup all-purpose flour

1¼ teaspoons baking powder

¾ teaspoon plus a pinch of salt

½ cup finely ground semolina flour

4 large whole eggs, separated, plus 1 large egg white

¾ cup sliced almonds with skins

3 tablespoons packed light brown sugar

1¼ cups granulated sugar

⅓ cup almond paste

½ teaspoon vanilla extract

⅔ cup whole milk

1. Preheat oven to 350°F. Generously butter a 9-inch springform pan. Sift all-purpose flour, baking powder, and ¾ teaspoon salt together into a bowl; whisk in semolina flour.

2. In a small bowl, whisk 1 egg white vigorously until foamy. Transfer 2 teaspoons whisked egg white to a medium bowl; discard remainder. Stir almonds, brown sugar, and a pinch of salt into egg white.

3. With an electric mixer, beat butter, 1 cup granulated sugar, and the almond paste until pale and fluffy, 3 to 4 minutes. Add egg yolks and vanilla; mix until well blended, about 2 minutes.

4. With mixer on low speed, mix in reserved flour mixture in 3 batches, alternating with 2 batches of milk. Mix until no traces of flour or milk remain, about 2 minutes. Transfer cake batter to a large bowl.

5. In a clean mixer bowl, with mixer on medium-high speed, whisk remaining 4 egg whites until foamy. Gradually whisk in remaining ¼ cup granulated sugar until soft peaks form, about 2 minutes. Using a flexible spatula, fold half of egg-white mixture into batter. Gently fold in remaining egg-white mixture.

6. Transfer batter to prepared pan; smooth top with an offset spatula. Bake until cake begins to turn golden but center is still wobbly, 15 to 20 minutes. Remove cake from oven; scatter reserved almond mixture evenly over top.

7. Return cake to oven; bake until topping is golden brown and a cake tester comes out clean, about 25 minutes. (Check cake 10 to 15 minutes beforehand; if almond topping is browning too quickly, tent loosely with foil.) Transfer pan to a wire rack to cool completely. Run a thin knife around edge of cake to loosen; remove side of pan. Using two spatulas, transfer cake to a serving platter or a cake stand. (Cake can be stored at room temperature, covered, up to 4 days.)

Chocolate-Cherry-Stout Cake

Sometimes a simple technique, like stenciling, can produce a striking effect. You can find cake stencils at crafts and baking-supply stores, or cut out your own. The glaze, made with cornstarch, sets to a firm finish ideal for stenciling; let it dry completely before you apply designs with cocoa powder or confectioners' sugar. **SERVES 8 TO 10**

FOR THE CAKE

Unsalted butter, for pans

1 cup all-purpose flour

$3/4$ teaspoon baking soda

$1/2$ teaspoon coarse salt

6 ounces ($1/2$ bottle) dark stout, such as Guinness

3 tablespoons unsulfured molasses

3 ounces dried cherries (about $2/3$ cup)

$1/4$ cup plus 3 tablespoons unsweetened Dutch-process cocoa powder, sifted, plus more for stencils (optional)

1 large egg, room temperature

$1/2$ cup granulated sugar

$1/4$ cup packed dark brown sugar

$1/2$ cup canola or safflower oil

$3/4$ teaspoon vanilla extract

$1/4$ cup plus 2 tablespoons sour cream

Confectioners' sugar, for stencils (optional)

FOR THE GLAZE

1 tablespoon plus $1/2$ teaspoons granulated sugar

$1/8$ teaspoons cornstarch

2 tablespoons plus $1/2$ teaspoons water, plus more as needed

3 ounces bittersweet chocolate (preferably at least 61 percent cacao), finely chopped

1. Make the cake: Preheat oven to 350°F. Butter an 8-inch round cake pan; line with a parchment round, and butter parchment. Whisk together flour, baking soda, and salt in a medium bowl.

2. Simmer stout, molasses, and cherries in a saucepan, stirring occasionally, until cherries are plump, about 5 minutes. Strain, reserving liquid. Let cherries cool completely. Return liquid to pan, and bring to a boil. Remove from heat, and whisk in $1/4$ cup plus 2 tablespoons cocoa until smooth. Transfer to a bowl, and let cool slightly.

3. With an electric mixer on medium-high speed, beat egg and both sugars until combined, 2 to 3 minutes. Reduce speed to low. Gradually beat in stout mixture. Raise speed to medium, and beat until combined. Reduce speed to low, and beat in oil and vanilla. Add flour mixture in 3 batches, alternating with 2 batches of sour cream, and beat until combined. Toss cherries with remaining tablespoon cocoa, and gently fold into batter.

4. Transfer batter to prepared pan. Gently tap pan on counter. Bake until a cake tester comes out clean, about 50 minutes. Transfer pan to a wire rack to cool 20 minutes. Run a knife around edge of cake to loosen, and turn out onto rack to cool completely. Using a serrated knife, trim top of cake to level. Transfer, cut side down, to a wire rack set over a baking sheet.

5. Make the glaze: Heat sugar, cornstarch, and the water in a large saucepan over medium, whisking until sugar has dissolved. Add chocolate, and bring to a simmer, whisking constantly and scraping down sides of pan as needed. Cook until smooth and thick, 4 to 5 minutes. Remove from heat. If needed, whisk in more water, 1 teaspoon at a time, until glaze is thick but pourable.

6. Ladle glaze onto center of cake. Spread to the edge with an offset spatula. Refrigerate until set, at least 1 hour, or let stand, uncovered, at room temperature overnight. Place a stencil on top of cake, and sift cocoa over top. Carefully remove stencil, and serve.

Almond Torte with Pears

This cake is no less delicious for what it lacks—namely, flour and butter. The method used to prepare the batter—beating the egg yolks with sugar and flavorings, then folding in ground nuts and stiffly beaten egg whites—is standard for Eastern European tortes such as this. All in all, it's lighter than most cakes, even with the poached pears and a dollop of creamy topping. **SERVES 8**

FOR THE CAKE

1¼ cups whole natural almonds (about 6 ounces), toasted (see page 344)

1 teaspoon cornstarch

4 large eggs, separated

¾ cup sugar

2 teaspoons finely grated lemon zest (from 1 lemon)

½ teaspoon vanilla extract

½ teaspoon coarse salt

FOR THE POACHED PEARS

4 cups water

¾ cup sugar

1 cinnamon stick

5 wide strips lemon zest (from 1 lemon)

4 firm, ripe Anjou or Bartlett pears, peeled, cored, and quartered

FOR THE TOPPING

1 cup heavy cream

¼ cup sour cream

2 tablespoons sugar

1. Make the cake: Preheat oven to 350°F. In a food processor, blend almonds and cornstarch until finely ground, about 15 seconds. With an electric mixer on medium-high speed, beat egg yolks, sugar, lemon zest, vanilla, and salt until pale and thick, 4 to 5 minutes. Using a flexible spatula, gently fold in almond mixture.

2. In another large bowl, whisk egg whites until stiff peaks form. Fold one third of the egg whites into almond mixture; fold almond mixture into remaining whites just until combined. Pour batter into a 9-inch springform pan. Bake until a cake tester comes out clean, 25 to 30 minutes. Transfer pan to a wire rack to cool completely.

3. Make the poached pears: In a large saucepan, bring the water, sugar, cinnamon, and lemon zest to a boil. Reduce to a simmer, add pears, and cover pan with a piece of parchment to keep pears submerged. Cook until pears are tender when pierced with a paring knife, about 15 minutes. With a slotted spoon, transfer to a plate. Bring liquid to a boil; reduce until thick and syrupy, 15 to 20 minutes. Remove from heat; let cool completely.

4. Make the topping: In a large bowl, whisk heavy cream until soft peaks form. Whisk in sour cream and sugar; continue to whisk until soft peaks return.

5. Serve cake with pears, syrup, and whipped cream topping.

Citrus Cake

You may very well be tempted to serve this delectably tender buttermilk cake with just the lemony icing—it would be a perfect everyday treat. But the candied-orange-peel garnish takes it from simple to extra special.

SERVES 8 TO 10

½ cup (1 stick) unsalted butter, plus more for pan

1½ cups cake flour (not self-rising), plus more for pan

¾ teaspoon baking powder

¼ teaspoon baking soda

¾ teaspoon salt

1 cup granulated sugar

2 large eggs

Zest of 2 lemons

½ cup buttermilk

1 cup confectioners' sugar

2 tablespoons plus 1½ teaspoons fresh lemon juice

1½ cups candied orange peel, cut into ¼-inch strips (see page 326)

1. Preheat oven to 350°F. Butter a 9-inch round cake pan; line with a parchment round, and butter parchment. Dust with flour, tapping out excess. Into a medium bowl, sift together flour, baking powder, baking soda, and salt.

2. With an electric mixer on medium-high speed, beat butter until creamy, about 3 minutes. Gradually add granulated sugar, and beat until pale and fluffy, 1 to 2 minutes. Add eggs, 1 at a time, beating until incorporated after each. Add lemon zest. Add flour mixture in 3 batches, alternating with 2 batches of buttermilk; beat until combined.

3. Transfer batter to prepared pan. Bake until golden brown and a cake tester comes out clean, about 30 minutes. Transfer pan to a wire rack to cool completely. Turn out cake onto a serving platter.

4. Whisk together confectioners' sugar and lemon juice until smooth and opaque. Spread glaze over top of cake with an offset spatula, allowing glaze to drip over side of cake. Garnish with candied orange peel, and serve.

Banana Pecan Cake

Though it's on the small side, this cake feels substantial nevertheless. (To make it in a 9-by-5-inch pan, double the ingredients and bake 55 minutes.) It's similar to banana bread but not as dense, thanks to cake flour and buttermilk in the batter. Brown sugar lends a hint of caramel flavor.

SERVES 4 TO 6

- 4 tablespoons unsalted butter, room temperature, plus more for pan
- 1 cup sifted cake flour (not self-rising), plus more for pan
- ½ teaspoon baking soda
- ¼ teaspoon baking powder
- ¼ teaspoon salt
- ¼ teaspoon ground cinnamon
- Pinch of ground cloves
- 1 very ripe large banana, mashed (about ½ cup)
- ¼ cup buttermilk
- ½ teaspoon vanilla extract
- ½ cup packed dark brown sugar
- 1 large egg
- ⅓ cup chopped toasted pecans (see page 344)
- Confectioners' sugar, for dusting

1. Preheat oven to 350°F. Butter a 6-by-2-inch round cake pan; line with a parchment round, and butter parchment. Dust with flour, tapping out excess. Into a bowl, sift together flour, baking soda, baking powder, salt, cinnamon, and cloves. In another bowl, whisk together banana, buttermilk, and vanilla.

2. With an electric mixer on medium-high speed, beat butter and brown sugar until pale and fluffy, 3 to 5 minutes. Beat in egg. Add flour mixture in 2 batches, alternating with banana mixture and beginning and ending with the flour; beat until just combined. Stir in pecans.

3. Transfer batter to prepared pan. Bake until golden brown, about 45 minutes. Transfer pan to a wire rack to cool 10 minutes. Run a knife around edge of cake to loosen; turn out onto rack to cool completely. Dust with confectioners' sugar before serving.

Pumpkin Spice Cake

A cake that requires no mixer—for the batter or the frosting—deserves a special spot in any home baker's collection of back-pocket recipes. This one is made with canned pumpkin purée for even greater ease. To bake the cake in a 9-by-5-inch loaf pan, increase the cooking time by twenty-five to thirty minutes. **SERVES 9**

FOR THE CAKE

- ½ cup (1 stick) unsalted butter, melted, plus more for pan
- 2½ cups all-purpose flour
- 2 teaspoons baking soda
- ½ teaspoon salt
- 1 tablespoon pumpkin-pie spice (or see note)
- 2 large eggs
- 1½ cups sugar
- 1 can (15 ounces) solid-pack pumpkin (not pie filling)

FOR THE FROSTING

- ½ cup (1 stick) unsalted butter, room temperature
- 8 ounces (1 bar) cream cheese, room temperature
- ¼ cup honey

1. Make the cake: Preheat oven to 350°F. Butter a 9-inch square baking pan. In a medium bowl, whisk together flour, baking soda, salt, and pumpkin-pie spice. In a large bowl, whisk together eggs, sugar, butter, and pumpkin until combined. Add flour mixture and mix until smooth.

2. Transfer batter to prepared pan; smooth top with an offset spatula. Bake until a cake tester comes out with just a few crumbs attached, 45 to 50 minutes. Transfer pan to a wire rack to cool 10 minutes. Turn out cake onto rack to cool completely.

3. Make the frosting: In a medium bowl, whisk together butter, cream cheese, and honey until smooth. With an offset spatula, spread frosting over top of cooled cake. To serve, cut into squares.

NOTE: To make your own pumpkin-pie spice, combine 1½ teaspoons ground cinnamon, ¾ teaspoon ground ginger, ½ teaspoon freshly grated nutmeg, and ⅛ teaspoon each ground allspice and cloves.

Cheesecakes

No wonder cheesecake is so irresistible: It has its origins in ancient Rome, so chefs and home cooks have had thousands of years to tinker with its basic components and their proportions, and to develop new interpretations too numerous to count. Today's cheesecakes entice us with luscious fillings, crisp cookie crusts, vibrant fruit toppings, and plenty of variations to suit every desire. Some people may argue that they're more tarts than cakes—but no one can disagree with the fact that they're delicious.

RASPBERRY-SWIRL CHEESECAKE, PAGE 175

New York–Style Cheesecake

New Yorkers are convinced that "their" cheesecake is the best, and indeed, this dessert—said to have made its debut at a city delicatessen in the 1920s—is the picture of smooth, creamy perfection. While there's no single definition of New York–style, the term generally refers to a classic, unadorned cheesecake. This luxurious version features a cream-cheese and sour-cream filling over a homemade cookie-dough crust.

SERVES 8 TO 10

FOR THE CRUST

½ cup (1 stick) unsalted butter, room temperature

½ cup sugar

2 large egg yolks

2¼ teaspoons vanilla extract

1¼ cups all-purpose flour, plus more for dusting

Pinch of salt

FOR THE FILLING

Unsalted butter, for pan

3½ pounds (seven 8-ounce bars) cream cheese, room temperature

2¼ cups sugar

½ cup all-purpose flour

5 large eggs, room temperature

1 cup sour cream, room temperature

1½ teaspoons vanilla extract

1. Make the crust: With an electric mixer on medium speed, beat butter and sugar until pale and fluffy, 3 to 5 minutes. Add yolks, 1 at a time, beating well after each and scraping down sides of bowl as needed. Beat in vanilla. Add flour and salt; beat until mixture comes together but still crumbles.

2. Preheat oven to 350°F. On a lightly floured surface, roll out dough to slightly more than ⅛ inch thick. Place the bottom of a 10-inch spring-form pan on top of dough; using a paring knife, cut out a round about ¼ inch larger in diameter than the pan. Transfer dough to a baking sheet; freeze 15 minutes. Bake until golden, 12 to 15 minutes. Transfer crust to a wire rack to cool completely.

3. Make the filling: Set a kettle of water to a boil. Replace bottom of springform pan, butter side, and insert bottom crust. With an electric mixer on medium speed, beat cream cheese until fluffy and smooth, about 3 minutes, scraping down sides of bowl as needed. In a small bowl, combine sugar and flour. Reduce mixer speed to low. Gradually add sugar mixture to cream cheese; beat until smooth. Add eggs, 1 at a time, beating until well incorporated after each and scraping down sides of bowl as needed. Mix in sour cream and vanilla.

4. Pour filling over crust. Wrap bottom and sides of springform pan in a double layer of foil; set springform pan in a large roasting pan. Carefully pour boiling water into roasting pan to reach halfway up side of springform pan. Bake cheesecake until set, 45 minutes; reduce oven temperature to 325°F. Continue to bake until cake is golden on top but still slightly wobbly in center, about 30 minutes more. Turn off oven; leave cake in oven with door slightly ajar 1 hour.

5. Remove from water bath; transfer to a wire rack to cool completely. Refrigerate, uncovered, at least 6 hours or up to overnight. Run a knife around edge of cake to loosen before unmolding.

Cheesecake with Poached Apricots

This cheesecake really makes a statement, thanks to its unexpected square shape and the neat rows of gorgeous, glossy poached apricots. There's no crust—you just mix the batter and bake it in a square pan, then turn out the cake onto a platter and top it with the apricots, letting some of their delicately spiced poaching syrup drip down the sides.

SERVES 8

FOR THE POACHED APRICOTS

- 2⅔ cups water
- 1 cup sugar
- 2 strips (about 2 inches long) fresh lemon peel, pith removed
- 2 thin slices peeled fresh ginger
- 5 cardamom pods, cracked
- 1 vanilla bean, split lengthwise and scraped
- 8 small ripe apricots (about 1 pound), halved and pitted

FOR THE CHEESECAKE

- Unsalted butter, for pan
- 1½ pounds (three 8-ounce bars) cream cheese, room temperature
- ¾ cup sugar
- ½ cup sour cream, room temperature
- 1 teaspoon vanilla extract
- 3 large eggs, room temperature
- 1 tablespoon fresh lemon juice

1. Poach the apricots: In a 3- to 4-quart pot over medium heat, combine the water with sugar, lemon peel, ginger, cardamom, and vanilla seeds. Bring mixture to a boil. Cook until sugar dissolves, then reduce heat to low. Simmer, uncovered, until liquid has thickened slightly, about 10 minutes.

2. Add apricots to the pot. Rinse a double thickness of cheesecloth (you can use a parchment round in its place) under cold water; drape it over apricots so all the fruit is covered by the cloth and submerged in liquid. Continue simmering until apricots soften slightly, 2 to 4 minutes. Remove from heat; cool completely. Use immediately, or transfer apricots and poaching liquid to an airtight container, making sure apricots are completely submerged in liquid. Refrigerate until ready to use, up to 4 days.

3. Make the cheesecake: Preheat oven to 400°F. Butter an 8-inch square baking pan; line with parchment. Set a kettle of water to a boil.

4. With an electric mixer on medium speed, beat cream cheese until fluffy and smooth, about 3 minutes. Mix in sugar, sour cream, and vanilla. Add eggs, 1 at a time, beating until each is fully incorporated before adding the next. Beat in lemon juice.

5. Transfer cream-cheese mixture to prepared pan; smooth top with an offset spatula. Set pan in a large roasting pan. Carefully pour boiling water into roasting pan to reach halfway up sides of baking pan. Bake until cheesecake is just set in the center and lightly browned on top, about 35 minutes.

6. Transfer pan to a wire rack to cool 30 minutes. Invert cheesecake onto serving platter. Refrigerate, covered, overnight.

7. To serve, arrange poached apricot halves, cut side down, on top of cheesecake, allowing juice to pool on surface and drizzle down edges.

Strawberries-and-Cream Cheesecake

Two contrasting layers of cheesecake—one white, one flecked with intensely flavored oven-roasted strawberries—make this dessert truly pretty in pink. For a neat line, use an offset spatula to spread small dollops of the plain cheese mixture gently over the berry base. If you prefer, you can fold the strawberries into all of the mascarpone-cream cheese mixture and skip the layered effect. **SERVES 8 TO 10**

FOR THE BERRIES

- 1½ pounds fresh strawberries, hulled
- 3 tablespoons light corn syrup

FOR THE CRUST

- 12 graham cracker sheets (6 ounces), finely ground (1½ cups)
- 3 tablespoons sugar
- 3 tablespoons unsalted butter, melted

FOR THE FILLING

- 1½ pounds (three 8-ounce bars) plus 5 ounces cream cheese, room temperature
- 1 cup sugar
- ¼ teaspoon salt
- 2 large eggs, room temperature
- 1 vanilla bean, split lengthwise and scraped, pod reserved for another use
- 1 container (about 8 ounces) mascarpone cheese, room temperature

1. Roast the berries: Preheat oven to 300°F. Spread strawberries in a single layer on a rimmed baking sheet. Drizzle with corn syrup, and toss gently to coat. Bake until syrup thickens and strawberries turn deep red and shrink slightly, about 1 hour 30 minutes. Transfer strawberries and syrup to a medium bowl; mash with a potato masher. Let cool completely.

2. Make the crust: Raise oven temperature to 350°F. In a small bowl, stir together graham-cracker crumbs, sugar, and butter. Press mixture evenly into the bottom of a 9-inch springform pan. Bake until crust is set and has just darkened, about 10 minutes. Transfer pan to a wire rack to cool completely.

3. Make the filling: Reduce oven temperature to 325°F. Wrap exterior of springform pan with a double layer of foil. Set a kettle of water to a boil. With an electric mixer on medium-low speed, beat cream cheese until fluffy and smooth, about 3 minutes. Gradually beat in sugar and salt. Add eggs, 1 at a time, mixing well after each addition and scraping down sides of bowl as necessary. Mix in vanilla seeds and mascarpone until very creamy and no lumps remain, about 3 minutes.

4. Add 5 cups cream-cheese mixture to bowl with mashed strawberries; stir to combine. Pour strawberry-cream cheese mixture over crust; smooth with an offset spatula. Carefully spoon dollops of plain cream-cheese mixture on top, smoothing with offset spatula.

5. Set springform pan in a large roasting pan. Carefully pour boiling water into roasting pan to reach halfway up side of springform pan. Bake cheesecake until set, 60 to 70 minutes. Remove springform pan from water bath; transfer springform pan to a wire rack and remove foil; let cool completely. Refrigerate until cold, at least 4 hours or up to overnight.

Lemon-Swirl Cheesecake

No one will ever guess how easy it is to achieve this swirled, two-tone effect. The secret? A wooden skewer. Dollop a second component (such as lemon curd, pictured opposite, or raspberry sauce, shown below) on top of the cheesecake batter, and drag the skewer through to make the pattern. See other variations on the pages that follow. **SERVES 8 TO 10**

FOR THE CRUST

- 8 graham cracker sheets (5 ounces), finely ground (1 cup)
- 2 tablespoons unsalted butter, melted
- 2 tablespoons sugar

FOR THE FILLING

- 2 pounds (four 8-ounce bars) cream cheese, room temperature
- 1½ cups plus 2 tablespoons sugar
- Pinch of salt
- 1 teaspoon vanilla extract
- 4 large eggs, room temperature
- 1 cup Lemon Curd (page 332)

1. Preheat oven to 350°F. Line bottom of a 9-inch springform pan with a parchment round.

2. Make the crust: Stir together graham-cracker crumbs, melted butter, and sugar in a medium bowl. Press crumb mixture firmly onto bottom of pan. Bake until set, about 10 minutes. Transfer pan to wire rack to cool completely.

3. Make the filling: Reduce oven temperature to 325°F. Wrap exterior of a 9-inch springform pan with a double layer of foil. Set a kettle of water to a boil. With an electric mixer on medium speed, beat cream cheese until fluffy and smooth, about 3 minutes. Reduce to low speed; add sugar in a slow, steady stream. Add the salt and vanilla; beat until well combined. Add eggs, 1 at a time, beating after each until just combined (do not overmix). Pour cream cheese filling over crust.

4. Drop lemon curd in small dollops over top of cream-cheese filling. With a wooden skewer or toothpick, swirl into filling.

5. Set springform pan inside a large, shallow roasting pan. Carefully pour boiling water into roasting pan to reach halfway up side of springform pan. Bake until cake is set but still slightly wobbly in center, about 75 minutes.

6. Transfer springform pan to a wire rack and remove foil; let cool completely. Refrigerate, uncovered, at least 24 hours. Run a knife around edge of cake to loosen before unmolding.

SWIRLING THE CHEESECAKE

Four More Cheesecakes

CARAMEL-SWIRL CHEESECAKE

Make crust and filling as directed in Lemon-Swirl Cheesecake recipe (page 172); omit lemon curd. Transfer one third of cheesecake mixture to a bowl; add 1 cup Caramel Sauce (page 333), while still warm. Pour half of plain filling over crust; dollop half of caramel-cheesecake mixture over filling. Swirl with a wooden skewer or toothpick. Repeat with remaining plain filling and caramel mixture. Bake, cool, and refrigerate as directed.

CHOCOLATE–PEANUT BUTTER BULL'S-EYE CHEESECAKE

Make crust and filling as directed in Lemon-Swirl Cheesecake recipe (page 172); omit lemon curd. Divide filling in half. Stir $1/2$ cup creamy peanut butter into one half of filling; stir 4 ounces melted semisweet chocolate into other half. Ladle 1 cup peanut-butter filling into center of crust. Tap pan on counter to settle filling; ladle 1 cup chocolate filling directly on top. Repeat. Switch to $1/2$ cup; continue adding filling to center of crust, alternating peanut butter and chocolate, until all filling is used. Bake about 80 minutes; let cool and refrigerate at least 6 hours or overnight. If desired, spoon Chocolate Glaze (page 331) over cooled cheesecake.

PUMPKIN-SWIRL CHEESECAKE

Make crust and filling as directed in Lemon-Swirl Cheesecake recipe (page 172); omit lemon curd. Transfer one third of cheesecake mixture to a bowl; add 1 cup solid-pack pumpkin purée, $\frac{1}{2}$ teaspoon ground cinnamon, and $\frac{1}{4}$ teaspoon freshly grated nutmeg. Pour plain filling over crust. Drop $\frac{1}{4}$-cup dollops of pumpkin-cheesecake mixture over filling; swirl with a wooden skewer. Bake, cool, and refrigerate as directed.

RASPBERRY-SWIRL CHEESECAKE

Purée 6 ounces raspberries (about $1\frac{1}{2}$ cups) until smooth, about 30 seconds. Pass purée through a fine sieve into a small bowl; discard solids. Whisk in 2 tablespoons sugar. Make crust and filling as directed in Lemon-Swirl Cheesecake recipe (page 172); omit lemon curd. Pour filling over crust. In step 5, drop purée by the teaspoon on top; swirl with a wooden skewer. Bake 70 to 80 minutes; let cool and refrigerate at least 6 hours or overnight.

Blood-Orange No-Bake Cheesecake

Blood-orange glaze adds a brilliant pop of color—and flavor—to this ricotta cheesecake. The fruit, in season from December through March, has a balanced, sweet taste that really shines. Before you begin, drain ricotta in a cheesecloth-lined sieve over a bowl in the refrigerator for at least 3 hours, preferably overnight. **SERVES 8 TO 10**

FOR THE CRUST

- 4 tablespoons unsalted butter, melted, plus more, room temperature, for pan
- 6 graham cracker sheets (3 ounces), finely ground (¾ cup)
- 2 tablespoons sugar

FOR THE FILLING

- 2 cups whole-milk ricotta cheese, drained (see note)
- 3 tablespoons fresh lemon juice
- ¾ teaspoon unflavored powdered gelatin
- 4 large egg yolks
- ½ cup plus 2 tablespoons milk
- ¾ cup plus 2 tablespoons sugar
  Pinch of salt
- 2 teaspoons finely grated blood-orange zest
- 1 teaspoon vanilla extract
- 4 ounces cream cheese, room temperature
- ½ cup heavy cream, whipped to soft peaks

FOR THE GLAZE

- ¼ teaspoon unflavored powdered gelatin
- 7 tablespoons strained blood-orange juice (from 1 to 2 oranges)
- 2 tablespoons sugar
- 1 candied blood-orange slice (see page 326)

1. Make the crust: Preheat oven to 350°F. Brush bottom and side of a 7-inch springform pan with butter; line with a parchment round. Combine graham-cracker crumbs and sugar in a small bowl. Stir in melted butter with a fork until crumbs are moistened. Press into bottom of pan, and bake until set, about 10 minutes. Transfer pan to a wire rack to cool completely.

2. Make the filling: Place lemon juice in a small bowl, and sprinkle gelatin over the surface. Set aside for a few minutes to soften.

3. In a saucepan, beat egg yolks until smooth. Whisk in milk. Gradually whisk in sugar. Add salt. Cook over low heat, stirring constantly, until mixture coats the back of a spoon, about 7 minutes. (Do not boil.) Transfer to a bowl, and stir in softened gelatin, orange zest, and vanilla, mixing until gelatin is completely dissolved.

4. Purée ricotta in a food processor until smooth. Add cream cheese, and process until smooth. With machine running, add custard, and process just long enough to combine. Transfer to a bowl, and fold in whipped cream. Pour over crust, cover, and refrigerate overnight.

5. Make the glaze: In a small bowl, sprinkle gelatin over 2 tablespoons juice; let stand a few minutes until soft. In a small saucepan, bring sugar and remaining 5 tablespoons juice to a boil. Remove from heat; stir in softened gelatin. Cool to lukewarm, 1 to 2 minutes. Place candied orange slice in center of cheesecake. Pour glaze over top, tipping cake pan to cover completely. Refrigerate until glaze is set, about 1 hour.

6. To unmold, wrap a hot towel around pan to help release cake, run a knife around edge of crust, and carefully remove outside of pan. Run an offset spatula underneath crust to loosen. Carefully slide cake onto a serving plate, and refrigerate until ready to serve.

Ricotta Cheesecake

The Italian fresh cheese gives this dessert—also known as ricotta pie and often enjoyed on Easter—a wonderfully light, fluffy texture. It's exceptionally easy to make: It takes just fifteen minutes to assemble and doesn't need to bake in a water bath as many other cheesecakes do. A vanilla-scented citrus topping is excellent alongside, but in the summer, serve fresh berries instead. **SERVES 10 TO 12**

FOR THE CHEESECAKE

Unsalted butter, for pan

¾ cup sugar, plus more for pan

1½ pounds (3 cups) whole-milk ricotta cheese

6 large eggs, separated, room temperature

⅓ cup all-purpose flour

1 packed tablespoon finely grated orange zest

¼ teaspoon salt

FOR THE CITRUS-VANILLA COMPOTE

1 red or pink grapefruit, washed well

1 navel orange, washed well

¼ cup water, plus more for boiling

¼ cup sugar

½ vanilla bean, split lengthwise and scraped, pod reserved

Pinch of salt

1. Make the cheesecake: Preheat oven to 350°F. Generously butter a 9-inch springform pan; dust with sugar to coat. Whisk together ricotta, egg yolks, flour, 6 tablespoons sugar, the zest, and salt in a large bowl.

2. With an electric mixer on low speed, whisk egg whites until foamy. Raise speed to high, and gradually add remaining 6 tablespoons sugar, whisking until stiff, glossy peaks form, 3 to 4 minutes. Gently fold one third of the whites into ricotta mixture, using a flexible spatula, until just combined. Gently fold in remaining whites until just combined.

3. Pour batter into prepared pan, and bake until center is firm and top is deep golden brown, about 60 minutes. Transfer pan to a wire rack to cool 10 minutes. Run a knife around edge of cake to loosen; release side to remove from pan, and cool completely. (Cheesecake can be refrigerated, covered loosely with plastic wrap, up to 3 days. Let stand at room temperature 20 minutes before serving.)

4. Meanwhile, make the compote: Cut peels from grapefruit and orange. Cut pith from peels, and slice peels into very thin strips. Slice fruit along membranes to release segments into a bowl. Squeeze juice from membranes into bowl; discard membranes. Pour ¼ cup juice through a fine sieve into a small bowl.

5. Bring a saucepan of water to a boil. Cook citrus peels 1 minute; drain. Bring ¼ cup water, the sugar, and vanilla seeds and pod to a boil in a clean saucepan, stirring until sugar dissolves. Reduce heat to low. Add reserved juice and peels and the salt; cook 2 minutes. Remove from heat; cool completely.

6. Discard vanilla pod. Toss syrup with reserved fruit. If not serving immediately, refrigerate compote, covered, up to 2 days. Serve cheesecake with compote.

Margarita Cheesecake

This dessert takes inspiration from the classic Tex-Mex cocktail—right down to the salt on the rim of the glass (in this case, a salted-pretzel crust). Tequila and orange-flavored liqueur make this ultra-creamy cheesecake an adults-only treat (or replace the liquor with lime juice for an alcohol-free version). **SERVES 8 TO 10**

FOR THE CRUST

- 4 ounces salted pretzels (4 cups)
- 1/3 cup sugar
- 4 tablespoons unsalted butter, melted

FOR THE FILLING

- 1 1/2 pounds (three 8-ounce bars) cream cheese, room temperature
- 1 cup sour cream, room temperature
- 3/4 cup sugar
- 2 tablespoons Grand Marnier, Triple Sec, or other orange-flavored liqueur
- 1 tablespoon tequila
- 1 tablespoon plus 2 teaspoons grated lime zest (from about 3 limes)
- Pinch of salt
- 4 large eggs, room temperature
- Key limes or small Persian limes, very thinly sliced, for garnish

1. Make the crust: Preheat oven to 375°F, with rack in center. In a food processor, pulse pretzels until fine crumbs form (you will have a little more than 1 cup). Add sugar and melted butter; process until combined. Press evenly in bottom and 1 inch up side of a 9-inch springform pan. Bake until golden brown, about 9 minutes. Transfer to wire rack to cool completely.

2. Make the filling: Reduce oven temperature to 325°F. Wrap exterior of springform pan with a double layer of foil. Set a kettle of water to a boil. With an electric mixer on medium-high speed, beat cream cheese until fluffy and smooth, about 3 minutes, scraping down sides of bowl as needed. Reduce speed to medium. Mix in sour cream, sugar, Grand Marnier, tequila, lime zest, and salt; beat until well incorporated. Add eggs, 1 at a time, beating well after each.

3. Pour cream-cheese mixture over cooled crust (filling will come up higher than crust). Set springform pan in a roasting pan. Carefully pour boiling water into roasting pan to reach halfway up side of springform pan.

4. Bake on center rack until cake is set and slightly firm to the touch, about 65 minutes. Transfer springform pan to a wire rack, and remove foil; let cool completely. Refrigerate until chilled, at least 6 hours or up to overnight. Run a knife around edge of cake to loosen before unmolding. Garnish with lime slices.

No-Bake Spiderweb Cheesecake

This Halloween-worthy dessert is really just a supereasy cheesecake with a deep, dark cookie crust. Serve it any time of the year without the spiderweb design. **SERVES 12 TO 14**

FOR THE CRUST

- ¾ cup (1½ sticks) unsalted butter, melted, plus more for pan
- 2 boxes (each 9 ounces) chocolate wafer cookies, finely ground (4½ cups)
- ¼ cup plus 2 tablespoons sugar
- 1 teaspoon coarse salt

FOR THE GANACHE

- 4 ounces bittersweet chocolate, finely chopped
- ½ cup heavy cream

FOR THE FILLING

- 2 pounds (four 8-ounce bars) cream cheese, room temperature
- 1½ cups sugar
- ¼ teaspoon coarse salt
- 3 tablespoons fresh lemon juice
- 1½ cups cold heavy cream

1. Make the crust: Butter a 10-inch springform pan. Mix cookies, sugar, butter, and salt in a medium bowl. Pat mixture into prepared pan, pressing firmly into bottom and all the way up side. Cover and refrigerate until ready to fill.

2. Make the ganache: Place chocolate in a food processor. Bring cream to a simmer in a small saucepan; pour over chocolate. When chocolate begins to melt, process until smooth. Reserve 2 tablespoons ganache for decorating; spread the remainder evenly over bottom and up sides of crust. Refrigerate until ready to fill.

3. Make the filling: With an electric mixer on medium speed, beat cream cheese until fluffy and smooth, about 3 minutes. Reduce speed to low; slowly add sugar and salt. Raise speed to medium-high; beat until very fluffy, about 3 minutes. Beat in lemon juice.

4. In a separate bowl, whisk cream until medium-stiff peaks form. Whisk one quarter of the whipped cream into cream cheese mixture, then fold in remaining whipped cream. Pour filling into crust; spread evenly. Gently tap bottom of pan on counter.

5. Transfer reserved ganache to a pastry bag fitted with a small round tip (such as #3). Starting in center of cheesecake, pipe a spiral, spacing lines about ½ inch apart. Pull the tip of a paring knife in a gently curved line from the center of the spiral to outer edge. Wipe knife clean; repeat every inch or so to form a web.

6. Cover; freeze at least 3 hours or overnight. Unmold cheesecake, and serve immediately.

FORMING THE SPIDERWEB

Maple Cheesecake with Roasted Pears

Cheesecake's comfort-food status makes it a wonderful treat in the fall. Add the seasonal sweetness of maple syrup and roasted pears, and you've got a dessert that's downright irresistible, and one that would be a welcome option at Thanksgiving. Slicing the pears lengthwise—stems, seeds, and all—leaves their shape intact, making them an especially pretty garnish. **SERVES 8 TO 10**

FOR THE CRUST

46 vanilla wafer cookies (6 ounces)

3 tablespoons granulated sugar

1/4 teaspoon coarse salt

5 tablespoons unsalted butter, melted

FOR THE FILLING

1 pound (two 8-ounce bars) cream cheese, room temperature

1/2 cup pure maple syrup

1 cup cold heavy cream

2 tablespoons confectioners' sugar

FOR THE TOPPING

2 medium pears, such as Bosc or Bartlett, sliced lengthwise 1/8 inch thick

1/4 cup pure maple syrup

Vegetable oil cooking spray

1. Make the crust: Preheat oven to 350°F. In a food processor, pulse cookies until finely ground (you should have about 1½ cups). Add granulated sugar, salt, and butter; pulse until combined. Firmly press crumb mixture into bottom and evenly up side of a 9-inch springform pan. Bake until crust is dry and set, about 12 minutes. Transfer pan to a wire rack to cool completely.

2. Make the filling: With an electric mixer on high speed, beat cream cheese until fluffy and smooth, about 3 minutes. Add ½ cup maple syrup; beat until smooth. In a clean bowl, beat cream and confectioners' sugar on high until soft peaks form, about 3 minutes. With a flexible spatula, stir about one third whipped cream into cream-cheese mixture, then fold in remainder. Pour filling over crust and refrigerate until firm, at least 3 hours (or overnight).

3. Make the topping: Preheat oven to 450°F. Coat a parchment-lined rimmed baking sheet with cooking spray. Arrange pear slices in a single layer on sheet; brush with 2 tablespoons maple syrup. Roast until pears are soft, about 20 minutes. Remove from oven, then heat broiler. Brush pears with remaining 2 tablespoons maple syrup; broil until browned in spots, about 4 minutes, rotating sheet frequently. Transfer baking sheet to a wire rack to cool completely.

4. To serve, unmold cheesecake, and arrange pear slices, overlapping slightly, on top.

Chocolate Cheesecake

Chocolate times three: Melted bittersweet chocolate, cocoa powder, and a cookie crust make this cheesecake the ultimate indulgence for the chocolate lover. **SERVES 8 TO 10**

FOR THE CRUST

22 chocolate wafer cookies (from one 9-ounce box), finely ground (1 cup)

4 tablespoons unsalted butter, melted

3 tablespoons sugar

FOR THE FILLING

8 ounces best-quality bittersweet chocolate, chopped

1½ pounds (three 8-ounce bars) cream cheese, room temperature

1 cup sugar

Pinch of salt

¾ cup sour cream, room temperature

3 tablespoons unsweetened cocoa powder

2 teaspoons vanilla extract

3 large eggs, room temperature

1. Make the crust: Preheat oven to 350°F. Stir together cookie crumbs, melted butter, and sugar in a medium bowl. Press crumb mixture firmly onto bottom and up 1 inch on side of a 9-inch springform pan. Bake until set, about 10 minutes. Transfer to a wire rack to cool completely. Wrap springform pan in a double layer of foil. Set a kettle of water to a boil.

2. Make the filling: In a medium heatproof bowl set over (not in) a pan of simmering water, melt chocolate, stirring, about 2 minutes. Let cool.

3. With an electric mixer on medium speed, beat cream cheese until fluffy, about 3 minutes. Reduce speed to low. Beat in sugar in a slow, steady stream. Add salt; beat until combined. Add sour cream, cocoa, vanilla, and melted chocolate; beat until combined. Add eggs, 1 at a time, beating after each until just combined (do not overmix). Pour filling over crust.

4. Set springform pan in a large roasting pan. Carefully pour boiling water in roasting pan to reach halfway up side of springform pan. Bake cheesecake until set but still slightly wobbly in center, 50 to 60 minutes. Transfer pan to a wire rack to cool completely. Refrigerate, uncovered, 6 hours or overnight. Run a knife around edge of cake to loosen before unmolding.

PRESSING CRUST INTO PAN

Gingerbread Cheesecake

With spices and molasses in the crust and filling, and gingerbread men dancing across the top, this cake is ready for any winter celebration. The cheesecake pictured is topped with two types of gingerbread for color variation. If you prefer, you can make all the cookies from the dough used for the crust. **SERVES 10**

All-purpose flour, for dusting

½ recipe Molasses-Gingerbread Cookie Dough (page 342; use remaining dough to make gingerbread men or reserve for another use)

4 tablespoons unsalted butter, melted

1¾ cups sugar

2 pounds (four 8-ounce bars) cream cheese, room temperature

1 teaspoon vanilla extract

4 large eggs, room temperature

¼ cup unsulfured molasses

¼ teaspoon salt

1½ teaspoons ground ginger

1 teaspoon ground cinnamon

1 teaspoon freshly grated nutmeg

¼ teaspoon ground cloves

½ teaspoon finely grated lemon zest

6 Gingerbread Men, for decorating (see page 342)

1. Preheat oven to 350°F. On a generously floured piece of parchment, roll dough to a 13-by-10-inch rectangle, about ¼ inch thick. Brush off excess flour. Slide dough and parchment onto a baking sheet. Bake until firm and golden brown, about 14 minutes. Transfer sheet to a wire rack to cool completely. Break into large pieces, then pulse in a food processor until finely ground.

2. Combine butter, ¼ cup sugar, and 2 cups cookie crumbs in a bowl. Press mixture firmly and evenly into bottom and one third of the way up side of springform pan. Bake until set, about 10 minutes. Transfer pan to a wire rack to cool completely.

3. Reduce oven temperature to 325°F. Wrap exterior of a 9-inch springform pan with a double layer of foil. Set a kettle of water to a boil. With an electric mixer on medium speed, beat cream cheese until fluffy and smooth, about 3 minutes. Beat in remaining 1½ cups sugar and the vanilla, scraping down sides of bowl as needed. Reduce speed to low. Add eggs, 1 at a time, beating well after each and scraping down sides of bowl as needed. Beat in molasses, salt, spices, and zest. Pour filling into cooled crust.

4. Set springform pan in a large, shallow roasting pan. Carefully pour boiling water into roasting pan to reach halfway up side of springform pan. Bake cheesecake until set but still slightly wobbly in center, 60 to 65 minutes. Transfer springform pan to a wire rack to cool completely. Refrigerate, uncovered, at least 8 hours (preferably overnight).

5. Before serving, run a knife around edge of cheesecake to loosen; remove sides of pan. Arrange gingerbread cookies in center of cake in a circle.

No-Bake Cheesecakes with Pomegranate

Individual-size cheesecakes made in muffin tins are just as cute—and irresistible—as cupcakes. The homemade pomegranate jelly makes a festive and tasty topping. If desired, you can substitute any other flavor.

MAKES 6

FOR THE CRUST

- 3 tablespoons granulated sugar
- 13 graham cracker sheets (7 ounces)
- 1/2 cup (1 stick) unsalted butter, melted

FOR THE FILLING

- 10 ounces cream cheese, room temperature
- 6 ounces crème fraîche
- 2/3 cup sifted confectioners' sugar
- 1 cup heavy cream

FOR THE JELLY

- 2/3 cup pomegranate juice
- 1 teaspoon fresh lemon juice
- 1 cup sugar
- 1 tablespoon plus 1 1/2 teaspoons liquid pectin

    Pomegranate seeds, for garnish

1. Make the crust: Line six cups of a jumbo muffin tin with plastic wrap. Pulse granulated sugar and graham crackers in a food processor until very finely ground. Transfer to a small bowl, and stir in melted butter. Press into prepared muffin tin. Place in freezer while preparing filling.

2. Make the filling: With an electric mixer on medium speed, beat cream cheese, crème fraîche, and confectioners' sugar until combined. In another bowl, beat heavy cream just until medium-stiff peaks form; fold into cream cheese mixture. Spoon into crusts; freeze until firm, about 30 minutes.

3. Make the jelly: Combine pomegranate juice, lemon juice, and sugar in a saucepan. Bring to a rolling boil, stirring until sugar is dissolved. Add liquid pectin; return to a rolling boil, and cook 1 minute, stirring occasionally. Transfer jelly to a large bowl set over an ice-water bath until cool but pourable. (If not using immediately, jelly can be refrigerated in an airtight container up to 1 month; heat over low until smooth before using.)

4. When ready to serve, lift out cheesecakes by gently pulling up on the plastic wrap. Carefully remove plastic; set cakes on serving plates. Drizzle each with jelly, and garnish with pomegranate seeds.

Icebox

Our nostalgically named icebox cakes are those that are chilled in the refrigerator or freezer. The best-known version is made from chocolate wafer cookies and whipped cream; layered together and refrigerated overnight, they meld into a strikingly striped cake. Here, you will find several variations on that technique, as well as bright-as-rainbows ice-cream cakes, semifreddo (an Italian take on the tradition), and other cool creations.

STRIPED ICE-CREAM CAKE, PAGE 195

Striped Ice-Cream Cake

Some desserts make you smile before you even take the first bite. This cheerful cake features layers of brightly colored sorbet, vanilla ice cream, blueberry jam, and angel-food sheet cake. Feel free to use different flavors of ice cream or jam than are suggested here. **SERVES 36**

FOR THE ANGEL-FOOD CAKE

- 12 large egg whites, room temperature
- ½ teaspoon cream of tartar
- 1¼ cups superfine sugar
- 1 cup all-purpose flour
  Pinch of salt
  Vegetable oil cooking spray

FOR ASSEMBLING

- 1 cup blueberry jam
- 2 pints vanilla ice cream
- 2 pints raspberry sorbet
- 1 pint peach sorbet

1. Make the angel-food cake: Preheat oven to 350°F. Coat a 13-by-17-inch rimmed baking sheet with cooking spray, line with parchment, and coat parchment with spray. With an electric mixer on medium speed, whisk egg whites and cream of tartar until soft peaks form. Slowly add ¾ cup superfine sugar; whisk until stiff, glossy peaks form, about 3 minutes.

2. Sift remaining ½ cup superfine sugar, the flour, and salt over egg-white mixture; fold gently until just combined, being careful not to deflate whites. Spread batter evenly onto prepared baking sheet. Bake until golden and set, about 20 minutes. Transfer sheet to a wire rack to cool completely. (Cake should pull away from sides easily.) Slide cake out from sheet, right side up; cut in half crosswise to form two 8½-by-13-inch pieces. Carefully remove parchment from cake. (Cake can be stored at room temperature, wrapped in plastic, up to 2 days.)

3. Assemble the ice-cream cake: Line a 9-by-13-inch baking dish with plastic wrap. Place half the baked angel-food cake in bottom of dish. Spread jam over top. Microwave ice cream to soften, about 20 seconds (or leave at room temperature 10 minutes), then transfer to a bowl and beat with an electric mixer on medium speed until smooth and spreadable, about 30 seconds. Spread ice cream over jam. Freeze until firm, about 1 hour.

4. Soften raspberry sorbet as above and beat until smooth, then spread over ice-cream layer. Freeze until firm, about 1 hour.

5. Soften peach sorbet as above and beat until smooth, then spread over raspberry layer; top with remaining angel-food cake. Wrap in plastic; freeze overnight (or up to 1 week).

6. To serve, remove plastic from top of cake, and turn out cake onto a cutting board. Peel off plastic wrap, and trim edges of cake. Cut into long thin slices, then cut crosswise into squares, wiping knife between slices.

SPREADING FRUIT SORBET

Chocolate–Peanut Butter Icebox Cake

We took the original chocolate-wafer icebox cake and turned it on its side—literally. The wafers are usually lined up with whipped cream in between them, forming a log shape. Here, six flat layers make a more traditional layer-cake shape, with the rounded edges of the cookies giving a pretty petal-like effect. We also added peanut butter to the filling for a sweet-salty contrast to the chocolate. If you've never made a cake like this before, you'll be surprised at how soft and sliceable the cookies become as they meld with the cream. To make the classic version, as shown on the table of contents, omit the peanut butter; you could also flavor the plain whipped cream with a quarter teaspoon of peppermint extract instead. **SERVES 8**

2 cups heavy cream, well chilled

⅓ cup confectioners' sugar

⅓ cup smooth natural-style peanut butter (not unsalted)

1 box (9 ounces) chocolate wafer cookies

1. With an electric mixer on medium speed, whisk 1½ cups cream with the confectioners' sugar until soft peaks form. In another bowl, whisk peanut butter until soft and smooth; whisk in remaining ½ cup cream until light and fluffy. Fold peanut-butter mixture into whipped cream until incorporated.

2. Dab the bottom of 7 cookies with a very small amount of cream mixture; arrange 6 in a circle on a serving plate, with 1 cookie in the middle. Carefully spread ⅔ cup cream mixture over cookies, leaving a slight border. Repeat to form 5 more layers (staggering the cookie layers), ending with cream. Cut 3 cookies in half; decorate top of cake with cookie halves.

3. Refrigerate at least 8 hours (or overnight). To serve, cut into wedges with a serrated knife.

LAYERING WAFERS AND CREAM

Mint Chocolate-Chip Cake

Start with a winning ice-cream flavor, and add chocolate cake. What's not to love? The ice cream in this cake serves as both filling and frosting. For contrasting stripes, alternate layers of green and white mint chocolate-chip ice cream, as shown here. When you're ready to serve, soften the cake in the refrigerator for thirty minutes; run a sharp knife under hot water for a few seconds, dry the knife, and cut the cake. Repeat, rinsing knife between cuts. **SERVES 8**

FOR THE CAKE

- $\frac{3}{4}$ cup (1$\frac{1}{2}$ sticks) unsalted butter, melted, plus more for pans
- 2 cups all-purpose flour, plus more for pans
- 1$\frac{1}{2}$ cups sugar
- $\frac{3}{4}$ cup unsweetened cocoa powder
- $\frac{1}{2}$ teaspoon salt
- 1$\frac{1}{2}$ teaspoons baking powder
- $\frac{3}{4}$ teaspoon baking soda
- 1 large whole egg plus 1 large egg white, room temperature
- 1 teaspoon vanilla extract
- 1$\frac{1}{3}$ cups strong hot coffee

FOR ASSEMBLING

- 4 cups white mint chocolate-chip ice cream
- 4 cups green mint chocolate-chip ice cream

1. Make the cake: Preheat oven to 325°F. Butter two 8-inch square baking pans; line with parchment, and butter parchment. Dust with flour, tapping out excess. With an electric mixer on low speed, whisk all ingredients except hot coffee until combined, about 1 minute. Slowly add the coffee; mix until smooth, about 1 minute. Transfer batter to prepared pans; smooth tops with an offset spatula. Bake until a cake tester comes out clean, 25 to 30 minutes. Transfer pans to a wire rack to cool completely.

2. Assemble the ice-cream cake: Trim cake layers to 6-inch squares. Slice each layer in half horizontally, making a total of 4 layers. Place 1 cake layer on a serving platter. Microwave white ice cream to soften, about 20 seconds (or leave at room temperature 10 minutes), then transfer to a bowl and beat with an electric mixer on medium speed until smooth and spreadable, about 30 seconds. Using an offset spatula, evenly spread 2 cups white ice cream over the cake. Place another cake layer on top of ice cream. Freeze cake 20 minutes. (Return white ice cream to freezer.)

3. Soften green ice cream as above, and beat until smooth and spreadable. Evenly spread 2 cups green ice cream over cake. Place third cake layer on top. Return cake to freezer for 20 minutes more. (Return green ice cream to freezer.)

4. Spread remaining 2 cups white ice cream over cake layer; place fourth cake layer on top. Freeze and chill until firm, about 1 hour.

5. With a long serrated knife, trim ¼ inch from all sides of cake, making them even. Use an offset spatula to quickly spread remaining 2 cups green ice cream over top and sides of cake. Return cake to freezer; freeze until completely hardened, at least 2 hours (or overnight). Cut into slices, wiping knife between slices.

Chocolate-Chestnut Mousse Cake

Chestnuts are a luxurious touch and make this a do-ahead dessert for any celebration. The idea of roasting chestnuts over an open fire sounds lovely, but it is much easier to buy them already roasted and peeled.

SERVES 8

Canola or safflower oil, for pan

1 jar (7.4 ounces) peeled roasted chestnuts

3 large egg yolks

1 tablespoon cornstarch

¼ cup plus 1 tablespoon light brown sugar

1 cup whole milk

Pinch of coarse salt

1 teaspoon vanilla extract

1 tablespoon unsalted butter, room temperature

2 ounces bittersweet chocolate (preferably 61 percent cacao), melted and slightly cooled, plus more for curls (see page 328)

1½ cups heavy cream, well chilled

24 chocolate wafer cookies (from one 9-ounce box)

1. Lightly coat an 8-inch round cake pan with oil and line with plastic, leaving a 4-inch overhang. Finely grind chestnuts in a food processor.

2. Whisk together yolks, cornstarch, and 2 tablespoons sugar in a medium heatproof bowl. Heat chestnuts, milk, remaining 3 tablespoons brown sugar, and the salt in a saucepan over medium-high, stirring occasionally, until bubbles form at edge. Slowly add hot chestnut mixture to yolk mixture, whisking constantly. Return to pan; cook over medium-low heat, whisking constantly, until thick, about 2 minutes.

3. Transfer to a mixing bowl. Add vanilla and butter. With an electric mixer on medium speed, beat until cool, about 5 minutes. Stir half the chestnut mixture into melted chocolate.

4. In another bowl, whisk 1¼ cups cream on medium speed until soft peaks form. Gently fold half the whipped cream into plain chestnut mixture and the other half into chocolate-chestnut mixture.

5. Pour chestnut mousse into prepared pan. Cover with 12 chocolate wafers, working in a circular pattern. Top with chocolate-chestnut mousse and remaining 12 chocolate wafers. Fold plastic over top to cover cake. Refrigerate overnight.

6. To serve, remove plastic from top of cake. Invert onto a serving platter; peel off plastic wrap. Whisk remaining ¼ cup cream until soft peaks form; spread on top of cake. Garnish with chocolate curls.

Chocolate, Banana, and Graham Cracker Icebox Cake

Kids and grown-ups alike will surely go bananas for this take on icebox cake. It evokes two other beloved treats—old-fashioned banana pudding and chocolate-covered bananas—but has a playful personality all its own. Use a serrated knife to trim the graham crackers to fit your loaf pan.

SERVES 10

Canola or safflower oil, for pan

15 ounces milk chocolate, chopped

5 large egg yolks

Pinch of salt

3 cups heavy cream

20 graham cracker sheets (10 ounces)

4 or 5 ripe bananas, very thinly sliced lengthwise

Whipped Cream, for serving (page 333)

1. Lightly coat a 9-by-5-inch loaf pan with oil and line with plastic wrap, leaving overhang on both long sides. Place chocolate in a heatproof bowl. Combine yolks and salt in another heatproof bowl.

2. Bring cream to a simmer in a medium saucepan. Slowly pour cream into bowl with yolks, whisking constantly; return mixture to saucepan. Cook over low heat, stirring constantly, until mixture is thick enough to coat the back of a wooden spoon, about 8 minutes (do not let boil). Immediately strain through a fine sieve into bowl with chocolate; stir until chocolate melts and mixture is smooth. Refrigerate, stirring occasionally, until thick enough to spread, about 4 hours.

3. Spread 1 cup chocolate mixture evenly into bottom of prepared pan. Top with a layer of 4 graham crackers, trimmed to fit. Spread ½ cup chocolate over tops; cover with some banana slices. Carefully spread ½ cup chocolate over bananas; top with a layer of 4 trimmed graham crackers. Repeat with remaining chocolate, bananas, and graham crackers (alternating between bananas and crackers) until you reach the top of the pan; finish with graham crackers. Fold plastic over top to cover cake. Refrigerate overnight (or up to 2 days).

4. To serve, remove plastic from top of cake; unmold onto a platter. Peel off plastic wrap. Spread whipped cream over top of cake with an offset spatula. Cut into slices, wiping knife between slices.

Lemon-Blackberry Semifreddo Roll

Here, an easy sponge cake is rolled around a frozen mousse known as semifreddo (in Italian, literally "half cold"). Lemon and blackberries give it bright flavor and color. **SERVES 8 TO 10**

⅔ cup sifted cake flour (not self-rising), plus more for pan

Pinch of salt

3 large whole eggs plus 2 large egg yolks

¾ cup granulated sugar

¼ cup (½ stick) unsalted butter, melted and cooled

Confectioners' sugar, for dusting

¼ cup water

¼ cup limoncello (Italian lemon liqueur)

Lemon-Blackberry Semifreddo (page 343), slightly firm

Blackberries, for serving

Vegetable oil cooking spray

1. Preheat oven to 450°F. Coat a 12-by-17-inch rimmed baking sheet with cooking spray. Line with parchment; coat with cooking spray. Dust with flour, tapping out excess. Whisk flour and salt in a bowl.

2. Combine whole eggs, yolks, and ½ cup granulated sugar in a large heatproof bowl set over (not in) a pan of simmering water; whisk until sugar has dissolved and mixture is warm to the touch. Remove bowl from heat. With an electric mixer on medium-high speed, whisk 2 minutes. Raise speed to high. Beat until mixture is pale and thick enough to hold a ribbon on its surface, about 4 minutes more.

3. Sift flour mixture over egg mixture. Using a large flexible spatula, carefully fold into egg mixture. When almost incorporated, pour melted butter down side of bowl; gently fold to incorporate completely.

4. With a large offset spatula, spread batter evenly in sheet. Bake until golden brown and springy to the touch, about 6 minutes. Run a small knife around sides of sheet; invert onto a wire rack. Remove parchment. Transfer cake to a dish towel dusted with confectioners' sugar; roll up, starting at a short end. Let cool completely.

5. Heat remaining ¼ cup granulated sugar and the water in a small saucepan over medium-high heat, stirring frequently, until sugar has dissolved. Bring to a boil. Let simple syrup cool completely.

6. Stir together limoncello and simple syrup in a small bowl. Unroll cake, remove towel, and place on parchment on the back of a rimmed baking sheet. Brush with limoncello syrup. Spread with semifreddo, leaving a 2-inch border on one short side and a ½-inch border on the long sides. Freeze until semifreddo is firm, about 25 minutes.

7. Starting at the short side that has semifreddo spread to the edge, roll cake, using parchment to help roll it. Transfer rolled cake, seam side down, to a platter; freeze until semifreddo is hard, at least 3 hours or up to overnight. Let stand at room temperature about 30 minutes. Dust with confectioners' sugar, before serving, then cut into slices, wiping knife between each, and serve with blackberries.

ROLLING THE CAKE

Chocolate Baked Alaskas

Baked Alaskas sound impossible—ice cream in the oven?—but a layer of meringue over the tops insulates them so the ice cream doesn't melt. The meringue gets golden and crisp like a toasted marshmallow (you can brown it with a kitchen torch instead). These mini versions are a spin on the classic dessert, said to have been named at New York restaurant Delmonico's in the 1860s to commemorate the Alaska Purchase. **MAKES 6**

FOR THE CAKE LAYERS

- 2 cups sugar
- 1⅓ cups all-purpose flour
- 1 cup unsweetened Dutch-process cocoa powder
- 2 teaspoons baking powder
- 2 teaspoons baking soda
- 1 teaspoon salt
- 1 cup canola or safflower oil
- ⅔ cup warm water (about 100°F)
- 2 teaspoons vanilla extract
- 6 large eggs, room temperature, separated

FOR ASSEMBLING

- 6 cups chocolate ice cream (3 pints)
  Vegetable oil cooking spray

FOR THE MERINGUE

- 12 large egg whites, room temperature
- 3 cups sugar
  Pinch of cream of tartar

1. Make the cake layers: Preheat oven to 350°F. Line two 12-by-17-inch rimmed baking sheets with parchment. Sift 1⅓ cups sugar, the flour, cocoa powder, baking powder, baking soda, and salt into a bowl. In another bowl, combine oil, the warm water, and vanilla.

2. With a mixer on medium-high speed, whisk egg yolks until pale and thick, about 5 minutes. With mixer on medium-low, slowly pour oil mixture into yolks, then add sugar mixture.

3. In a clean mixing bowl, whisk egg whites on medium-high speed, gradually adding remaining ⅔ cup sugar, until medium-stiff peaks form. Mix one third of the whites into cake batter, then gently fold in remaining whites.

4. Divide batter evenly between baking sheets; spread with an offset spatula. Bake until cakes are set and spring back when touched, 18 to 20 minutes. Transfer sheets to wire racks to cool completely.

5. Assemble the baked Alaskas: Coat six 10-to-12-ounce bowls or ramekins with cooking spray; line with plastic wrap, leaving an overhang. Cut out 6 cake rounds to fit in bottoms of bowls (we used a 2½-inch round cookie cutter), and place in each bowl. Microwave ice cream to soften, about 20 seconds (or leave at room temperature 10 minutes), then transfer to a bowl and beat with an electric mixer on medium speed until smooth and spreadable, about 30 seconds. Top each with ⅓ cup chocolate ice cream, smoothing surface with an offset spatula. Cut out 6 cake rounds to fit on top of ice cream (we used a 3½-inch round cookie cutter), and place on ice cream. Freeze until set, about 30 minutes. (Return ice cream to freezer.)

(CONTINUES)

BAKED ALASKA

Slicing into a baked Alaska has an element of surprise: Only then is the cake-and-ice cream filling revealed. These miniature versions break from tradition by offering a double dose of chocolate (cake and ice cream) and three layers of cake; they would be just as delicious with other ice creams, especially hazelnut, mint chocolate chip, or tried-and-true vanilla. For the most classic baked Alaska, layer a variety of ice creams and/or sorbets atop a single cake base. There's no end to the flavor combinations you can use. Some of our favorites include cherry and pistachio ice creams (excellent with chocolate cake); vanilla ice cream layered with raspberry and blueberry sorbets (perfect for a Fourth of July celebration); a Neapolitan mix of chocolate, strawberry, and vanilla; and coconut paired with either mango, for a tropical twist, or rum raisin.

6. Top each cake with another ⅓ cup ice cream, smoothing surface. Cut out 6 cake rounds to fit in bowl (we used a 4-inch round cookie cutter), and place on ice cream. (This should fit just at the top of the bowl.) Cover assembled cakes with plastic overhang, and freeze at least 4 hours (or up to 3 days).

7. Unmold: Remove plastic wrap from top, flip cakes onto a baking sheet, and peel off plastic wrap. Freeze cakes while making meringue.

8. Make the meringue: Preheat oven to 500°F. Heat egg whites, sugar, and cream of tartar in a heatproof bowl set over (not in) a pan of simmering water, whisking, until sugar dissolves and mixture is warm to the touch, about 2 minutes. With an electric mixer on medium-high, whisk until meringue is cool and forms stiff peaks, about 10 minutes.

9. Use an offset spatula to spread each assembled cake with 1 cup meringue, swooping it into peaks. Bake until meringue is browned in spots, 2 to 3 minutes. Alternatively, hold a small kitchen torch at a 90-degree angle, 3 to 4 inches from surface of meringue, moving flame back and forth until meringue is browned and caramelized. Serve immediately.

BROWNING MERINGUE

Raspberry Ice-Cream Cake

This delicious and easy dessert proves that keeping it simple can be a very good thing. Start with a plain pound cake, layer it with ice cream (in any flavor) and fresh fruit, and voilà! Dessert is served. **SERVES 8**

1 loaf Pound Cake (page 17), sliced horizontally into thirds

1 pint vanilla ice cream, softened

1½ cups fresh raspberries (6 ounces)

Confectioners' sugar, for dusting

1. Place bottom layer of cake on a large piece of foil or in a loaf pan of equal size. Spread about ⅔ cup ice cream over bottom layer; sprinkle half the raspberries on top. Spread ⅓ cup ice cream over berries; top with second cake layer. Repeat, layering ⅔ cup ice cream, remaining berries, and remaining ⅓ cup ice cream; top with third cake layer.

2. Wrap with plastic, and freeze at least 4 hours (or up to overnight). Remove cake from freezer about 30 minutes before serving; dust with confectioners' sugar.

Chocolate-Chip-Cookie Icebox Cake

Want a guaranteed crowd-pleaser? Make a cake out of dozens of everybody's favorite cookie. Though chocolate wafers are the most common foundation of an icebox cake, they're not the only option. In fact, any cookies will do, as long as they're nice and crisp. These chocolate-chip cookies are stacked with a luscious mix of whipped cream and mascarpone cheese. **SERVES 10 TO 12**

FOR THE COOKIES

2¼ cups all-purpose flour

1 teaspoon baking soda

1¼ teaspoons salt

1 cup (2 sticks) unsalted butter, room temperature

1½ cups packed light brown sugar

¾ cup granulated sugar

2 large eggs

2 teaspoons vanilla extract

12 ounces semisweet chocolate chips or chunks (2 cups)

FOR THE CREAM

4 cups heavy cream, well chilled

8 ounces mascarpone cheese

2 tablespoons granulated sugar

1 tablespoon whiskey (optional)

Chocolate curls, for garnish (see page 328)

1. Make the cookies: Preheat oven to 350°F. Line 2 large baking sheets with parchment paper. Sift flour, baking soda, and salt into a bowl. With an electric mixer on medium-high speed, beat butter and both sugars until pale and fluffy, about 3 minutes. Reduce speed to low. Add eggs, 1 at a time, beating until combined after each and scraping down sides of bowl as needed. Add flour mixture in 3 batches, then beat in vanilla. Fold in chocolate chips.

2. Using a 1¼-inch ice-cream scoop (or a tablespoon), scoop dough onto prepared baking sheets, spacing them 2 inches apart. Bake until edges are golden brown and centers are set, 14 to 16 minutes. Transfer sheets to wire racks to cool 5 minutes. Transfer cookies to racks to cool completely.

3. Make the cream: With an electric mixer on medium speed, whisk 3 cups cream and the mascarpone in a chilled bowl until soft peaks form. Add granulated sugar and whiskey (if using). Whisk on medium-high speed until medium-stiff peaks form. Refrigerate until ready to use.

4. Dab the bottom of 11 cookies with a very small amount of cream mixture; arrange 9 in a circle on a serving plate, with 2 cookies in the middle. Carefully spread 1 cup cream mixture evenly over cookies, leaving a slight border. Repeat to form 7 more layers (staggering cookies), ending with cookies (you'll have a few cookies left over). Refrigerate, lightly draped with plastic wrap, overnight.

5. To serve, whisk remaining 1 cup cream until soft peaks form, and spread over top of cake. Garnish with curls. Cut into wedges with a serrated knife.

Chocolate-Berry Ice-Cream Cake

Here's a cool trick: Bake a chocolate cake and top it, right in the same pan, with ice-cream layers. Fitting the pan with a parchment collar allows you to create a cake with more height. For neat slices, run your knife under hot water between cuts. **SERVES 8 TO 10**

¼ cup unsweetened cocoa powder

½ cup all-purpose flour

½ cup sugar

½ teaspoon baking soda

¼ teaspoon baking powder

¼ teaspoon coarse salt

1 large egg yolk

¼ cup buttermilk

¼ cup warm water

1 tablespoon canola or safflower oil

½ teaspoon vanilla extract

1 cup fresh or thawed frozen blackberries (5 ounces)

1 pint vanilla ice cream

1 pint raspberry sorbet

Vegetable oil cooking spray

1. Preheat oven to 350°F. Lightly coat an 8-inch springform pan with cooking spray. In a large bowl, whisk together cocoa powder, flour, sugar, baking soda, baking powder, and salt. Whisk in egg yolk, buttermilk, the warm water, oil, and vanilla. Pour batter into prepared pan, and bake until cake pulls away from side and a cake tester comes out clean, about 15 minutes. Transfer pan to a wire rack to cool completely, 1½ hours.

2. Cut 1 or 2 strips of parchment 1 inch taller than side of pan; place between sides of cake and inside of pan, overlapping if necessary, to form a collar (parchment should fit snugly around entire circumference of cake).

3. In a medium bowl, lightly mash blackberries with a fork. Microwave ice cream to soften, about 20 seconds (or leave at room temperature 10 minutes), then transfer to a bowl and beat with an electric mixer on medium speed until smooth and spreadable, about 30 seconds. Stir in berries. With a small offset or flexible spatula, spread ice-cream mixture in an even layer over cooled cake. Freeze until ice cream is very firm, about 2 hours.

4. Soften sorbet as above and beat until smooth, then spread evenly over ice-cream layer; freeze until set, 1 hour (or up to 1 week, covered). To serve, unmold cake and remove parchment.

Frozen Espresso Cheesecake

Take a few of the components of tiramisù—espresso, chocolate, and mascarpone—and turn them into frozen cheesecake. Nuggets of torrone, an Italian nougat candy, make this dessert even more *delicioso*. Use a food processor to grind the wafer cookies. **SERVES 10**

1½ cups finely ground chocolate wafer cookies (8 ounces; about 35 cookies)

4 tablespoons unsalted butter, melted

½ cup plus 2 tablespoons sugar

4 large egg yolks

4½ teaspoons good-quality instant espresso powder (such as Medaglia d'Oro)

Pinch of salt

1½ pounds mascarpone cheese, room temperature

1½ teaspoons vanilla extract

12 ounces hard torrone (Italian nougat), cut into ¼-inch pieces

½ cup heavy cream, well chilled

Canola or safflower oil

1. Stir together cookie crumbs, melted butter, and 3 tablespoons sugar in a medium bowl.

2. In a heatproof bowl, combine egg yolks, ¼ cup sugar, the espresso, and the salt. Set bowl over (not in) a pan of simmering water; whisk until thick, about 2 minutes. With an electric mixer on medium speed, beat 2 minutes. Stir in mascarpone and vanilla by hand until smooth. Stir in torrone.

3. In another bowl, whisk cream with remaining 3 tablespoons sugar on medium speed until soft peaks form. Fold into mascarpone mixture until incorporated. Refrigerate until ready to use.

4. Lightly coat a 10-by-5-inch loaf pan with oil and line with plastic wrap and parchment, leaving an overhang on sides. Pour one third of mascarpone mixture into lined pan; smooth with an offset spatula. Top with half of crumb mixture; press crumbs to adhere. Repeat to make a second layer of mascarpone mixture and crumbs. Top with remaining mascarpone mixture. Loosely fold over parchment and plastic wrap. Freeze at least 3 hours (or up to 3 days).

5. To serve, let cake stand at room temperature 10 minutes. Set loaf pan in a larger pan; pour tap water into pan to reach three quarters of the way up sides of loaf pan. Let stand 10 seconds. Holding parchment, lift out cake. Unmold onto a serving plate; peel off parchment and plastic. Cut into slices, wiping knife between slices.

LAYERING IN PAN

Chocolate-Hazelnut Ice-Cream Cake

Sometimes more is better. This extravagant dessert has everything: ice cream, nuts, fluffy marshmallow, and enough satisfyingly cakey bits to hold it all together. SERVES 10 TO 12

FOR THE CAKE

Unsalted butter, for pans

²/₃ cups all-purpose flour, plus more for pans

²/₃ cup sugar

½ cup unsweetened cocoa powder

1 teaspoon baking powder

1 teaspoon baking soda

½ teaspoon coarse salt

½ cup canola or safflower oil

⅓ cup warm water

1 teaspoon vanilla extract

3 large eggs, room temperature, separated

FOR THE MARSHMALLOW SWIRL

4 large egg whites, room temperature

1 cup sugar

¼ teaspoon cream of tartar

1 teaspoon vanilla extract

FOR ASSEMBLING

3 pints chocolate ice cream (6 cups), softened

1 cup chopped toasted skinned hazelnuts (see page 344)

1. Make the cake: Preheat oven to 350°F. Butter two 10-inch spring-form pans (or one 10-inch springform pan and one 10-inch round cake pan); line with parchment rounds, and butter parchment. Dust with flour, tapping out excess. Whisk together ⅓ cup sugar, the flour, cocoa powder, baking powder, baking soda, and salt in a bowl. Mix oil, water, and vanilla in another bowl.

2. With an electric mixer on medium-high speed, beat egg yolks until pale and thick, about 5 minutes. Gradually add oil mixture, beating until combined. Gradually beat in flour mixture until combined.

3. In a clean mixer bowl, beat egg whites on medium-high speed until foamy. Gradually add remaining ⅓ cup sugar, beating until medium-stiff peaks form. Fold one third of the egg whites into yolk mixture with a flexible spatula, then gently fold in remaining whites.

4. Divide batter evenly between prepared pans; spread with an offset spatula. Bake until cakes are set and spring back when touched, 10 to 12 minutes. Transfer pans to a wire rack to cool completely. Remove cake from 1 pan (the cake pan, if using), and crumble.

5. Make the marshmallow swirl: Place egg whites, sugar, and cream of tartar in a bowl set over (not in) a pan of simmering water. Whisk constantly until sugar dissolves and mixture is warm, 3 to 4 minutes. Remove from heat. Beat with an electric mixer, starting on low speed and gradually raising to high, until stiff, glossy peaks form, 5 to 7 minutes. Beat in vanilla until thoroughly combined. Use immediately.

6. Assemble cake: Meanwhile, stir together ice cream and hazelnuts in a large bowl. Fold in three quarters of the marshmallow swirl and all the crumbled cake. Just barely fold in remaining marshmallow swirl, and spread over cake in springform pan, swirling top. Freeze until firm, at least 6 hours (or overnight). Remove side of pan, and let sit at room temperature 5 minutes before serving.

Gingerbread Icebox Cake

To give the familiar icebox cake a holiday feel, use homemade gingerbread cookies and top it with sweet-tart blood-orange compote. You will need a 2⅜-inch fluted round cutter to cut out the cookies.

SERVES 8 TO 10

FOR THE CAKE

All-purpose flour, for dusting

Molasses-Gingerbread Cookie Dough (page 342)

4 cups heavy cream, well chilled

¼ cup confectioners' sugar

1 teaspoon vanilla extract

FOR THE TOPPING

4 blood oranges, very thinly sliced into rounds

2 cups granulated sugar

2 cups water

1. Make the cake: Preheat oven to 350°F. Generously dust a piece of parchment with flour; on parchment, roll out dough to ¹⁄₁₆ inch thick. Brush off excess flour. Slide dough and parchment onto baking sheets; freeze 10 minutes. Using a 2⅜-inch fluted cutter, cut out 72 rounds. Transfer to parchment-lined baking sheets; freeze 10 minutes.

2. Bake cookies 5 minutes. Remove sheets from oven; tap them firmly on counter to flatten cookies. Return to oven, rotating sheets; bake until cookies are set and edges have darkened slightly, about 5 minutes more. Transfer sheets to wire racks to cool completely.

3. With an electric mixer on medium-high speed, whisk cream, confectioners' sugar, and vanilla just until stiff peaks form. Dab the bottom of 8 cookies with a very small amount of cream mixture; arrange 7 in a circle on a serving plate, with 1 cookie in the middle. Carefully spread ¾ cup whipped cream evenly over cookies, leaving a slight border. Repeat to form 8 more layers, ending with cream. Refrigerate 1 hour.

4. Meanwhile, make the topping: Bring a large pot of water to a boil. Add orange slices; cook until semitranslucent, about 5 minutes. Using a slotted spoon, transfer to a baking sheet.

5. Cut a round of parchment to fit in a large, shallow saucepan. Bring sugar and the 2 cups water to a boil, stirring until sugar has dissolved. Carefully add orange slices; place parchment directly on surface. Reduce heat, and simmer gently until oranges have softened and liquid is syrupy, about 30 minutes. Remove from heat; let oranges cool in syrup. Halve or quarter some of the orange slices, if desired. (Oranges can be refrigerated in syrup in an airtight container up to 1 week; bring to room temperature before serving.)

6. Spoon some of the oranges and their syrup over top of cake. Serve remaining oranges on the side.

Cakes with Fruit

When you see a perfect pineapple or plump, ripe peach or basket of juicy berries, bring it home to bake something that tastes unmistakably fresh and of the season. Upside-down cakes showcase the fruit (it ends up on top!), but you can also stir it into a batter or pile it on a finished cake. Whichever recipe you choose, the fruit you pick up at the farmers' market or in the produce aisle really has occasion to shine.

PINEAPPLE UPSIDE-DOWN CAKE, PAGE 224

Cranberry Upside-Down Cake

Though cakes aren't always contenders for the Thanksgiving buffet, this one would be welcome at the holiday feast, with maple-soaked cranberries atop a soft, almond-scented cake. Of course, you needn't serve it just once a year; enjoy this dessert throughout the fall and winter, when cranberries are readily available. **SERVES 8**

3/4 cup (1½ sticks) unsalted butter, room temperature, plus more for pan

3/4 cup all-purpose flour, plus more for pan

2¾ cups fresh or thawed frozen cranberries

1/2 cup plus 1 tablespoon pure maple syrup

1/2 teaspoon ground cinnamon

1 teaspoon baking powder

1/4 teaspoon salt

1/4 cup plus 2 tablespoons coarse yellow cornmeal

1/4 cup almond paste

3/4 cup plus 2 tablespoons sugar

3 large eggs, separated, room temperature

1/4 teaspoon vanilla extract

1/4 teaspoon almond extract

1/2 cup milk

1. Butter an 8-inch round cake pan; dust with flour, tapping out excess. In a large skillet, heat 6 tablespoons butter over medium until sizzling. Add cranberries; cook until shiny, about 2 minutes. Add maple syrup and cinnamon. Cook, stirring frequently, until cranberries soften but still hold their shape, 3 to 5 minutes. Remove from heat.

2. With a slotted spoon, transfer cranberries to a baking sheet to cool slightly before arranging in prepared cake pan. Return skillet to medium heat and cook until syrup boils and thickens, 3 to 4 minutes; do not overcook. Immediately pour syrup over cranberries; let cool, about 10 minutes.

3. Preheat oven to 350°F, with rack in center. Whisk flour, baking powder, and salt in a bowl. Whisk in cornmeal with a fork.

4. With an electric mixer on medium, beat remaining 6 tablespoons butter and the almond paste until well combined, about 30 seconds. Gradually add ¾ cup sugar; beat until creamy, about 2 minutes. Add egg yolks; beat until well combined. Beat in vanilla and almond extracts. Add flour mixture in 2 batches, alternating with the milk and beginning and ending with the flour; beat until just combined.

5. In a clean bowl, with an electric mixer on medium-low, whisk egg whites until foamy. Slowly add remaining 2 tablespoons sugar. Raise speed to high and beat until soft peaks form, about 5 minutes. Whisk one third of the whites into batter; fold in remaining whites.

6. Carefully spread batter over cranberries. Bake until a cake tester comes out clean, about 45 minutes. Transfer to a wire rack to cool 2 hours before inverting onto a serving plate.

Pineapple Upside-Down Cake

Forget old-fashioned examples made with canned pineapple and maraschino cherries. This take on the all-American dessert starts with a whole fresh pineapple. With its spiky top and spiny sides, the fruit can be a little intimidating, but it's easy to prepare: First, cut off the pineapple's top and bottom. Stand it on end, and, with downward strokes, cut the skin off in wide strips, removing the "eyes." Then cut the fruit into rounds, and use a paring knife (or small round cookie cutter) to cut out the core in the center. **SERVES 8 TO 10**

FOR THE CAKE

- 1½ cups all-purpose flour
- 2 teaspoons baking powder
- ¼ teaspoon salt
- 6 tablespoons unsalted butter, room temperature
- 1 cup sugar
- 2 large eggs
- 1 teaspoon vanilla extract
- ½ cup milk

FOR THE TOPPING

- ⅔ cup sugar
- 3 tablespoons unsalted butter, cut into small pieces
- 6 thin rounds cored pineapple (from 1 small pineapple), cut into halves

1. Make the cake: Preheat oven to 350°F. In a large bowl, combine flour, baking powder, and salt.

2. With an electric mixer on medium-high speed, beat butter and sugar until pale and fluffy, 3 to 5 minutes. Add eggs and vanilla; beat until combined. Add flour mixture in 3 batches, alternating with 2 batches of milk. Mix just until combined.

3. Make the topping: Pour sugar into a 10-inch ovenproof skillet (preferably cast-iron). Heat over medium until sugar begins to liquefy; cook, stirring with a wooden spoon, until sugar is fully melted and golden, 2 to 3 minutes. If sugar browns too quickly, remove pan from heat briefly before continuing. Remove pan from heat, and stir in butter. Arrange pineapple halves in pan, overlapping slightly if necessary to fit.

4. Carefully spoon batter over pineapples in skillet. Bake until a cake tester comes out clean, about 38 minutes. Transfer pan to a wire rack to cool 5 minutes. Run a knife around edge of cake to loosen, then carefully invert onto a platter. Serve warm or at room temperature.

PREPARING PINEAPPLE

Stone Fruit Upside-Down Cakes

Keep this recipe in mind for a summer party when stone fruit is at its peak. Nectarines, plums, and apricots all work wonderfully here; use one type of fruit per cake, or mix and match. If making two 9-inch cakes, decrease the amount of fruit to about two pounds and bake for about 70 minutes.

MAKES FIVE 6-INCH OR TWO 9-INCH CAKES

FOR THE TOPPING

- 1 cup (2 sticks) unsalted butter, room temperature
- 3 tablespoons maple syrup
- 1 teaspoon dark rum
- 2 cups packed light brown sugar
- 1/2 teaspoon vanilla extract
- 1/2 teaspoon coarse salt
- 10 to 15 nectarines, plums, or apricots (2 1/2 pounds), pitted and sliced into 1/4-inch wedges
- Vegetable oil cooking spray

FOR THE CAKES

- 1 1/2 cups all-purpose flour
- 1 1/2 cups cake flour (not self-rising)
- 1 tablespoon baking powder
- 1 teaspoon salt
- 1 cup (2 sticks) unsalted butter, room temperature
- 1 3/4 cups granulated sugar
- 4 large eggs
- 2 teaspoons vanilla extract
- 1 1/4 cups milk

1. Preheat oven to 350°F. Make the topping: With an electric mixer on medium speed, beat butter, maple syrup, rum, brown sugar, vanilla, and salt until well blended.

2. Coat five 6-by-3-inch or two 9-by-2-inch round cake pans with cooking spray, line with parchment rounds, and spray parchment. Divide topping evenly among pans, smoothing with an offset spatula. Starting from the center and working outward, arrange fruit slices in an overlapping fan shape over topping in pans.

3. Make the cakes: In a medium bowl, sift together both flours, the baking powder, and salt. With an electric mixer on medium-high speed, beat butter and granulated sugar until pale and fluffy, 3 to 4 minutes, scraping down sides of bowl as needed. Beat in eggs, 1 at a time, then beat in vanilla. Reduce mixer speed to low. Add flour mixture in 3 batches, alternating with 2 batches of milk; beat until combined after each addition.

4. Divide batter evenly among prepared pans; smooth tops with an offset spatula. Bake, rotating halfway through, until cakes are golden brown and a cake tester comes out clean, 35 to 40 minutes. Transfer pans to wire racks to cool 30 minutes. Run a small knife around edges of cakes to loosen, then invert onto racks or serving plates. Serve warm or at room temperature.

Coconut-Lime-Berry Cake

Buttermilk and coconut make this snacking cake especially moist. A touch of rum lends a tropical flavor, but you can substitute orange juice instead. Use whichever berries look best at the market, whether one type or a colorful mix like the one shown here. **SERVES 12**

¾ cup (1½ sticks) unsalted butter, room temperature, plus more for baking dish

1¾ cups plus 1 tablespoon all-purpose flour, plus more for baking dish

2 teaspoons baking powder

½ teaspoon coarse salt

1 cup packed sweetened shredded coconut

1 cup plus 1 tablespoon sugar

3 large eggs

¾ cup buttermilk

2 teaspoons finely grated lime zest plus 2 tablespoons fresh lime juice

3 cups berries, such as raspberries, blackberries, and blueberries (about 1 pound)

3 tablespoons rum or orange juice

1. Preheat oven to 350°F. Butter a 9-by-13-inch baking dish; dust with flour, tapping out excess. In a large bowl, whisk together 1¾ cups flour, the baking powder, salt, and coconut.

2. With an electric mixer on high speed, beat butter and 1 cup sugar until pale and fluffy, scraping down sides of bowl as needed, about 4 minutes. Add eggs, 1 at a time, and beat until combined. Reduce mixer speed to low. Add flour mixture in 3 batches, alternating with 2 batches of buttermilk; beat until combined. Stir in lime zest and juice. Transfer batter to prepared dish; smooth with an offset spatula.

3. In a medium bowl, toss berries with remaining 1 tablespoon flour and 1 tablespoon sugar, and the rum. Scatter berry mixture over batter. Bake until cake is golden at edges and a cake tester inserted in center comes out clean, about 35 minutes. Transfer pan to a wire rack to cool 20 minutes; serve warm or at room temperature. (Cooled cake can be refrigerated, wrapped in plastic, up to 5 days.)

Mandarin Orange and Vanilla Upside-Down Cake

Orange slices atop this cake bring to mind bright slices of sunshine. We left the rind on for a deliciously tart taste. Satsuma mandarins— small, slightly flattened oranges that are symbols of good fortune in Chinese New Year celebrations—are excellent here, but you can use other varieties as well. Since the whole fruit is used, seek out organic, pesticide-free oranges and wash them well before using. **SERVES 8 TO 10**

4 to 5 medium mandarins, preferably Satsuma (1½ pounds), thinly sliced, seeds removed

1 cup (2 sticks) unsalted butter, room temperature

1 vanilla bean, halved lengthwise and scraped, pod reserved for another use

1½ cups sugar

1 tablespoon finely grated mandarin zest plus 3 tablespoons fresh mandarin juice (from 1 mandarin)

1⅓ cups plus 1 tablespoon all-purpose flour

1½ teaspoons baking powder

½ teaspoon coarse salt

2 large eggs

½ cup whole milk

1. Preheat oven to 350°F. Bring a large pot of water to a boil. Add mandarin slices; boil 3 minutes. Drain. Arrange slices in a single layer on paper towels.

2. Place ½ cup butter in a 9-by-2-inch round cake pan. Mix half the vanilla seeds and ½ cup sugar; sprinkle over butter. Place pan in oven until butter melts, about 7 minutes. Remove from oven; carefully whisk in 2 tablespoons mandarin juice.

3. Whisk together flour, baking powder, and salt in a medium bowl. With an electric mixer on medium-high speed, beat zest and remaining ½ cup butter, 1 cup sugar, and vanilla seeds until pale and fluffy, 3 to 5 minutes. With mixer running, add eggs, 1 at a time, beating well after each addition. Reduce mixer speed to low. Add flour mixture in 2 batches, alternating with the milk and remaining 1 tablespoon juice.

4. Arrange mandarin slices over sugar mixture in pan, starting in the center and spiraling outward, overlapping slices slightly. (Use slices that are completely intact.) Gently spoon batter on top of mandarins; spread evenly with an offset spatula. Bake until cake is golden brown and a cake tester comes out clean, 45 to 50 minutes. Transfer pan to wire rack to cool 10 minutes. Run a knife around edge of cake to loosen, then invert onto a serving plate; let cool before serving. (Cake can be stored at room temperature, covered, for 1 day.)

Lemon-Fig Cake

Olive oil has a gentle fruitiness that works well in simple snacking cakes. Try this one for breakfast, with a cappuccino, or to accompany an afternoon cup of tea. You can use a 9-inch round cake pan instead of the tart pan; brush it with oil and line with a parchment round.

SERVES 8 TO 10

½ cup olive oil, plus more for pan

½ cup milk

1 large egg

1½ cups all-purpose flour

¾ cup sugar

½ teaspoon baking powder

¼ teaspoon salt

10 ounces dried figs, stemmed and coarsely chopped (about 1½ cups)

1½ teaspoons finely grated lemon zest

1. Preheat oven to 350°F. Brush a 9-inch tart pan with a removable bottom with oil.

2. In a medium bowl or liquid measuring cup, whisk together oil, milk, and egg. In a large bowl, whisk together flour, sugar, baking powder, and salt; add milk mixture, and stir with a flexible spatula just until smooth (do not overmix). Gently fold in figs and lemon zest.

3. Transfer batter to prepared pan; set pan on a rimmed baking sheet. Bake until golden and a cake tester comes out clean, 35 to 40 minutes. Transfer pan to a wire rack to cool 15 minutes. Turn out cake onto rack to cool completely. (Cake can be stored at room temperature, wrapped in plastic, up to 1 day.)

Apple Pie Upside-Down Cake

Borrow the flavors of the all-American pie for a cake that's equally at home at a harvest picnic or a Thanksgiving dinner. Its low profile is the result of baking it in a 12-inch tart pan; if you don't have one, you could use a pizza pan of the same size instead. **SERVES 10 TO 12**

1¼ cups (2½ sticks) unsalted butter, room temperature, plus more for pan

1½ cups packed light brown sugar

3 tablespoons Calvados

¾ teaspoon plus a pinch of salt

3 whole cinnamon sticks

6 Braeburn or McIntosh apples (about 2½ pounds), peeled, cored, and cut into ¼-inch-thick rings

2¼ cups all-purpose flour

½ teaspoon baking soda

½ teaspoon baking powder

¾ teaspoon ground cinnamon

1½ cups granulated sugar

3 large eggs

1½ teaspoons vanilla extract

½ cup sour cream

1. Preheat oven to 375°F, with rack in lower third of oven. Butter a 12-inch round tart pan with a removable bottom; line with a parchment round, and butter parchment. Wrap exterior of pan with foil.

2. With an electric mixer on medium-high speed, beat ½ cup (1 stick) butter, the brown sugar, Calvados, and a pinch of salt until pale and fluffy, 2 to 3 minutes. Spread mixture in prepared pan. Arrange apple rings in pan (you may not need all the apple rings; use the prettiest ones), and press them gently into mixture. Place cinnamon sticks in gaps. Sift together flour, baking soda, baking powder, remaining ¾ teaspoon salt, and the ground cinnamon into a bowl.

3. With mixer on medium-high speed, beat remaining ¾ cup (1½ sticks) butter and the granulated sugar in a clean bowl until pale and fluffy, 2 to 3 minutes. Beat in eggs, 1 at a time, and vanilla. Reduce speed to low. Add flour mixture in 2 batches, alternating with the sour cream and beginning and ending with the flour; beat until just combined. Spread batter evenly over apples.

4. Bake until cake is golden brown and a cake tester comes out clean, about 45 minutes. Transfer to a wire rack to cool 15 minutes, then carefully invert onto a serving plate. (Cake can be stored at room temperature, covered, up to 1 day.)

Rhubarb Upside-Down Cake

Rhubarb lends its sweet-tart flavor and rosy color to this springtime treat. Sliced stalks are tossed with sugar in a cake pan; batter and streusel are layered on top (of course, the streusel will be the bottom of the cake once it's inverted). It's important to let the cake cool for ten minutes before turning it out: The rhubarb will be too hot to handle right after baking, but if it sits too much longer, it may stick. **SERVES 8 TO 10**

FOR THE STREUSEL

- 4 tablespoons unsalted butter, melted
- ½ cup all-purpose flour
- ¼ cup sugar
- ¼ teaspoon coarse salt

FOR THE CAKE

- ¾ cup (1½ sticks) unsalted butter, room temperature, plus more for pan
- 1 pound rhubarb, trimmed and cut on a very sharp diagonal about ½ inch thick
- 1¾ cups sugar
- 1½ cups all-purpose flour
- 1½ teaspoons baking powder
- 1½ teaspoons coarse salt
- ½ teaspoon finely grated orange zest plus 1 tablespoon fresh orange juice
- 2 large eggs
- 1 cup sour cream

1. Preheat oven to 350°F. Make the streusel: Stir together butter, flour, sugar, and salt until moist and crumbly.

2. Make the cake: Butter a 9-by-2-inch round cake pan. Dot with 4 tablespoons butter (cut into pieces). Toss rhubarb with ¾ cup sugar; let stand 2 minutes. Toss again; spread in pan.

3. Whisk together flour, baking powder, and salt. With an electric mixer on medium speed, beat butter and 1 cup sugar until pale and fluffy, 3 to 5 minutes. Beat in zest and juice. Add eggs, 1 at a time, beating until incorporated after each and scraping down sides of bowl as necessary. Add flour mixture in 3 batches, alternating with 2 batches of sour cream, and beating until smooth. Spread evenly over rhubarb. Crumble streusel over batter.

4. Bake until a cake tester comes out clean and top springs back when touched, about 60 minutes. Transfer pan to a wire rack to cool 10 minutes. Run a knife around edge of cake to loosen, then invert onto rack to cool completely.

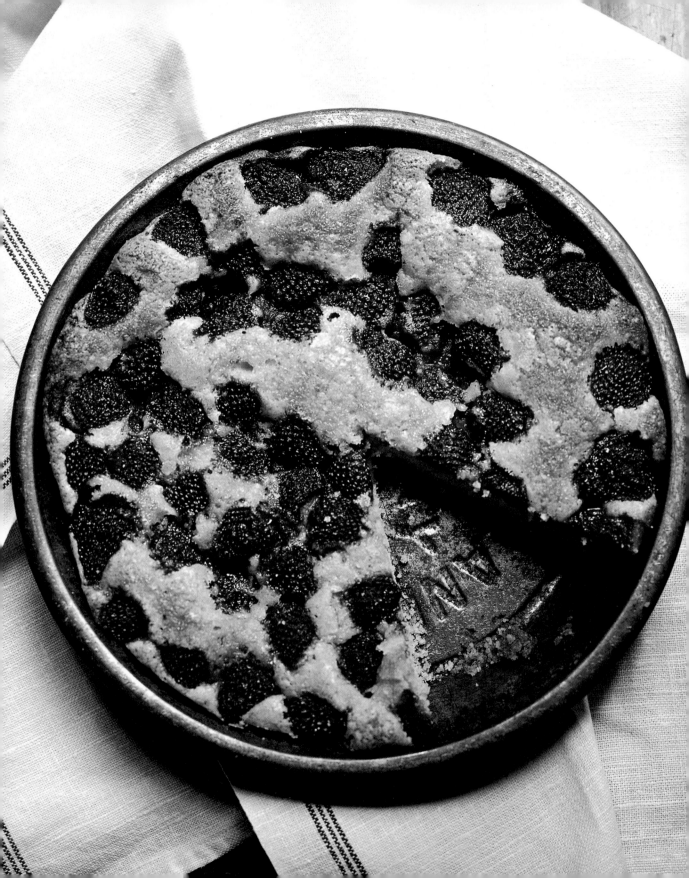

Strawberry Cake

Baked in a pie tin and bursting with berries, this homespun dessert offers an excellent excuse to go strawberry picking (as if you need an excuse). Take it with you on a picnic or to a backyard potluck, and serve it straight from the pan. You can bake it in a 9-inch cake pan if you prefer.

SERVES 8 TO 10

6 tablespoons unsalted butter, room temperature, plus more for pie plate

1½ cups all-purpose flour

1½ teaspoons baking powder

½ teaspoon salt

1 cup plus 2 tablespoons sugar

1 large egg

½ cup milk

1 teaspoon vanilla extract

1 pound fresh strawberries, hulled and halved

1. Preheat oven to 350°F. Butter a 10-inch pie plate. Sift together flour, baking powder, and salt into a medium bowl.

2. With an electric mixer on medium-high speed, beat butter and 1 cup sugar until pale and fluffy, about 3 minutes. Reduce speed to medium-low; mix in egg, milk, and vanilla.

3. Reduce speed to low; gradually add flour mixture. Transfer batter to prepared pie plate. Arrange strawberries on top of batter, cut sides down and as close together as possible. Sprinkle remaining 2 tablespoons sugar over berries.

4. Bake cake 10 minutes. Reduce heat to 325°F, and continue to bake until cake is golden brown and firm to the touch, about 60 minutes more. Transfer pie plate to a wire rack to cool completely. (Cake can be stored at room temperature, loosely covered, up to 2 days.)

Pear Pavlova

This light, airy dessert, named for Russian ballerina Anna Pavlova, comes to us from Down Under—in fact, both New Zealand and Australia have claimed it as their own. Traditionally the meringue is topped with passion fruit, strawberries, or kiwi; our pears poached in spiced red wine are an autumnal twist. When making the meringue, be sure the egg whites are free of any yolk and that the bowl is spotless and dry; even a small trace of fat can prevent meringue from whipping properly. **SERVES 6**

FOR THE PEARS

- 1 bottle (750 ml) dry red wine, such as Cabernet or Zinfandel
- 3 cups water
- 1 cup granulated sugar
- 1 teaspoon whole black peppercorns
- 3 dried bay leaves
- 2 cinnamon sticks
- 3 to 6 ripe Bosc pears

FOR THE MERINGUE BASE

- 4 large egg whites, room temperature
- Pinch of salt
- 3/4 cup packed light brown sugar
- 1/4 cup superfine sugar
- 1 teaspoon distilled white vinegar
- 1 teaspoon vanilla extract

FOR THE TOPPING

- 1 cup heavy cream
- 2 tablespoons superfine sugar

1. Poach the pears: Combine wine, the water, sugar, peppercorns, bay leaves, and cinnamon sticks in a large saucepan. Bring to a boil; stir until sugar has dissolved. Reduce heat to a gentle simmer.

2. Carefully peel pears, leaving stems intact. Add to pan; cover, and cook, rotating pears occasionally, until bases of pears are easily pierced with a paring knife, 20 to 25 minutes, depending on ripeness of fruit. Meanwhile, prepare an ice-water bath.

3. Using a large slotted spoon, carefully transfer pears to a large metal bowl set in the ice-water bath. Pour poaching liquid through a fine sieve into bowl with pears; let cool completely. Cover with plastic wrap; refrigerate overnight to let pears absorb the poaching liquid.

4. Make the meringue base: Preheat oven to 300°F with rack in center. Line a baking sheet with parchment. Using an overturned bowl or cake pan as a guide, trace an 8-inch circle on the parchment; turn parchment over, marked side down.

5. With an electric mixer on low speed, whisk egg whites, salt, and brown sugar until combined and no lumps of sugar remain. Raise speed to medium; beat until soft peaks form, about 9 minutes. With mixer running, gradually add superfine sugar. Continue beating until peaks are stiff and glossy, about 2 minutes more. Beat in vinegar and vanilla.

6. Using a flexible spatula, spread meringue onto the marked 8-inch circle on prepared baking sheet; form peaks around the edge and a well in the center (see photo on page 242). Bake meringue until crisp around the edge and just set in the center, about 75 minutes. Transfer baking sheet to a wire rack until meringue is cool enough to handle. Carefully peel off parchment; let meringue cool completely on rack.

(CONTINUES)

PAVLOVA

This version of pavlova has a caramel-like flavor and slightly chewy texture, thanks to the addition of brown sugar in the meringue. For a crisper, more classic shell, use only superfine sugar (keep the total quantity the same). Among pavlova's appeals is its endless versatility; feel free to swap out the fruit here with fresh, macerated, poached, or even roasted fruits (or a combination of these), depending on the season. Passion fruit, strawberries, and kiwi are all traditional, given the dessert's origin. Try rhubarb and raspberries in the spring, stone fruits and other berries in the summer, quince or apples in the fall, and citrus or mango in the winter. You can also change up the whipped cream by folding in pastry cream or mascarpone, or replacing it with crème fraîche, fruit curd, pudding or other custard, mousse, even ice cream or sorbet. Consider sprinkling the assembled dessert with chopped toasted nuts (pistachios are especially nice with fresh fruit).

7. Make the topping: In a small bowl, whip heavy cream and superfine sugar until stiff peaks form. Cover with plastic wrap; refrigerate until ready to use.

8. Slice pears in half lengthwise. Remove seeds and stems with a spoon or melon baller; discard. Cut pears into ¾-inch pieces; place in a bowl, and cover with plastic wrap until ready to use.

9. Bring 3 cups poaching liquid to a boil in a medium saucepan, and prepare another ice-water bath. Reduce heat; simmer until syrupy and reduced to about 1 cup, 20 to 25 minutes. Pour syrup into a clean bowl set in the ice-water bath; stir frequently until cool and thickened.

10. To assemble, carefully place meringue on a serving platter. Spoon whipped cream on top, then add pears. Serve, sliced into wedges and drizzled with syrup.

SPREADING MERINGUE

Olive-Oil Cake with Red Grapes

Grapes make this Italian cake—traditionally served to celebrate the start of the harvest season—unexpected and special. **SERVES 9**

- ½ cup extra-virgin olive oil, plus more for pan
- 1 cup all-purpose flour, plus more for pan
- ½ cup finely ground toasted almonds (see page 344)
- ¼ cup quick-cooking polenta or coarse yellow cornmeal
- 1½ teaspoons baking powder
- ½ teaspoon salt
- 2 large eggs
- ⅔ cup sugar
- 2 teaspoons finely grated lemon zest
- ⅓ cup milk
- 2 cups red seedless grapes

1. Preheat oven to 350°F. Brush an 8-inch square pan with oil; dust with flour, tapping out excess. In a medium bowl, whisk together flour, almonds, polenta, baking powder, and salt.

2. With an electric mixer on high speed, beat eggs, sugar, and zest until pale and fluffy, 3 to 5 minutes. Reduce speed to low; slowly add oil. Add flour mixture in 3 batches, alternating with 2 batches of milk; beat until just combined.

3. Transfer batter to prepared pan; scatter 1 cup grapes over top. Bake 15 minutes. Scatter remaining 1 cup grapes over cake. Bake until cake is golden and a cake tester comes out clean, 25 to 27 minutes more. Transfer pan to a wire rack to cool 15 minutes. Turn out cake, and cut into squares to serve.

Plum Skillet Cake

This cake is quick and easy enough to whip up for a last-minute brunch or weeknight dinner. Slide the cake into the oven as you sit down to eat, and it will be ready for dessert when you are. **SERVES 6**

- 4 tablespoons unsalted butter, room temperature, plus more for skillet
- 1 cup all-purpose flour, plus more for skillet
- ½ teaspoon baking powder
- ¼ teaspoon baking soda
- ½ teaspoon coarse salt
- ¾ cup plus 2 tablespoons sugar
- 1 large egg
- ½ cup buttermilk
- 2 ripe medium plums, thinly sliced

1. Preheat oven to 375°F. Butter an 8-inch ovenproof skillet (preferably cast-iron); dust with flour, tapping out excess. Whisk together flour, baking powder, baking soda, and salt. With an electric mixer on medium speed, beat butter and ¾ cup sugar until pale and fluffy, 3 to 5 minutes. Beat in egg. Add flour mixture in 3 batches, alternating with 2 batches of buttermilk; beat until just combined.

2. Transfer batter to prepared skillet; smooth top with an offset spatula. Arrange plums on top, fanning the slices; sprinkle with remaining 2 tablespoons sugar. Bake until golden brown and a cake tester comes out clean, 35 to 40 minutes. Transfer to a wire rack to cool slightly before serving.

Strawberry-Basil Shortcake

Make a summer classic even better (yes, it's possible!) with the addition of basil, another of the season's signature flavors. Be sure to cover the cream with plastic wrap while the basil is steeping. SERVES 8 TO 10

2¼ cups cold heavy cream, plus 2 tablespoons, for brushing

20 large basil leaves, plus ⅓ cup small or torn basil leaves

3 cups all-purpose flour

½ cup granulated sugar, plus more if needed

1 tablespoon plus 1½ teaspoons baking powder

¾ teaspoon salt

1 cup (2 sticks) plus 2 tablespoons cold unsalted butter, cut into small pieces

2 large eggs, lightly beaten

½ teaspoon vanilla extract

1¼ pounds (4½ cups) sliced strawberries

3 tablespoons confectioners' sugar

1. Bring 1½ cups cream to a gentle simmer in a small saucepan over medium heat. Bruise large basil leaves by hitting them repeatedly with the dull side of a knife, and stir into cream. Remove from heat, cover tightly, and let steep 25 minutes. Strain through a fine sieve, pressing solids to extract liquid. Refrigerate in an airtight container at least 5 hours (or up to 1 day).

2. Preheat oven to 400°F. Whisk together flour, 3 tablespoons granulated sugar, the baking powder, and salt. Cut in butter with a pastry blender or rub in with your fingers. (The largest pieces should be the size of small peas.)

3. Whisk together ¾ cup heavy cream, the eggs, and vanilla. Stir into flour mixture using a fork until ingredients are moistened but not fully incorporated (do not overmix).

4. Turn dough out onto a parchment-lined baking sheet; pat into a 9½-inch round. Brush dough with remaining 2 tablespoons heavy cream; sprinkle with 1 tablespoon granulated sugar.

5. Bake until light golden brown and just cooked through, about 25 minutes. Transfer baking sheet to a wire rack to cool completely, about 2 hours. (The shortcake is best served within 4 hours of baking, but untopped shortcake can be stored at room temperature, wrapped in plastic, up to 8 hours.)

6. Meanwhile, combine strawberries with remaining ¼ cup granulated sugar, adding more sugar if needed, depending on sweetness. Let macerate, stirring occasionally, at least 1 hour and up to 3 hours.

7. Toss berries with small basil leaves. With an electric mixer on high speed, whisk basil cream with confectioners' sugar in a chilled bowl until soft peaks form. To serve, mound basil cream on shortcake; spoon berries and basil leaves with juice over top.

Peach and Cornmeal Upside-Down Cake

An upside-down cake with a Southern accent, this dessert features peaches and cornmeal—two regional favorites. The lavender is optional but brings a lovely, subtle fragrance and flavor to the delicious dessert.

SERVES 8 TO 10

½ cup plus 3 tablespoons unsalted butter, room temperature

1 cup sugar

3 ripe peaches (about 1¼ pounds), skins on, pitted and cut into ¾-inch wedges

1 cup coarse yellow cornmeal or polenta

¾ cup all-purpose flour

1 teaspoon baking powder

2 teaspoons chopped fresh lavender, or 1½ teaspoons dried lavender (optional)

1¼ teaspoons coarse salt

3 large eggs

½ teaspoon vanilla extract

½ cup heavy cream

1. Preheat oven to 350°F. Melt 3 tablespoons butter in a 10-inch ovenproof skillet (preferably cast-iron) over medium heat, using a pastry brush to coat sides with butter as it melts. Sprinkle ¼ cup sugar evenly over bottom of skillet; cook until sugar starts to bubble and turn golden brown, about 3 minutes. Arrange peaches in a circle at edge of skillet, on top of sugar; arrange remaining wedges in center to fill. Reduce heat to low; cook until juices are bubbling and peaches begin to soften, 10 to 12 minutes. Remove from heat.

2. Whisk together cornmeal, flour, baking powder, lavender if using, and salt. With an electric mixer on high speed, beat remaining ½ cup butter and ¾ cup sugar until pale and fluffy, about 3 minutes. Reduce speed to medium. Add eggs, 1 at a time, beating well after each addition and scraping down sides of bowl as needed. Mix in vanilla and cream. Reduce speed to low, and beat in cornmeal mixture in 2 additions.

3. Drop large spoonfuls of batter over peaches; spread evenly using an offset spatula. Bake until golden brown and a cake tester comes out clean, 20 to 22 minutes. Transfer skillet to a wire rack to cool 10 minutes. Run a knife or spatula around edge of cake to loosen. Quickly invert cake onto a cutting board or serving platter. Tap bottom of skillet to release peaches; carefully remove skillet. If necessary, reposition peach slices on top of cake. Let cool slightly before serving.

SPREADING BATTER OVER PEACHES

Blackberry Cornmeal Cake

This rustic summer specialty makes it worth turning on the oven—even on a hot day. Its preparation couldn't be more carefree: Just pour the batter into a skillet, scatter berries over the top, and pop it in the oven.

SERVES 8

1¼ cups all-purpose flour

½ cup coarse yellow cornmeal or polenta

2 teaspoons baking powder

1 teaspoon salt

1 cup plus 2 tablespoons sugar, plus ¼ cup for sprinkling

½ cup buttermilk

2 large eggs

7 tablespoons unsalted butter, melted, plus 1 tablespoon for skillet

2 containers (5 ounces each) fresh blackberries

1. Preheat oven to 375°F. In a large bowl, whisk together flour, cornmeal, baking powder, salt, and 1 cup plus 2 tablespoons sugar. In another bowl, whisk together buttermilk, eggs, and melted butter; pour over flour mixture, whisking to combine.

2. In a 10-inch ovenproof skillet (preferably cast-iron), heat remaining tablespoon butter in the oven until melted and skillet is hot, about 5 minutes. Remove from oven; swirl to coat bottom of pan. Transfer batter to skillet, scatter blackberries on top, and sprinkle with remaining ¼ cup sugar.

3. Bake, with a baking sheet on rack below (to catch any drips), until top is evenly browned, 45 to 50 minutes. Transfer to a wire rack to cool 30 minutes. Before serving, run a knife around edge of cake to loosen; serve warm or at room temperature.

Gingerbread-Pear Upside-Down Cake

Dress up a holiday favorite with pears in a rich brandy syrup. Ginger is used in two forms: fresh and ground. The easiest way to grate ginger is with a ceramic grater (often found in Asian grocery stores) or a rasp-style grater. **SERVES 8 TO 10**

- ½ cup plus 2 tablespoons butter (1¼ sticks), room temperature, plus more for pan
- 5 large ripe Bartlett pears, peeled, cored, and quartered
- 2 tablespoons fresh lemon juice
- ¼ cup granulated sugar
- ¼ cup plus 2 tablespoons brandy
- 1 cup all-purpose flour
- 1 tablespoon ground ginger
- 1 teaspoon ground cinnamon
- ¼ teaspoon ground cloves
- ¼ teaspoon freshly grated nutmeg
- ¼ teaspoon salt
- ¼ cup packed dark brown sugar
- 3 large eggs
- ½ cup unsulfured molasses
- 1 tablespoon freshly grated peeled ginger
- 1 teaspoon baking soda
- 2 tablespoons boiling water

1. Preheat oven to 350°F. Butter a 9-inch round cake pan. In a large bowl, toss pears with lemon juice. In large skillet over medium-high heat, melt 2 tablespoons butter; sprinkle with 2 tablespoons granulated sugar. Add half the pears, cut sides down, in a single layer; cook, flipping once, until browned on both sides, 2 to 3 minutes per side. Using a slotted spoon, transfer cooked pears to a plate. Cook remaining pears; transfer to a baking sheet, leaving juices behind.

2. Add brandy to skillet, and sprinkle with remaining 2 tablespoons granulated sugar. Cook, stirring, until reduced to a syrup, about 1 minute. Pour into cake pan; swirl to coat. Arrange pears in pan in a single layer, with the tapered sides all facing the same direction.

3. In a medium bowl, whisk together flour, ground ginger, cinnamon, cloves, nutmeg, and salt. With an electric mixer on medium-high speed, beat remaining ½ cup butter until fluffy, about 2 minutes. Add brown sugar; continue beating until pale and fluffy, about 3 minutes more. Add eggs; beat to combine. Beat in molasses and grated ginger.

4. Reduce speed to low. Mix in half of flour mixture. In a small bowl, combine baking soda and the boiling water; beat into batter. Beat in remaining flour mixture until combined. Transfer to pan; bake 25 minutes. Reduce heat to 325°F; bake until cake is springy to the touch, 15 to 20 minutes more. Transfer to a wire rack to cool 1 hour. Run a knife around edge of cake to loosen, then invert cake onto a serving plate. If necessary, reposition pears on top of cake.

Chocolate-Cherry Upside-Down Cakes

Individual upside-down cakes turn deep, dark, and delicious with a chocolate batter baked over a brown sugar and sour cherry combo. They taste like cherry-flavored truffles—with a finishing touch of rum-spiked whipped cream. If you can't find jarred sour cherries, substitute frozen sour cherries, thawed and drained, and use one teaspoon fresh lemon juice in place of the cherry juice in step one. **MAKES 2**

4 tablespoons unsalted butter, room temperature

1/3 cup plus 3 tablespoons packed light brown sugar

1 1/2 cups drained jarred sour cherries (1 teaspoon juice reserved)

1/3 cup all-purpose flour

1/4 cup unsweetened cocoa powder

1/4 teaspoon baking powder

1/4 teaspoon coarse salt

1 large egg yolk

3 tablespoons whole milk

1/4 cup heavy cream

2 teaspoons rum

1. Preheat oven to 350°F. Place 1 tablespoon butter, 1 tablespoon brown sugar, and 1/2 teaspoon cherry juice in the bottom of each of two 8-ounce ramekins. Bake until butter and brown sugar are melted and bubbling, about 1 minute. Arrange cherries in a tightly packed layer in bottom of each ramekin.

2. Whisk together flour, cocoa, baking powder, and salt. In another bowl, stir together remaining 2 tablespoons butter and 1/3 cup brown sugar with a wooden spoon until pale and fluffy, about 3 minutes. Stir in egg yolk, then flour mixture and milk. Divide between ramekins.

3. Place ramekins on a rimmed baking sheet. Bake until a cake tester comes out with only a few crumbs attached, about 30 minutes. Transfer ramekins to a wire rack to cool 20 minutes.

4. Meanwhile, with an electric mixer, beat heavy cream, remaining 1 tablespoon brown sugar, and the rum until soft peaks form. Run a knife around edges of cakes to loosen, then invert onto serving plates. If necessary, reposition cherries on top of cakes. Serve cakes with rum whipped cream.

Layer Cakes

We all have memories of frosting-swirled layer cakes from childhood birthdays, Grandma's kitchen, or the neighborhood bakery—and they are often among the most meaningful. The more than two dozen recipes in this chapter include ultimate versions of the most delectable cakes and frostings, as well as some delightful new flavor combinations. Use them to build on favorite traditions—or to start new ones of your own.

BUTTERMILK CAKE WITH CHOCOLATE FROSTING, PAGE 259

Buttermilk Cake with Chocolate Frosting

Close your eyes and make a wish—for the quintessential birthday cake. With these golden buttermilk layers generously covered in dark chocolate frosting, your wish comes true. **SERVES 10 TO 12**

1 cup (2 sticks) unsalted butter, room temperature, plus more for pans

3 cups all-purpose flour, plus more for pans

1 tablespoon baking powder

1 teaspoon baking soda

½ teaspoon salt

2 cups sugar

4 large eggs, lightly beaten

1¼ cups buttermilk

1½ teaspoons vanilla extract

Rich Chocolate Frosting (page 337)

White nonpareils, for decorating (optional)

1. Preheat oven to 350°F. Butter two 8-by-2-inch round cake pans; line with parchment rounds, and butter parchment. Dust with flour, tapping out excess. Sift together flour, baking powder, baking soda, and salt into a medium bowl.

2. With an electric mixer on medium speed, beat butter until softened, 1 to 2 minutes. Gradually add sugar; continue beating until pale and fluffy, 3 to 4 minutes, scraping down sides of bowl as needed. Add eggs, a little at a time, beating well after each addition and scraping down sides of bowl once or twice, about 5 minutes.

3. Reduce speed to low. Slowly add flour mixture in 2 batches, alternating with the buttermilk and beginning and ending with the flour; beat until just incorporated. Beat in vanilla.

4. Divide batter evenly between prepared pans. Bake, rotating halfway through, until golden brown and a cake tester comes out clean, 35 to 45 minutes. Transfer pans to wire racks to cool 15 minutes. Turn out cakes onto racks to cool completely.

5. Place bottom cake layer on a cake stand or platter, and spread evenly with about 1 cup chocolate frosting. Place remaining layer, top side down, on top of first; press down slightly. Spread remaining frosting over top and sides of cake, using an offset spatula to create large swirls. Sprinkle with nonpareils, if desired. Refrigerate cake until frosting sets, about 10 minutes (or up to 3 days), before serving.

Chiffon Cake with Strawberries and Cream

Love strawberry shortcake? Don't miss this twist on the springtime favorite. The cake is similar in texture to an angel-food cake, but richer, thanks to the addition of egg yolks. The filling is simply whipped cream and strawberries that have been halved and tossed with sugar, lemon juice, and a pinch of salt. **SERVES 10 TO 12**

FOR THE CAKE

- 2¼ cups cake flour (not self-rising)
- 1½ cups granulated sugar
- 2¼ teaspoons baking powder
- ¾ teaspoon salt
- ½ cup canola or safflower oil
- 7 large egg yolks plus 9 large egg whites, room temperature
- ¾ cup milk
- ½ teaspoon cream of tartar
- 1 whole vanilla bean, split lengthwise and scraped (pod reserved for another use), or 2 teaspoons vanilla extract

FOR THE FILLING

- 2 pounds fresh strawberries, hulled and halved or quartered (about 5 cups), plus more for serving
- ½ cup granulated sugar
- 1 tablespoon fresh lemon juice
- Pinch of salt
- 2 cups cold heavy cream
- ¼ cup confectioners' sugar, plus more for dusting

1. Make the cake: Preheat oven to 325°F. Whisk together flour, ¾ cup granulated sugar, the baking powder, and salt in a medium bowl. Whisk together oil, egg yolks, and milk in a large bowl. Whisk flour mixture into egg-yolk mixture.

2. With an electric mixer on high speed, beat egg whites until frothy. Add cream of tartar and vanilla seeds or extract; beat until soft peaks form. Gradually add remaining ¾ cup granulated sugar, beating until stiff, glossy peaks form, about 5 minutes. Whisk one third of egg-white mixture into batter. Gently but thoroughly fold in remaining egg-white mixture with a flexible spatula.

3. Transfer batter to a 9½-inch tube pan. Bake until top of cake springs back when touched, 52 to 55 minutes. Invert pan onto its legs or over the neck of a glass bottle to cool 1 hour.

4. Make the filling: While cake is baking and cooling, in a bowl combine strawberries, granulated sugar, lemon juice, and salt, and let sit, stirring occasionally, 1 hour. Just before assembling, with an electric mixer beat cream and confectioners' sugar until medium peaks form.

5. Slide a paring knife around edge of cake to loosen; release cake from pan. With a serrated knife, split cake horizontally into 3 layers. Transfer bottom layer to a cake plate or platter. Spread with half the berries; drizzle with juices. Spread half the whipped cream over berries; add middle cake layer. Spread with remaining berries and whipped cream. Top with remaining cake layer. Refrigerate cake 1 hour. Dust with confectioners' sugar and serve with more berries.

Coconut-Pecan Cake with Milk Chocolate Ganache

Combine the sweet, nutty taste of coconut with toasted pecans and milk chocolate, and you've got a flavor reminiscent of a favorite candy bar. Creamed coconut is available at natural-foods stores and online; it's not the same as "cream of coconut," which has added sugar. If you can't find it, use unsalted butter in its place. **SERVES 10 TO 12**

¾ cup (1½ sticks) unsalted butter, room temperature, plus more for pans

2¼ cups all-purpose flour, plus more for pans

1 cup firmly packed sweetened shredded coconut

¾ cup pecan halves (3 ounces), toasted (see page 344)

2 cups sugar

1 tablespoon baking powder

¾ teaspoon salt

¼ cup creamed coconut or 4 tablespoons (½ stick) unsalted butter

4 large eggs

1 tablespoon coconut extract

1 cup plus 2 tablespoons unsweetened coconut milk (9 ounces)

Coconut-Cream Filling (page 340)

Milk Chocolate Ganache (page 339)

2 cups toasted shaved coconut (see page 344), for decorating (optional)

1. Preheat oven to 350°F. Butter two 9-inch round cake pans; line with parchment rounds, and butter parchment. Dust with flour, tapping out excess.

2. In a food processor, finely grind shredded coconut; transfer to a bowl. Finely grind pecans with 2 tablespoons sugar. Into a large bowl, sift together flour, baking powder, and salt; stir in ground coconut and pecans.

3. With an electric mixer on medium-high speed, beat butter, creamed coconut, and remaining sugar until pale and fluffy, about 4 minutes. Beat in eggs and extract. Add flour mixture in 3 batches, alternating with 2 batches of coconut milk; beat until just combined.

4. Divide batter evenly between prepared pans; smooth tops with an offset spatula. Bake until golden and a cake tester comes out clean, about 35 minutes. (If tops begin to brown too quickly, tent loosely with foil.) Transfer pans to a wire rack to cool 30 minutes. Run a knife around edges of cakes to loosen; turn out onto rack to cool completely.

5. Line 2 rimmed baking sheets with parchment; fit 1 with a cooling rack. With a serrated knife, trim tops of cake layers to level, if desired. Transfer bottom layer to baking sheet with rack; spread with coconut filling. Place remaining cake layer on top, cut side down.

6. Using an offset spatula, spread the chilled ganache over sides of cake; smooth over cake, coating completely. Transfer cake and rack to second prepared baking sheet; refrigerate until set, about 5 minutes.

7. Coat the cake with the room-temperature ganache. Refrigerate until nearly set, about 5 minutes. Press toasted coconut onto sides of the cake, if desired. Keep at room temperature until ready to serve.

Candied-Pecan Cake with Browned-Butter Pears

Here, cake layers are studded with candied nuts, sandwiched with caramelized pears, and capped off with bourbon-spiked whipped cream. All the components are uncomplicated and can be made in stages, for a dessert that's fancy but far from fussy. **SERVES 10**

FOR THE CANDIED PECANS

- 2 cups chopped pecans
- 3 tablespoons unsalted butter, melted
- 1/4 cup packed light brown sugar
- 1 tablespoon vanilla extract
- 2 teaspoons ground cinnamon
- 1/4 teaspoon freshly grated nutmeg

FOR THE CAKE

- 3/4 cup (1 1/2 sticks) unsalted butter, room temperature, plus more for pans
- 3 cups all-purpose flour, plus more for pans
- 2 teaspoons baking powder
- 1/2 teaspoon coarse salt
- 1 3/4 cups granulated sugar
- 1 cup plus 2 tablespoons milk
- 3 large egg whites

FOR THE FILLING

- 4 Anjou pears
- 1 tablespoon fresh lemon juice
- 4 tablespoons unsalted butter

FOR THE TOPPING

- Whipped Cream (bourbon variation; see page 333)
- 1/3 cup chopped toasted pecans (see page 344), for garnish

1. Make the candied pecans: Preheat oven to 400°F. Toss pecans with butter, brown sugar, vanilla, cinnamon, and nutmeg on a rimmed baking sheet. Toast, stirring to coat halfway through, until fragrant, about 10 minutes. Transfer baking sheet to a wire rack to cool completely.

2. Make the cake: Reduce oven temperature to 350°F. Butter three 8-inch round cake pans; dust with flour, tapping out excess. Sift flour, baking powder, and salt into a bowl. With an electric mixer on medium, beat butter and 1 1/4 cups granulated sugar until pale and fluffy, about 3 minutes. Add flour mixture in 3 batches, alternating with 2 batches of milk; beat until just combined. Stir in candied pecans.

3. In a clean mixer bowl, beat egg whites on high speed until frothy. Gradually add remaining 1/2 cup sugar; beat until stiff peaks form. Gently fold one third of the egg whites into the batter using a flexible spatula. Fold in remaining egg whites in 2 additions.

4. Divide batter among prepared pans. Bake until cakes are set and a cake tester comes out clean, about 30 minutes. Transfer pans to wire racks to cool 10 minutes. Turn out cakes onto racks to cool completely.

5. Meanwhile, make the filling: Peel and core pears; cut into 1/2-inch wedges, and toss with lemon juice. Cook butter in a skillet over medium heat until browned, about 5 minutes. Add pears; cook, stirring occasionally, until tender, about 6 minutes. Cool completely.

6. Using a serrated knife, trim tops of cakes to level. Transfer bottom cake layer to a cake stand or platter, and spread with half the pears. Add second layer, and spread with remaining pears. Top with remaining layer. (Assembled cake can be refrigerated, covered, up to 3 days.) Spread bourbon whipped cream over top, and garnish with pecans just before serving.

Tender Lemon Cake

Swirls of old-fashioned powdered-sugar frosting lend this cake some homespun charm; a crown of candied lemon peel is fit for a special occasion. When working with soft fillings, such as lemon curd, try this trick: First pipe a ring of frosting around the edge of each cake layer; it acts as a "dam" to keep the curd in place. If you don't have a pastry bag, make one by filling a large resealable plastic bag with frosting and snipping off one corner. **SERVES 10 TO 12**

1¼ cups (2½ sticks) unsalted butter, room temperature, plus more for pans

3¾ cups all-purpose flour, plus more for pans

1 tablespoon plus ¾ teaspoon baking powder

¾ teaspoon salt

2½ cups sugar

5 large eggs

Finely grated zest of 1½ lemons

1¼ teaspoons vanilla extract

1¼ cups buttermilk

Lemon Curd (page 332)

Basic Buttercream Frosting (page 334)

Candied lemon peel, for garnish (optional; see page 326)

1. Preheat oven to 325°F. Butter three 8-inch round cake pans; line with parchment rounds, and butter parchment. Dust with flour, tapping out excess.

2. Whisk together flour, baking powder, and salt in a medium bowl. With an electric mixer on medium speed, beat butter and sugar until pale and fluffy, 3 to 5 minutes. Add eggs, 1 at a time, beating well after each addition and scraping down sides of bowl as necessary. Mix in zest and vanilla. With mixer on low speed, add flour mixture in 3 batches, alternating with 2 batches of buttermilk; beat until just combined.

3. Divide batter evenly among prepared pans, smoothing tops with an offset spatula. Bake until golden brown and a cake tester comes out clean, 40 to 45 minutes. Transfer pans to wire racks to cool 15 minutes. Turn out cakes onto racks to cool completely.

4. With a serrated knife, trim tops of cake layers to level. Place bottom layer on a cake stand or platter. Using a pastry bag fitted with a coupler or a resealable plastic bag with one corner snipped off, pipe a dam of frosting around edge of cake. Fill with ¾ cup lemon curd, spreading with an offset spatula. Repeat with second layer, frosting dam, and another ¾ cup lemon curd; top with third layer. Spread remaining frosting over top and sides of cake, using an offset spatula to create large swirls. Arrange candied lemon peel on top of cake, if desired.

Red Velvet Cake

What has long been considered a Southern specialty has become a favorite across the country. And it's no wonder: The deep red layers are striking, and the delicate texture and mild chocolate flavor of the cake are the perfect match for a tangy cream-cheese frosting. **SERVES 8 TO 10**

Unsalted butter, for pans

2½ cups cake flour (not self-rising), plus more for pans

¼ cup unsweetened cocoa powder

1 teaspoon salt

1½ cups sugar

1½ cups canola or safflower oil

2 large eggs

1 tablespoon red food coloring

1 teaspoon vanilla extract

1 cup buttermilk

1½ teaspoons baking soda

2 teaspoons white vinegar

Cream-Cheese Frosting (page 335)

1. Preheat oven to 350°F. Butter two 9-by-2-inch round cake pans; line with parchment rounds, and butter parchment. Dust with flour, tapping out excess. In a medium bowl, whisk together flour, cocoa, and salt.

2. With an electric mixer on medium speed, beat sugar and oil until well combined. Add eggs, 1 at a time, beating well after each addition. Add food coloring and vanilla; beat until well combined. Add flour mixture in 2 batches, alternating with the buttermilk and beginning and ending with the flour; beat until just combined, scraping sides of bowl as needed.

3. In a small bowl, mix baking soda and vinegar. Add to batter; beat 10 seconds. Divide batter evenly between prepared pans. Bake until a cake tester comes out clean, 30 to 35 minutes. Transfer pans to a wire rack to cool 15 minutes. Turn out cakes onto rack to cool completely.

4. Place bottom cake layer on a cake stand or platter, and spread evenly with about 1½ cups cream-cheese frosting. Place second layer on top; spread and swirl remaining frosting over cake. Cake can be refrigerated up to 6 hours; bring to room temperature before serving.

Chocolate Truffle Cake

It's hard to imagine a cake more luxurious than this one: layer upon layer of chocolate cake, chocolate ganache filling, and gorgeous swirls of chocolate frosting. Unless, of course, you top it with chocolate curls. Alternatively, you could replace the frosting with the poured variation of the ganache (page 339) for a sleek finish. **SERVES 10**

1 cup (2 sticks) plus 2 tablespoons unsalted butter, room temperature, plus more for pans

½ cup plus 1 tablespoon best-quality unsweetened cocoa powder, plus more for pans

¼ cup plus 2 tablespoons boiling water

¾ cup milk

2¼ cups sifted cake flour (not self-rising)

¾ teaspoon baking soda

½ teaspoon salt

1¾ cups sugar

2 teaspoons vanilla extract

3 large eggs, lightly beaten

Whipped Bittersweet Chocolate Ganache (page 339)

Rich Chocolate Frosting (page 337)

Chocolate curls, for decorating (optional; see page 328)

1. Preheat oven to 350°F. Butter three 9-by-2-inch round cake pans; line with parchment rounds, and butter parchment. Dust with cocoa, tapping out excess. Sift cocoa into a medium bowl. Stir in the boiling water until smooth; gradually whisk in milk. Set aside to cool.

2. Whisk together flour, baking soda, and salt in a bowl. With an electric mixer on low, beat butter until fluffy, 3 to 5 minutes. Gradually beat in sugar, scraping down sides of bowl twice. Beat in vanilla.

3. Add eggs in 3 batches, beating well after each addition. With mixer on low speed, add flour mixture and reserved cocoa mixture a little at a time in alternate batches, starting and ending with the flour; beat until just combined.

4. Divide batter evenly among prepared pans; smooth tops with an offset spatula. Bake, rotating halfway through, until a cake tester comes out clean, 20 to 25 minutes. Transfer pans to wire racks to cool 15 minutes. Turn out cakes onto racks to cool completely.

5. With a serrated knife, trim tops of cakes to level. Place bottom cake layer on a cake stand or platter, and spread evenly with about 1¼ cups whipped ganache; top with second layer and 1¼ cups ganache. Top with third layer. Spread remaining whipped ganache over top and sides of cake to form a crumb coat; refrigerate until ganache is firm, about 30 minutes.

6. Spread chocolate frosting over top and sides of cake, using an offset spatula to create large swirls. Top with chocolate curls, if using. Refrigerate cake until frosting sets, about 10 minutes, before serving. Bring to room temperature before serving.

Citrus-Poppy Seed Cake

Lemon and poppy seeds make a well-matched pair. Here, we do the pairing one—or make that two—better, with the addition of orange and lime zests. We also doubled up on the icings, with cream-cheese filling between the layers and a lemony glaze drizzled over the top. **SERVES 12**

FOR THE CAKE

- 1½ cups (3 sticks) unsalted butter, room temperature, plus more for pans
- 3¾ cups all-purpose flour, plus more for pans
- 2½ teaspoons baking powder
- ¾ teaspoon salt
- 2½ cups granulated sugar
- 7 large eggs, lightly beaten
- 1½ teaspoons vanilla extract
- 1 cup milk
- ½ teaspoon each finely grated lemon, orange, and lime zests
- ⅓ cup poppy seeds

FOR THE FILLING

- 12 ounces cream cheese, room temperature
- 6 tablespoons unsalted butter, room temperature
- 3 cups confectioners' sugar

FOR THE TOPPINGS

- Lemon Glaze (poppy-seed variation; see page 331)
- Poppy seeds, for sprinkling
- Lemon and orange peel, cut into thin strips, for garnish

1. Make the cake: Preheat oven to 350°F. Butter three 8-by-2-inch cake pans; line with parchment rounds, and butter parchment. Dust with flour, tapping out excess. Sift together flour, baking powder, and salt into a bowl.

2. With an electric mixer on medium-low speed, beat butter until fluffy, 2 to 3 minutes. Gradually add granulated sugar; beat until pale and fluffy, 3 to 4 minutes, scraping down sides of bowl once or twice. With mixer running, gradually drizzle eggs into bowl, beating until well incorporated; continue to beat until smooth and fluffy, about 5 minutes, scraping down sides of bowl as needed. Beat in vanilla. Reduce speed to low. Add flour mixture in 3 batches, alternating with 2 batches of milk; beat until just combined, scraping down sides of bowl once or twice. Beat in citrus zests and poppy seeds.

3. Divide batter evenly among prepared pans. Bake, rotating halfway through, until a cake tester comes out clean, 35 to 40 minutes. Transfer pans to wire racks to cool 15 minutes. Turn out cakes onto racks to cool completely.

4. Make the filling: With an electric mixer on medium-low speed, beat cream cheese until smooth, about 1 minute. Add butter; beat until smooth, 2 minutes. Reduce speed to low; beat in confectioners' sugar. Raise speed to medium and beat until mixture is smooth and fluffy, about 1 minute. (If filling is too soft, refrigerate in an airtight container until firm before using.)

5. Save the prettiest layer for top. Place bottom layer on a cake stand or platter, and spread evenly with about 1½ cups filling. Add second layer; spread with remaining filling. Place reserved layer on top. Refrigerate, loosely covered with plastic wrap, 1 hour.

6. Just before serving, pour glaze over top of cake, letting it run down sides. Sprinkle glaze with poppy seeds and garnish with citrus peel.

One-Bowl Chocolate Cake with Mocha Buttercream

Try this once and it will become your go-to chocolate cake recipe (and everyone needs one of those!). It's dark, rich, and almost impossibly moist. It's easy to mix in a single bowl, so cleanup is a breeze. And it's versatile: We like the batter for a layer cake, but it also makes great cupcakes and sheet cakes. And you can certainly frost it with something other than the mocha buttercream pictured. Try it with Basic Buttercream Frosting (page 334), Milk Chocolate Frosting (page 338), or Cream-Cheese Frosting (page 335)—the possibilities are endless. **SERVES 10 TO 12**

Unsalted butter, room temperature, for pans

$3/4$ cup unsweetened cocoa powder, plus more for pans

$1\frac{1}{2}$ cups all-purpose flour

$1\frac{1}{2}$ cups sugar

$1\frac{1}{2}$ teaspoons baking soda

$3/4$ teaspoon baking powder

$3/4$ teaspoon salt

2 large eggs

$3/4$ cup buttermilk

$3/4$ cup warm water

3 tablespoons canola or safflower oil

1 teaspoon vanilla extract

Mocha Buttercream (page 337)

1. Preheat oven to 350°F. Butter two 8-by-2-inch round cake pans; dust with cocoa, tapping out excess. Sift together cocoa, flour, sugar, baking soda, baking powder, and salt into a mixing bowl. Beat on low speed until just combined. Raise speed to medium; add eggs, buttermilk, water, oil, and vanilla. Beat until smooth, about 3 minutes.

2. Divide batter evenly between prepared pans. Bake until a cake tester comes out clean, about 35 minutes. Transfer pans to wire racks to cool 15 minutes. Turn out cakes onto racks to cool completely. (Unfrosted cake layers can be stored, wrapped in plastic, at room temperature or refrigerated overnight.)

3. Place bottom layer on a cake stand or platter, and spread evenly with about 1 cup buttercream. Top with remaining layer; frost top and sides with another 2 cups buttercream, smoothing sides with an offset spatula. Divide remaining buttercream among pastry bags fitted with open and closed star tips, such as #16, #22, #30, and #35. Pipe swirls of buttercream on top of cake. Frosted cake can be refrigerated overnight; bring to room temperature before serving.

NOTE: For cupcakes, divide the batter evenly between 2 lined 12-cup muffin tins, filling each cup two thirds full. Bake, rotating pans halfway through, about 20 minutes. For a sheet cake, butter a 9-by-13-inch pan and dust with cocoa; bake about 35 minutes.

Lemon Meringue Cake

For this, one of Martha's favorite cakes, chiffon-cake layers are filled with tart lemon curd, then finished with a cloud-like layer of Swiss meringue.

SERVES 8 TO 10

FOR THE CAKE

- 1 cup plus 2 tablespoons sifted cake flour (not self-rising)
- 1½ teaspoons baking powder
- ¼ teaspoon salt
- 3 large eggs, separated, room temperature
- ¾ cup superfine sugar
- ¼ cup canola or safflower oil
- 1 teaspoon finely grated orange zest plus ¼ cup fresh orange juice
- 1 teaspoon finely grated lemon zest plus 2 tablespoons fresh lemon juice
- Pinch of cream of tartar
- Lemon Curd (page 332)

FOR THE MERINGUE

- 5 egg whites, room temperature
- ¾ cup granulated sugar
- 1 teaspoon vanilla extract

1. Make the cake: Preheat oven to 325°F. Sift together flour, baking powder, and salt twice into a medium bowl. With an electric mixer on medium-high speed, beat egg yolks until pale and foamy, 3 to 5 minutes. Gradually add ½ cup superfine sugar, beating until very pale and fluffy, 5 to 7 minutes. With mixer running, add oil in a steady stream. Add zests; beat 1 minute. Reduce speed to medium-low. Add flour mixture in 4 batches, alternating with juices in 3 batches; beat until just incorporated.

2. In a clean mixer bowl, whisk egg whites on low speed until foamy. Add cream of tartar. Raise speed to medium-high; beat until soft peaks form. Gradually add remaining ¼ cup superfine sugar; beat until whites are glossy and stiff peaks form, 1 to 2 minutes.

3. Stir one quarter of egg whites into yolk mixture. Carefully fold in remaining whites. Gently transfer batter to a 7-inch tube pan. Bake until cake is golden brown and a cake tester comes out clean, about 40 minutes. Invert pan onto its legs or over the neck of a glass bottle to cool completely. Run a knife around edges to loosen; remove from pan.

4. With a serrated knife, slice cake horizontally into 3 layers. Place bottom layer on a baking sheet. Spread half the lemon curd over bottom layer; add second layer and spread with remaining curd. Finish with domed top layer. Refrigerate, covered, until set, preferably overnight. Brush off excess crumbs with a dry pastry brush.

5. Make the meringue: Preheat oven to 400°F. Whisk together egg whites, granulated sugar, and vanilla in a heatproof bowl set over (not in) a pan of simmering water. Continue whisking until mixture feels hot to the touch. Remove from heat. With an electric mixer on high speed, whisk until whites are glossy and form stiff peaks.

6. Spread meringue over top and sides of cake, swirling with an offset spatula. Bake, watching carefully, until meringue is brown around edges and beginning to brown elsewhere, 2 to 3 minutes. (Alternatively, hold a small kitchen torch 3 to 4 inches from surface of meringue, and wave it back and forth until meringue is lightly browned all over.) Serve immediately.

Pumpkin Layer Cake

This spiced pumpkin cake is enhanced by layers of a delectably rich frosting that features cream cheese and goat cheese. Quince, available in the fall, has a fragrant, apple-like flavor. If you can't find fresh ones, use pears or apples instead. **SERVES 12**

1 cup (2 sticks) unsalted butter, room temperature, plus more for pans

2¾ cups all-purpose flour, plus more for pans

1½ teaspoons baking powder

1 teaspoon baking soda

1½ teaspoons ground cinnamon

¾ teaspoon freshly grated nutmeg

½ teaspoon salt

2 cups packed light brown sugar

3 large eggs

1½ cups solid-pack pumpkin (not pie filling)

1 teaspoon vanilla extract

¾ teaspoon grated peeled fresh ginger

½ cup buttermilk

Cream Cheese–Goat Cheese Frosting (page 335)

Quince-Ginger Compote (optional; page 341)

1. Preheat oven to 350°F. Brush two 8-inch round cake pans with butter; line with parchment rounds. Butter parchment; dust with flour, tapping out excess. Whisk together flour, baking powder, baking soda, cinnamon, nutmeg, and salt in a medium bowl.

2. With an electric mixer on medium speed, beat butter and brown sugar until pale and fluffy, 3 to 4 minutes. Beat in eggs, 1 at a time. Beat in pumpkin; add vanilla and ginger. Reduce speed to low. Add flour mixture in 3 batches, alternating with 2 batches of buttermilk; beat until just combined, scraping down sides of bowl as needed.

3. Divide batter evenly between prepared pans. Bake until cakes are golden brown, edges pull away from sides of pans, and a cake tester comes out clean, about 35 minutes. Transfer pans to wire racks to cool 15 minutes. Turn out cakes onto racks to cool completely.

4. Place bottom layer on a cake stand or platter, and spread evenly with half the frosting. Top with second layer, and spread remaining frosting over top. Top cake with some quince-ginger compote, and serve remainder on the side.

Sugar-and-Spice Cake

Mascarpone, a triple-cream cheese available at most grocery stores, adds a rich, silky component to this towering cake, also layered with jam (blackberry here, but any flavor will do). A sweet sprinkling of cinnamon-sugar on top is the finishing touch—and the reason for its name.

SERVES 10 TO 12

FOR THE CAKE

- 1 1/2 cups all-purpose flour
- 1 1/2 cups cake flour (not self-rising)
- 1 tablespoon baking powder
- 1 teaspoon ground cinnamon
- 1/4 teaspoon freshly grated nutmeg
- Pinch of ground cloves
- 1/2 teaspoon salt
- 1 cup (2 sticks) unsalted butter, room temperature
- 1 3/4 cups granulated sugar
- 3 large eggs
- 2 teaspoons vanilla extract
- 1 1/4 cups milk
- Vegetable oil cooking spray

FOR THE FROSTING AND FILLING

- 2 cups cold heavy cream
- 1 pound mascarpone cheese
- 1/2 cup confectioners' sugar, sifted
- 1 1/2 cups blackberry jam (from one 17.5-ounce jar)
- 2 tablespoons granulated sugar
- 1/2 teaspoon ground cinnamon

1. Make the cake: Preheat oven to 350°F. Coat two 8-inch round cake pans with cooking spray; line with parchment rounds, and coat parchment. Sift both flours, baking powder, cinnamon, nutmeg, cloves, and salt into a bowl.

2. With an electric mixer on medium speed, beat butter and granulated sugar until pale and fluffy, about 3 minutes. Beat in eggs, 1 at a time, then vanilla. Reduce speed to low. Add flour mixture in 3 batches, alternating with 2 batches of milk. Continue to beat until smooth, about 1 minute more.

3. Divide batter evenly between prepared pans. Bake until a cake tester comes out clean, about 40 minutes. Transfer pans to wire racks to cool 20 minutes. Turn out cakes onto racks to cool completely.

4. Make the frosting: With an electric mixer on medium-high speed, whisk heavy cream until stiff peaks form. In another bowl, whisk together mascarpone and confectioners' sugar until smooth. Fold whipped cream into mascarpone mixture.

5. With a large serrated knife, trim tops of cakes to level; split cakes in half horizontally. Transfer bottom layer to a cake stand or platter, and spread evenly with 1/2 cup jam, then spread 1 cup frosting over jam. Add another cake layer. Repeat layering cakes with jam and frosting, leaving top layer (bottom side up) uncovered. Spread remaining frosting on top of cake. Whisk together granulated sugar and cinnamon in a small bowl; dust top of cake with cinnamon-sugar. Refrigerate cake until frosting sets, 10 minutes, before serving. Bring to room temperature before serving.

Vanilla Layer Cake

Here's an all-purpose, foolproof yellow cake recipe that's easy to make and uses ingredients that are always on hand—a good thing since it's likely to become an instant favorite at your home (as it was in our test kitchens). The frosting is at first familiar—it's based on the basic buttercream from the side of the box—yet because cream cheese replaces some of the butter, it's ultra-creamy and not too sweet. Piped Swiss-dot details are simple to achieve with a plain round tip; follow our lead or create your own design (or omit altogether). **SERVES 10 TO 12**

½ cup (1 stick) unsalted butter, room temperature, plus more for pans

2 cups all-purpose flour, plus more for pans

1½ cups sugar

3 large eggs

1 tablespoon baking powder

½ teaspoon salt

1 cup milk

1 teaspoon vanilla extract

Creamy Vanilla Frosting (page 334)

1. Preheat oven to 350°F. Butter two 8-inch round cake pans; line with parchment rounds, and butter parchment. Dust with flour, tapping out excess. With an electric mixer on medium speed, beat butter and sugar until combined, 1 to 2 minutes. Add eggs and beat until well incorporated, scraping down sides of bowl as necessary. Add flour, baking powder, and salt; beat until just combined. Add milk and vanilla and beat until smooth.

2. Divide batter evenly between prepared pans, smoothing tops with an offset spatula. Bake until golden and a cake tester comes out clean, about 35 minutes. Transfer pans to a wire rack to cool 15 minutes. Turn out cakes onto rack to cool completely.

3. Place bottom layer on a cake stand or platter, and spread evenly with about 1 cup frosting. Place second cake layer on top. Fill a pastry bag fitted with a small round tip (such as #7) with ½ cup frosting. Spread remaining frosting over top and sides of cake; smooth with an offset spatula. Pipe a border of small dots along bottom and top edges, and small dots on top and sides of cake. Cake can be refrigerated, covered, up to 3 days; let sit at room temperature 30 minutes before serving.

Apple-Ginger Stack Cake

A down-home treat from Kentucky and its environs, this dessert is also known as Appalachian stack cake. Pioneers served it at weddings; neighbors and friends would bring layers and the hosts would add the filling. Here, dried apples are soaked in cider for double the flavor.

SERVES 10 TO 12

5 cups dried apples (about ¾ pound)

5 cups apple cider

1½ cups water

1⅔ cups granulated sugar

1 cup (2 sticks) unsalted butter, room temperature, plus more for pans

3 cups sifted all-purpose flour, plus more for pans

1 large egg

1 cup unsulfured molasses

1 cup buttermilk

1 teaspoon baking soda

1 teaspoon ground ginger

⅛ teaspoon ground cloves

½ teaspoon salt

Confectioners' sugar, for dusting

1. Bring apples and cider to a boil in a large pot. Reduce to a simmer; cook, stirring occasionally, until apples begin to soften and liquid has reduced, 40 to 50 minutes. Add 1 cup water; cook, mashing apples slightly, until liquid has reduced, about 10 minutes. Add ⅔ cup granulated sugar and remaining ½ cup water; simmer until apples are very soft and coated in syrup, about 15 minutes. Let cool completely.

2. Preheat oven to 375°F. Butter two 9-inch round cake pans; line with parchment rounds, and butter parchment. Dust with flour, tapping out excess.

3. With an electric mixer on medium-high, beat butter and remaining 1 cup sugar until creamy, about 3 minutes. Reduce speed to low; mix in egg, molasses, buttermilk, baking soda, flour, spices, and salt.

4. Divide batter evenly between prepared pans. Bake until a cake tester comes out clean and tops spring back when lightly touched, about 35 minutes. Transfer pans to a wire rack to cool 10 minutes. Run a knife around edges of pans to loosen; turn out cakes onto rack to cool completely.

5. Using a serrated knife, split each cake in half horizontally. Transfer 1 bottom layer to a cake stand or platter, and spread with one third of apple mixture. Stack 1 top layer on apples; top with another one third of apple mixture. Repeat with remaining cake bottom and apples, then add remaining cake top. Let stand at room temperature at least 1 hour. Before serving, sift confectioners' sugar over top of cake.

Hummingbird Cake

This Southern layer cake features a crowd-pleasing combination of banana, pineapple, and coconut. The name's origin remains something of a mystery: Some say it's because the cake is as sweet as nectar; others, that it makes you hum with happiness. **SERVES 10 TO 12**

Unsalted butter, for pans

3 cups all-purpose flour, plus more for pans

1 teaspoon baking soda

1 teaspoon ground cinnamon

½ teaspoon salt

1 cup canola or safflower oil

2 teaspoons vanilla extract

2 cups sugar

3 large eggs

2 cups mashed ripe banana (about 3 large)

1 can (8 ounces) crushed pineapple, drained

1 cup chopped walnuts or pecans

1 cup unsweetened shredded coconut

Cream-Cheese Frosting (page 335)

Candied pineapple slices (optional; see page 327)

1. Preheat oven to 350°F, with rack in center. Butter two 9-by-2-inch round cake pans; line with parchment rounds, and butter parchment. Dust with flour, tapping out excess. Whisk together flour, baking soda, cinnamon, and salt in a bowl.

2. With an electric mixer on medium speed, beat oil, vanilla, and sugar until combined, about 2 minutes. Add eggs, 1 at a time, beating until incorporated after each before adding the next. Beat until mixture is pale and fluffy, about 3 minutes.

3. In a bowl, mix together banana, pineapple, nuts, and coconut. Add to egg mixture; stir until combined. Add flour mixture; blend well.

4. Divide batter evenly between prepared pans. Bake, rotating halfway through, until golden brown and a cake tester comes out clean, 30 to 40 minutes. Transfer pans to a wire rack to cool 15 minutes. Run a knife around edges of cakes to loosen; turn out onto rack to cool completely. If not assembling right away, wrap each layer in plastic and freeze (thaw before using).

5. Place bottom layer on a cake stand or platter, and spread evenly with about 1½ cups frosting. Top with second layer. Spread remaining frosting over top and sides of cake. Arrange candied pineapple on top, if using. Cake can be refrigerated up to 3 days; serve at room temperature.

Devil's Food Cake

There is considerable debate about how this dessert got its name. Early versions may have been made with red food coloring, though the term "devil's food" has come to refer to any deep, dark chocolate cake. Regardless of its origin, this version, rich with sour cream and covered with pure white icing, is undeniably decadent and delicious. **SERVES 10 TO 12**

1½ cups (3 sticks) unsalted butter, room temperature, plus more for pans

1 cup unsweetened cocoa powder, plus more for pans

1 cup boiling water

1 cup sour cream

3 cups all-purpose flour

1 teaspoon baking powder

1 teaspoon baking soda

¾ teaspoon salt

2¼ cups sugar

4 large eggs

1 tablespoon plus 1 teaspoon vanilla extract

Seven-Minute Frosting (page 336)

Chocolate curls, for garnish (optional; see page 328)

1. Preheat oven to 350°F. Butter two 8-inch round cake pans; line with parchment rounds, and butter parchment. Dust pans with cocoa, tapping out excess. Whisk boiling water into cocoa in a medium bowl until smooth; whisk in sour cream. In another bowl, whisk together flour, baking powder, baking soda, and salt.

2. With an electric mixer on medium-high speed, beat butter and sugar until pale and fluffy, 3 to 5 minutes. Add eggs, 1 at a time, beating until incorporated after each. Reduce mixer speed to low. Add flour mixture in 3 batches, alternating with 2 batches of cocoa mixture; beat until combined. Beat in vanilla.

3. Divide batter evenly between prepared pans. Bake, rotating halfway through, until a cake tester comes out clean, 45 to 50 minutes. Transfer pans to wire racks to cool completely.

4. With a serrated knife, trim tops of cake layers to level, if desired. Place bottom layer on a cake stand or platter, and spread evenly with about 1 cup frosting. Stack second layer on top; use an offset spatula to swirl remaining frosting over top and sides of cake. Garnish with chocolate curls, if using.

Rum Rose Cake

This cake offers an easier way to pipe buttercream roses: Just one oversize star tip creates each bloom. The pastry bag is filled with two shades of frosting, half untinted and half pale pink. Underneath, four layers of sponge cake are brushed with a light-rum syrup and sandwiched with pastry cream. **SERVES 10 TO 12**

FOR THE CAKE

- 4 tablespoons unsalted butter, melted, plus more, room temperature, for pans
- 1½ cups cake flour (not self-rising), sifted, plus more for pans
- 9 large eggs, separated, room temperature
- 1½ cups sugar
- 1 teaspoon vanilla extract

  Pinch of salt

  Rum Syrup (page 341)

FOR ASSEMBLING

- 2 recipes Pastry Cream (page 340)

  Swiss Meringue Buttercream (page 336)

  Gel-paste food coloring in pink or red

PIPING THE BUTTERCREAM ROSES

1. Make the cake: Preheat oven to 350°F. Butter two 9-by-2-inch cake pans; line with parchment rounds. Butter parchment; dust with flour, tapping out excess. Whisk egg yolks and 1 cup sugar in a heatproof bowl set over (not in) a pan of simmering water until sugar has dissolved and mixture is warm, 3 to 4 minutes. Add vanilla and salt. Remove from heat. With an electric mixer on medium speed, whisk until mixture is pale and thick enough to hold a ribbon on its surface, 3 to 5 minutes. Transfer to a large bowl.

2. In a clean mixer bowl, whisk whites on medium-high speed until soft peaks form. Gradually add remaining ½ cup sugar, beating until stiff, glossy peaks form. Fold one third of egg-white mixture into yolk mixture. Fold in remaining egg-white mixture. Fold in flour, then melted butter, until just combined. Divide batter evenly between prepared pans. Bake until a cake tester comes out clean, 25 to 30 minutes. Turn out cakes onto a wire rack to cool.

3. With a serrated knife, split each in half horizontally. Place bottom layer on a cake stand or platter. Brush top with some syrup; spread with one third of the pastry cream. Repeat with 2 more cake layers, brushing each with syrup and spreading each with one third of the pastry cream. Top with final cake layer; brush with remaining syrup.

4. Spread a thin layer of buttercream over cake to form a crumb coat; refrigerate until firm, about 30 minutes. Spread a second layer of buttercream over cake, smoothing with an offset spatula.

5. Tint half of remaining buttercream pink with food coloring. Fit a pastry bag with an oversize open-star tip, such as Wilton #1M. From tip to cuff, fill half the bag with untinted buttercream; add pink buttercream to the other half. Pipe roses onto cake: Hold bag at a 90-degree angle to the cake, and pipe a tight, continuous spiral, decreasing pressure as you release. Serve immediately, or refrigerate, uncovered, up to 2 days; let cake come to room temperature before serving.

German Chocolate Cake

Here's our take on the universally appealing German chocolate cake—which just happens to be an American invention. It came about in 1957 when a Texas woman sent a cake recipe to her newspaper that used a product called German's Sweet Chocolate (which had been named for chocolate maker Sam German). And the rest, as they say, is history.

SERVES 10 TO 12

¾ cup (1½ sticks) unsalted butter, room temperature, plus more for pans

2 cups cake flour (not self-rising), plus more for pan

1 teaspoon baking soda

¾ teaspoon salt

1⅓ cups sugar

3 large eggs

1½ teaspoons vanilla extract

1 cup buttermilk

5 ounces semisweet chocolate, melted and cooled

Coconut-Pecan Frosting (page 338)

1 cup unsweetened shaved or flaked coconut, lightly toasted (see page 344), for decorating

1. Preheat oven to 350°F. Butter a 9-inch springform pan; line with a parchment round. Butter parchment; dust with flour, tapping out excess. Whisk together flour, baking soda, and salt in a medium bowl.

2. With an electric mixer on medium-high speed, beat butter and sugar until pale and fluffy, 3 to 5 minutes. Add eggs, 1 at a time, beating well after each addition. Beat in vanilla. Reduce speed to low. Add flour mixture in 3 batches, alternating with 2 batches of buttermilk; beat until just combined. Beat in chocolate.

3. Transfer batter to prepared pan; smooth top with an offset spatula. Bake until a cake tester comes out clean, 50 to 60 minutes. Transfer pan to a wire rack to cool 30 minutes. Turn out cake onto rack to cool completely. Wrap cooled cake in plastic; refrigerate until cold, at least 1 hour or up to overnight, to make it easier to slice.

4. Using a serrated knife, split cake horizontally into 3 layers. Transfer bottom layer to a cake stand or platter, and spread evenly with one third of frosting. Repeat, layering cake and frosting, finishing with frosting. Sprinkle toasted coconut over top.

Raspberry White Cake

In this ethereal dessert, egg whites serve as a leavener for the cake layers (and give the frosting all of its volume). Since sugar can slow the rate at which egg whites foam, it must be added very gradually to form the proper glossy peaks needed for the icing. **SERVES 10 TO 12**

Unsalted butter, for pans

2 cups sifted cake flour (not self-rising), plus more for pans

1 teaspoon salt

1 cup sugar

1 cup heavy cream

2 tablespoons milk

2 teaspoons baking powder

4 large egg whites, room temperature

1 teaspoon vanilla extract

¼ teaspoon almond extract

1½ cups raspberries (8 ounces)

⅔ cup raspberry jam

Seven-Minute Frosting (page 336)

½ cup unsweetened large-flake coconut, for decorating

1. Preheat oven to 325°F. Butter three 8-inch round cake pans; line with parchment rounds. Butter parchment; dust with flour, tapping out excess. Whisk together flour, salt, and ½ cup sugar in a medium bowl. With an electric mixer on medium-high speed, beat together cream, milk, baking powder, and egg whites until mixture thickens. Whisk in vanilla, almond extract, and remaining ½ cup sugar.

2. Fold flour mixture into batter. Fold in raspberries. Divide batter evenly among prepared pans. Bake until golden and top springs back when lightly touched, about 25 minutes. Transfer pans to wire racks to cool 30 minutes. Turn out cakes onto racks to cool completely.

3. Place bottom cake layer on a cake stand or platter, and spread evenly with half the jam. Top with second layer. Repeat with remaining jam and layer. Swirl frosting over top and sides of cake with an offset spatula; sprinkle top with coconut.

Double-Chocolate Cake

Candy-coated milk chocolates hint at the flavor of this four-layer beauty. The candies on top celebrate a seventh birthday, but you could also arrange them in colorful stripes or concentric circles. Look for specialty colors at candy stores and online. **SERVES 10 TO 12**

¾ cup unsalted butter, room temperature, plus more for pans

2¼ cups all-purpose flour, plus more for pans

1½ teaspoons baking soda

2½ teaspoons coarse salt

1 cup plus 2 tablespoons granulated sugar

⅓ cup packed light brown sugar

2 large whole eggs plus 1 large egg yolk

1 tablespoon vanilla extract

1½ cups sour cream

¾ cup milk

8 ounces bittersweet chocolate (61 to 70 percent cacao), finely chopped

Milk Chocolate Frosting (page 338)

8 ounces candy-coated chocolates, such as M&Ms, for decorating (optional)

1. Preheat oven to 350°F. Butter two 8-inch round cake pans; line with parchment rounds, and butter parchment. Dust with flour, tapping out excess. Whisk together flour, baking soda, and salt in a bowl.

2. With an electric mixer on medium-high speed, beat butter and both sugars until pale and fluffy, about 5 minutes. Beat in eggs and yolk, 1 at a time, beating well after each addition. Beat in vanilla. Gradually add flour mixture in 3 batches, alternating with sour cream and then milk, beginning and ending with flour; beat until just incorporated. Fold in chocolate.

3. Divide batter evenly between prepared pans; smooth tops with an offset spatula. Bake until deep golden brown and a cake tester comes out clean, about 40 minutes. Transfer pans to a wire rack to cool 20 minutes. Turn out cakes onto rack to cool completely.

4. With a serrated knife, cut each cake in half horizontally. Place bottom layer on a cake stand or platter, and spread evenly with about ¾ cup frosting. Repeat with second layer and another ¾ cup frosting. Place third layer on top, and spread with another ¾ cup frosting. Top with fourth layer. Spread remaining frosting over top and sides of cake, smoothing with an offset spatula. Arrange candies on top as desired. Cake can be refrigerated, uncovered, up to 2 days; let cake come to room temperature before serving.

1-2-3-4 Lemon Cake

The name of this old-fashioned cake comes from its simple measuring formula: one cup butter, two cups sugar, three cups flour, and four eggs. Our take on the classic offers layers of textures and tastes, with sweetened whipped cream, custardy lemon curd, and fresh mixed berries.

SERVES 8 TO 10

- 1 cup (2 sticks) unsalted butter, room temperature, plus more for pans
- 3 cups sifted all-purpose flour, plus more for pans
- 1 tablespoon baking powder
- 1 teaspoon baking soda
- 1/2 teaspoon salt
- 2 cups granulated sugar
- 4 large eggs, lightly beaten
- 1 1/4 cups buttermilk
- 1 1/2 teaspoons vanilla extract
- Zest of 2 lemons
- 2 recipes Lemon Curd (page 332)
- Whipped Cream (page 333)
- 12 ounces assorted fresh berries
- Confectioners' sugar, for dusting

1. Preheat oven to 350°F. Butter two 8-by-2-inch round cake pans; line with parchment rounds, and butter parchment. Dust with flour, tapping out excess. Sift together flour, baking powder, baking soda, and salt into a medium bowl.

2. With an electric mixer on medium speed, beat butter until softened, 1 to 2 minutes. Gradually add granulated sugar, and beat until pale and fluffy, 3 to 4 minutes, scraping down sides of bowl once or twice. Gradually add eggs; beat until incorporated after each addition, scraping down sides of bowl once or twice.

3. Slowly add the flour mixture in 3 batches, alternating with 2 batches of buttermilk; beat until just combined. Beat in vanilla and lemon zest.

4. Divide batter evenly between prepared pans. Bake, rotating halfway through, until a cake tester comes out clean, 35 to 45 minutes. Transfer pans to wire racks to cool 15 minutes. Turn out cakes onto racks to cool completely.

5. With a serrated knife, split each cake in half horizontally. Reserve the prettiest domed top for the top of the cake. Place the other top, dome-side down, on a cake stand or platter, and spread evenly with 1 cup lemon curd to within 1/2 inch of the edge. Top with second layer, and spread with another 1 cup curd. Repeat with third layer and remaining curd. Refrigerate cake to firm up lemon curd (or, if the kitchen is warm and the curd is too soft during assembly, refrigerate the layers as they are completed).

6. Just before serving, place the reserved domed layer on top of cake. Spoon whipped cream over top, and sprinkle with berries; dust with confectioners' sugar.

Carrot Cake

Grated carrots add earthy sweetness and flecks of color to dense, soft cake layers made with cinnamon, ginger, and nutmeg. For a garnish, tint marzipan orange and mold it into tiny carrot shapes; use the back of a paring knife to make lines, then insert a snipped carrot frond into the end of each one. **SERVES 10 TO 12**

1½ cups (3 sticks) unsalted butter, room temperature, plus more for pans

2½ cups all-purpose flour, plus more for pans

1 teaspoon baking powder

1 teaspoon baking soda

1 teaspoon ground cinnamon

¾ teaspoon coarse salt

½ teaspoon ground ginger

¼ teaspoon freshly grated nutmeg

1 cup packed light brown sugar

½ cup granulated sugar

3 large eggs

2 teaspoons vanilla extract

½ cup water

1 pound carrots (8 to 10 medium), peeled and shredded on the large holes of a box grater or in a food processor (about 2¾ cups)

1 cup toasted pecans (see page 344), finely chopped

Cream-Cheese Frosting (page 335)

Marzipan carrots, for decorating (optional; see note above)

1. Preheat oven to 350°F. Butter three 9-inch round cake pans; line with parchment rounds, and butter parchment. Dust with flour, tapping out excess. Whisk together flour, baking powder, baking soda, cinnamon, salt, ginger, and nutmeg in a medium bowl.

2. With an electric mixer on medium speed, beat butter and both sugars until pale and fluffy, 3 to 5 minutes. Add eggs, 1 at a time, beating well after each addition. Beat 3 minutes. Add vanilla, the water, and carrots. Beat until well combined, about 2 minutes. Reduce speed to low; add flour mixture, then pecans.

3. Divide batter evenly among prepared pans. Bake, rotating halfway through, until golden brown and a cake tester comes out clean, about 30 minutes. Transfer pans to wire racks to cool 15 minutes. Run a knife around edges of cakes to loosen; turn out cakes onto racks to cool completely.

4. With a serrated knife, trim tops of cake layers to level, if desired. Place bottom layer on a cake stand or platter, and spread evenly with 1 cup frosting. Top with second layer; spread with another 1 cup frosting. Top with remaining layer. Spread remaining frosting over top and sides of cake. Refrigerate 1 hour (or up to 1 day, covered) before serving.

Chestnut-Chocolate Layer Cake

Chestnuts are closely associated with the Christmas holiday. Here they make an excellent base for a rich and celebratory layer cake that is best served the day it is made. Bake it in the morning, and finish it later in the day; it can stand in a cool place for about three hours before serving.

SERVES 10 TO 12

FOR THE CAKE

- Unsalted butter, for pans
- 1 jar (14 ounces) chestnuts, drained
- 1 cup sugar
- 4 large eggs, separated, room temperature
- ½ teaspoon cream of tartar
- 1 cup sifted cake flour (not self-rising)
- 1 cup sifted chestnut flour
- 2 teaspoons baking powder
- ½ teaspoon ground cinnamon
- ¼ teaspoon salt
- ½ cup water
- ½ cup canola or safflower oil
- 1 teaspoon vanilla extract
- 6 ounces very finely chopped semisweet chocolate
- Pastry Cream (page 340)
- 8 marrons glacés, for garnish (optional)

FOR THE GANACHE

- 5 ounces semisweet chocolate, finely chopped
- ⅔ cup heavy cream

1. Make the cake: Preheat oven to 325°F. Butter two 9-by-2-inch round cake pans; line with parchment rounds, and butter parchment. Pulse drained chestnuts and 2 tablespoons sugar until very finely ground in the bowl of a food processor.

2. With an electric mixer on medium-low speed, whisk egg whites and cream of tartar until foamy, 5 to 6 minutes. With mixer running, slowly add ½ cup sugar. Raise speed to medium-high; beat until stiff peaks form, 6 to 7 minutes. Transfer egg-white mixture to a large bowl.

3. Sift cake flour, chestnut flour, baking powder, cinnamon, salt, and remaining 6 tablespoons sugar into a clean mixer bowl. Add egg yolks, the water, oil, and vanilla; beat on medium speed until smooth and well combined, about 1 minute.

4. Using a flexible spatula, carefully and gently fold flour mixture in 4 or 5 additions into the egg-white mixture until well combined. Gently fold in ground chestnuts and chocolate. Divide batter evenly between prepared pans. Bake, rotating halfway through, until golden and a cake tester comes out clean, about 55 minutes. Transfer pans to a wire rack to cool completely.

5. Place bottom layer on a cake stand or platter, and spread evenly with pastry cream to within ½ inch of edge. Top with second layer.

6. Make the ganache: Place chocolate in a heatproof bowl. Bring cream to a boil in a small saucepan. Pour boiling cream over chocolate; let sit several minutes; then stir until chocolate is completely smooth and melted. Set ganache aside in a cool place; let stand until thickened, 10 to 15 minutes.

7. Pour ganache over top of cake. Arrange marrons glacés on top of cake, if desired. Let set until ganache is firm.

Almond-Orange Layer Cake

Finely ground almonds and grated orange zest combine to give this cake its wonderful flavor; cake flour gives it a fine crumb. An ultra-smooth coating of pale yellow buttercream is a lovely canvas for delicate tendrils, budding blooms, and a monogram in disguise. It's perfect for Mother's Day or a special birthday. **SERVES 10 TO 12**

¾ cup (1½ sticks) unsalted butter, room temperature, plus more for pans

1 cup plus 2 tablespoons all-purpose flour, plus more for pans

1½ cups (7½ ounces) almonds, toasted (see page 344)

1 cup plus 2 tablespoons cake flour (not self-rising)

2¼ teaspoons baking powder

½ teaspoon coarse salt

¼ cup plus 2 tablespoons granulated sugar

¾ cup packed dark brown sugar

1 tablespoon orange zest (from 2 oranges)

1 tablespoon vanilla extract

1 cup plus 2 tablespoons milk

6 large egg whites, room temperature

Swiss Meringue Buttercream (page 336)

Gel-paste food coloring in yellow, pink, and peach

1. Preheat oven to 350°F. Butter two 8-inch round cake pans; line with parchment rounds, and butter parchment. Dust with flour, tapping out excess. In a food processor, finely grind almonds. Whisk together both flours, the baking powder, salt, and ground almonds in a bowl.

2. With an electric mixer on medium speed, beat butter, both sugars, and zest until pale and fluffy, 3 to 5 minutes. Beat in vanilla. Reduce speed to low. Add flour mixture in 3 batches, alternating with 2 batches of milk; beat until just combined.

3. In a clean mixer bowl, with mixer on medium speed, whisk egg whites until stiff peaks form. Fold egg whites into batter in 2 additions.

4. Divide batter evenly between prepared pans. Bake until a cake tester comes out clean, about 30 minutes. Transfer pans to a wire rack to cool completely.

5. Using a serrated knife, trim cake layers to level. Tint 4½ cups buttercream to yellow with gel-paste food coloring. Place bottom layer on a cake stand or platter, and spread evenly with about 1½ cups tinted buttercream; top with second layer. Spread a thin layer of buttercream over top and sides of cake to form a crumb coat; refrigerate until firm, about 30 minutes. Spread a second layer of buttercream over top and sides of cake, smoothing with an offset spatula.

6. Tint remaining buttercream to desired shades (here, light peach, dark peach, and pink). Use a pastry bag fitted with a small round tip, such as #3, and light peach buttercream to pipe monogram and vines. Switch to a small V-leaf tip, such as #349, and pink buttercream, and pipe leaves. Hold bag at a 45-degree angle to the cake, with the tip's pointed end facing up (with the V facing sideways); squeeze gently, pulling the bag up as you release pressure. Switch to a small standard leaf tip, such as #65, and dark peach buttercream, and pipe more leaves, moving tip back and forth slightly to create a ribbon effect. Serve immediately, or refrigerate, uncovered, up to 2 days; if refrigerated, let cake come to room temperature before serving.

Coconut Layer Cake

Coconut lovers, rejoice! This dessert is all about your favorite flavor. Six layers (or five, as shown) make a towering cake—and that means more coconut, inside and out. The layers are sweetened with flaked coconut, filled with coconut cream, and topped with seven-minute frosting. **SERVES 8**

FOR THE CAKE

- 3/4 cup (1 1/2 sticks) unsalted butter, room temperature, plus more for pans
- 2 cups sifted cake flour (not self-rising), plus more for pans
- 1/2 teaspoon baking powder
- 1/2 teaspoon baking soda
- 1/4 teaspoon salt
- 1 cup superfine sugar
- 4 large egg yolks, lightly beaten
- 2/3 cup sour cream
- 1 teaspoon vanilla extract
- 1/2 to 3/4 cup (about 2 ounces) sweetened flaked coconut
- 2 recipes Coconut-Cream Filling (page 340)

FOR THE FROSTING

- 2 large egg whites, room temperature
- 1 1/2 cups granulated sugar
- 2 teaspoons light corn syrup
- 1/4 teaspoon cream of tartar
- 5 tablespoons cold water
- 1/2 teaspoon pure vanilla extract
- 3 cups (about 9 ounces) sweetened flaked coconut

1. Make the cake: Preheat oven to 350°F. Butter three 6-by-2-inch round cake pans; line with parchment rounds, and butter parchment. Dust with flour, tapping out excess. Sift together flour, baking powder, baking soda, and salt into a medium bowl.

2. With an electric mixer on medium-low speed, beat butter until fluffy, 1 to 2 minutes. Gradually add superfine sugar; beat until mixture is pale and fluffy, about 3 minutes. Gradually drizzle in egg yolks, beating until well incorporated after each addition. Beat until mixture is fluffy again, about 3 minutes more.

3. Add flour mixture in 3 batches, alternating with 2 batches of sour cream; beat until just incorporated. Beat in vanilla. Divide batter evenly among prepared pans. Bake, rotating halfway through, until a cake tester comes out clean, 30 to 40 minutes. Transfer pans to wire racks to cool 15 minutes. Turn out cakes onto racks to cool completely.

4. With a serrated knife, split each layer in half horizontally. Reserve top with the prettiest dome to be used for final layer. Place 1 top half, dome-side down, on a cake stand or platter. Sprinkle 2 to 3 tablespoons of flaked coconut over cake. Spread a generous 1/2 cup coconut-cream filling over coconut flakes. Repeat with remaining layers, sprinkling 2 to 3 tablespoons coconut and spreading 1/2 cup cream on each; finish with reserved domed layer. Refrigerate cake until firm, about 1 hour.

5. Make the frosting: Combine egg whites, sugar, corn syrup, cream of tartar, and the cold water in a heatproof mixing bowl set over (not in) a pan of simmering water, stirring to dissolve sugar. Remove from heat. Beat egg mixture with an electric mixer on medium-low speed for 4 minutes; raise to high for an additional 3 to 4 minutes. Remove from heat. Add vanilla; continue to beat until icing holds its peaks, 3 to 5 minutes more (do not overmix).

6. Spread frosting over top and sides of cake. Sprinkle coconut flakes all over cake while frosting is soft; do not refrigerate.

Gluten-Free Chocolate Layer Cake

Skipping gluten shouldn't mean skipping out on all the birthday fun! Covered in pastel pink frosting, this sweet-looking layer cake rivals the best of those made with wheat flour. When possible, blend the flours instead of relying on packaged mixes, which often contain additives. We combined brown-rice, almond, and quinoa flours, all available at natural-foods stores and many supermarkets. **SERVES 8 TO 10**

1½ cups sugar

¾ cup brown-rice flour

½ cup almond flour

¾ cup unsweetened cocoa powder

¼ cup quinoa flour

2 teaspoons baking soda

1 teaspoon baking powder

¾ teaspoon coarse salt

2 large eggs

¾ cup warm water

¾ cup buttermilk

2 tablespoons unsalted butter, melted

1 teaspoon vanilla extract

Vegetable oil cooking spray

Seven-Minute Frosting (page 336)

Food coloring (preferably gel-paste) in pink or red (optional)

1. Preheat oven to 350°F. Lightly coat two 8-inch round cake pans with cooking spray. Line with parchment rounds; coat parchment.

2. Whisk together dry ingredients in a large bowl. Add eggs, the warm water, buttermilk, butter, and vanilla. Add and mix until smooth, about 3 minutes.

3. Divide batter evenly between prepared pans. Bake until edges pull away from sides of pans, about 60 minutes. Transfer pans to a wire rack to cool completely. (Cakes will keep, covered, up to 1 day.)

4. Tint frosting with food coloring, if desired. Spread about 2 cups frosting over bottom cake layer. Top with remaining cake layer. Spread remaining frosting over top and sides of cake. Cake is best eaten the same day.

Black Forest Cake

The Bavarian classic, featuring cherries and chocolate, is usually swathed in whipped cream, but we think it's more enticing this way, with the key components on display: Moist chocolate layers are brushed with a cherry brandy known as kirsch, then filled with pastry cream and cherries. Divine, glossy chocolate ganache is poured over the top. **SERVES 8 TO 10**

FOR THE CAKE

- 1 cup (2 sticks) plus 2 tablespoons unsalted butter, room temperature, plus more for pans
- 1 cup plus 2 tablespoons unsweetened cocoa powder, plus more for pans
- 2½ cups plus 2 tablespoons all-purpose flour
- 2 teaspoons baking soda
- ⅛ teaspoon salt
- 1 cup granulated sugar
- 1 cup packed dark brown sugar
- 3 large eggs, room temperature
- ¾ cup sour cream
- 1½ cups buttermilk
- 1 twelve-ounce jar (40 to 50) preserved cherries
- ¼ cup kirsch
- 2 recipes Pastry Cream (page 340)

FOR THE GANACHE

- 5 ounces semisweet chocolate, coarsely chopped
- ⅓ cup heavy cream
- 1 tablespoon honey

1. Make the cake: Preheat oven to 350°F. Butter three 8-inch cake pans; line with parchment rounds, and butter parchment. Dust with cocoa, tapping out excess. Into a large bowl, sift together flour, cocoa, baking soda, and salt.

2. With an electric mixer on medium speed, beat butter and granulated sugar until pale and fluffy, about 2 minutes. Add brown sugar; beat until fluffy, about 1 minute. Add eggs, 1 at a time, beating well after each addition. Mix in sour cream.

3. Reduce speed to low. Add flour mixture in 2 batches, alternating with buttermilk and beginning and ending with the flour; beat until just incorporated. Divide batter evenly among prepared pans. Bake, rotating halfway through, until cakes spring back when lightly touched and a cake tester comes out clean, 25 to 30 minutes. Transfer pans to wire racks to cool completely.

4. Drain cherries, reserving ¼ cup plus 2 tablespoons juice. Combine juice and kirsch in small bowl. With a serrated knife, trim tops of cakes to level. Brush each top with one third of kirsch mixture. Place bottom layer on cake stand or platter, and spread evenly with 1½ cups pastry cream. Arrange 15 drained cherries on top. Add second cake layer, brushed side up. Spread with remaining pastry cream; arrange 15 more cherries. Top with third cake layer, cut side down. (Cake may be assembled 3 to 4 hours ahead; refrigerate, wrapped loosely in plastic.)

5. Make the ganache: Pulse chocolate in food processor until finely chopped. In a small saucepan, stir together cream and honey; bring to a boil. With machine running, slowly drizzle hot cream over chocolate; process until combined. Transfer to a medium bowl. Refrigerate, stirring occasionally, until ganache is thickened and smooth, 45 to 60 minutes. Pour ganache onto center of top cake layer, and spread evenly with an offset spatula. Garnish with remaining cherries.

The Basics

Following a few trusted tips and guidelines will go a long way toward
helping you bake the best cakes. On the following pages, you'll find
a primer on essential equipment and ingredients, plus illustrated
step-by-step techniques for mixing, baking, and finishing. We've also
included recipes for the frostings used throughout this book, and page
upon page of garnishes, glazes, toppings, and other accompaniments.

Ingredients

BAKING STAPLES

FLOUR Although all-purpose flour is the most popular choice for baking cakes, other types—especially cake flour—are also common. All-purpose flour has more protein and produces cakes with a coarser crumb, while cake flour, which contains less protein, produces cakes with a finer texture (think angel-food and chiffon cakes). Do not substitute self-rising cake flour; it contains baking powder and salt. See page 320 for how to properly measure flour.

SUGAR Granulated white sugar, made from refined sugarcane or sugar beets, is the standard for baked goods. When a deeper flavor and moister texture are desired, a recipe might call for brown sugar, a combination of granulated sugar and molasses (dark brown sugar contains more molasses). Confectioners' sugar (also called powdered sugar) is made by grinding granulated sugar to a fine powder, then sifting in a small amount of cornstarch. It is primarily used to make frosting, or for dusting over finished cakes.

BUTTER AND OIL Fat is essential for adding moistness and producing cakes with the right texture. Unsalted butter has the purest flavor and is usually fresher than salted (because salt acts as a preservative). Most butter-cake recipes begin by creaming the butter and sugar; this creates air pockets in the batter that will result in a fluffy cake. Cakes made with vegetable oil are very moist, with a soft crumb; cakes made with oil tend to keep well. Use only neutral-tasting oils, such as canola or safflower, unless otherwise specified in the recipe.

EGGS Eggs play multiple roles in baking: The whites act as leaveners, especially when beaten to stiff peaks separately before being folded into batter, while yolks are emulsifiers, which enable fats and liquids to hold together. Eggs are easiest to separate when cold, but should generally be brought to room temperature before using in order to blend more easily with other ingredients; whites are best beaten when at room temperature for the most volume (or warm, as when making meringue and some buttercreams). Always use large eggs, unless otherwise specified in the recipe.

SALT The recipes in this book call for "salt" (table salt) or "coarse salt" (kosher salt). If substituting one for the other in a recipe, use a bit less table salt than the amount of coarse salt called for (and vice versa).

BAKING SODA AND BAKING POWDER Cakes rely on chemical leaveners—specifically baking soda and baking powder—for volume and lightness. The two are not interchangeable, but are often combined to produce the proper texture. Baking soda works in combination with an acid, and as such is often found in recipes containing buttermilk or sour cream. Baking powder has a small amount of acid (usually cream of tartar) mixed in. Store both in a cool, dry place, and note the use-by date on the label. To test for potency, stir $\frac{1}{4}$ teaspoon baking powder into $\frac{1}{2}$ cup hot water; the water should instantly bubble. For baking soda, add $\frac{1}{4}$ teaspoon white vinegar to the hot water before testing.

DAIRY Different kinds of dairy products contribute different flavors and textures: Heavy cream produces a more velvety crumb than whole milk, while buttermilk, sour cream, cream cheese, and yogurt (all acidic ingredients that react with baking soda, as mentioned above) add subtle flavor and moist texture. In a pinch, you can make your own buttermilk by adding 1 tablespoon white vinegar or lemon juice to 1 cup regular milk (adjust the amounts of each depending on how much buttermilk is called for); let sit 10 minutes, or until sufficiently thickened, before using. You can also purchase powdered buttermilk and mix just what you need for each recipe.

VANILLA EXTRACT You'll find this extract in almost every cake recipe, and for good reason: Its subtle essence complements a multitude of flavors, especially chocolate but also fruits and spices; it also shines on its own. Always use pure, not imitation, vanilla extract.

SPECIALTY INGREDIENTS

CHOCOLATE When used alone or in combination with cocoa powder, chocolate produces cakes that are moist and wonderfully dense. It also creates frostings that are rich and satiny. When buying chocolate for baking, look for the best-quality bar, block, or chips you can find; the higher the percentage of cacao (or chocolate liquor), the richer the taste. Milk chocolate must only contain 10 percent chocolate cacao, while dark chocolate (bittersweet and semisweet) has a higher cacao content—anywhere from 35 to 70 percent. (Unsweetened chocolate is 100 percent cacao; white chocolate contains none and is not technically considered to be chocolate.) Some premium brands to look for are Valrhona, Callebaut, El Rey, and Scharffen Berger.

COCOA POWDER Cocoa powder gives baked goods a deeper, rounder flavor than when made with solid chocolate alone. It's made by removing anywhere from 65 to 90 percent of the cocoa butter from chocolate, then finely grinding what remains. There are two types: natural (sometimes called "nonalkalized cocoa") and Dutch-process, which is treated with an alkaline solution that reduces cocoa's natural acidity and gives the powder a milder flavor and darker color. Unless a recipe specifies a particular type, you can use either. Before baking with cocoa powder, you may want to sift it with a small sieve to remove any lumps.

VANILLA BEANS Some of the recipes in this book call for vanilla beans instead of extract, as the seeds impart a more complex flavor and fragrance (you can generally substitute 1 tablespoon extract for 1 whole bean). To use a vanilla bean, lay it flat on a cutting board; holding one end, slice it open lengthwise with a paring knife, then run knife along each cut side to scrape out the seeds.

NUTS Nuts—either whole, chopped, or ground and used as flour—are often mixed into cake batters before baking; they are also arranged on top of frosted cakes for a decorative finish. Since they are naturally high in oils (which give them their rich taste), nuts can

turn rancid quickly. Buy them from a store with high turnover, and keep in an airtight bag or container in the freezer up to six months.

CORNMEAL Flour is not the only grain suitable for baking. Cornmeal, for example, imparts a delightful crunch and produces a cake with a crumbly texture. Semolina, nut flours, and gluten-free flours are other alternatives to try.

GRAHAM CRACKERS AND WAFER COOKIES When ground into crumbs and combined with butter and sugar, graham crackers and wafer cookies form the cookie crust common to most cheesecakes. They are also the foundation of traditional icebox cakes.

COCONUT The recipes in this book call for both sweetened and unsweetened shredded coconut (also sometimes called desiccated coconut). Large-flake coconut (usually unsweetened) makes a striking garnish, especially when toasted (see page 344).

MOLASSES, HONEY, AND MAPLE SYRUP Each of these liquid ingredients boasts its own distinct flavor and also adds moistness to cakes. Use unsulfured molasses and Grade B maple syrup for cooking and baking. Store molasses and honey at room temperature in their original containers up to one year, and maple syrup in the refrigerator up to six months.

SPICES Most recipes call for ground spices, not whole, although freshly grated nutmeg (see page 344) is preferred for its complex, nuanced flavor. Store ground and whole spices in airtight containers away from light and heat (do not store them above the stovetop). Most spices will lose their potency after about a year; mark the date of purchase on each bottle so you'll know when it's time to replace.

CITRUS FRUITS Use zest and juice both to flavor cakes, fillings, frostings, and glazes. Citrus slices and strips of zest, whether candied or plain, also make beautiful garnishes (see page 326).

Tools & Equipment

1. MIXING BOWLS A set of bowls in graduated sizes is the most practical; heatproof materials such as tempered glass or stainless steel are best.

2. OVEN THERMOMETER Oven temperature is critical to successful baking. Place an oven thermometer in the center of your oven to gauge the temperature, and adjust your oven's heat control accordingly.

3. PASTRY BAGS AND TIPS You will find pastry bags and tips sold separately or together in sets. Reusable bags are a good option for frequent pipers; choose ones that are 10 to 14 inches in size. Disposable ones are sold in bulk (good for piping multiple shades of frosting).

4. LIQUID MEASURING CUP Use a clear liquid measuring cup (preferably made of tempered glass) with a spout and a handle to measure liquids. Set the cup on a flat surface, and read measurements at eye level.

5. PARCHMENT This heat-resistant, nonstick, disposable paper is indispensable in the kitchen. Use it to line pans or baking sheets, or to cover a work surface for easy cleanup, especially when glazing cakes.

6. BENCH SCRAPER Often used to loosen pastry dough from a work surface, a bench scraper is also an excellent tool for smoothing the edge of a frosted cake and for making chocolate curls (see page 328).

7. WHISK A whisk lets you quickly and thoroughly incorporate dry ingredients, and whip heavy cream by hand.

8. RASP GRATER Use the small, sharp blades of a rasp grater to zest citrus fruits and to finely grate chocolate, nutmeg, and fresh ginger.

9. DRY MEASURING CUPS Measure dry ingredients (such as flour and sugar) and semisolid ingredients (such as sour cream and peanut butter) in graduated dry measuring cups, preferably long-handled stainless-steel ones. Level ingredients with a straightedge for the most accurate measurements.

10. MEASURING SPOONS Measure dry and liquid ingredients with a set of graduated measuring spoons. Level dry ingredients, such as salt, with a straightedge; pour liquids, such as vanilla extract, to the rim of the spoon. Don't measure directly over the bowl.

11. FLEXIBLE SPATULAS Use these kitchen staples for folding ingredients and scraping mixing bowls, as well as for tinting frostings with food colorings and filling pastry bags. A silicone version (which is heatproof) is good for stirring melted chocolate until smooth.

12. PASTRY BRUSH A small pastry brush evenly coats pans with butter to prevent cakes from sticking. Use a clean brush with firmly attached bristles; wash after every use in warm, soapy water, and let dry completely before storing. You can also use a pastry brush to sweep away excess crumbs from cake layers before frosting.

13. CAKE TESTER A cake tester—either a wooden skewer, toothpick, or specialty tool—is used to determine the doneness of most cakes.

14. OFFSET SPATULAS The thin metal blade and angled design of an offset spatula make it just right for spreading and smoothing batters and frostings.

15. SERRATED KNIFE Use a serrated knife and a sawing motion to trim cake layers' domed tops and to split cakes horizontally (see page 322).

16. COOLING RACK A raised wire rack allows air to circulate around baked goods as they cool. Choose one with a stainless-steel mesh grid and feet on the bottom.

17. SIEVE A fine-mesh sieve can be used to sift ingredients (such as flour or cocoa powder) into a bowl, or to dust confectioners' sugar or cocoa over the top of a baked cake for decoration.

18. PANS It is worth buying good-quality baking pans, as they will produce better results and last a lifetime. Choose straight-sided, light-colored pans made of heavy-duty aluminum, which conducts heat best.

Essential Techniques

MEASURING

A glass measuring cup is designed for liquids; set it on a flat surface and read it at eye level for accuracy. Graduated cups with handles are made for dry ingredients and solids; stainless-steel ones are best.

Decant flour into a wide-mouthed canister to make it easier to measure. Whisk flour (to aerate), spoon it into a measuring cup, and then use a straightedge to level the top, scraping excess into canister.

When a recipe calls for "packed" brown sugar, it should look compact (as shown, right). Compress it tightly with your fingers so that the sugar is level with the top of the measuring cup.

MIXING BATTER

To cream butter and sugar, beat them with an electric mixer until the mixture is pale and fluffy—lightened in both color and texture. For most recipes, this will take 3 to 5 minutes; in a few cases, such as when making pound cake, you will need to beat longer in order to incorporate as much air as possible.

When beating egg whites, start with room-temperature whites and a spotless stainless-steel bowl. As the whites are beaten they will first begin to look foamy, then form soft peaks, which droop slightly when the whisk is lifted, and finally glossy stiff peaks, which hold their shape; do not beat past this point or the whites may curdle.

To combine egg whites with a heavier base, gently fold in one third at a time: Cut a flexible spatula through the center of the mixture, sweep up the side of the bowl, and turn spatula over (making a J-shape). Repeat, rotating bowl as you go, until just combined.

PREPARING PANS

To cut a square of parchment into a round, fold it into quarters, then a triangle, then in half again; repeat until triangle is about 1 inch wide. Hold the point at the center of a cake pan; snip off the end. Unfold.

Softened butter is better than melted for coating pans. Use a pastry brush to spread butter and to coat hard-to-reach spots. If lining with parchment, lay parchment over butter, then butter parchment.

To coat with flour, dust pan; rotate and tap edge of pan to distribute evenly. Tap out excess flour. When making a chocolate cake, dust the pan with cocoa powder instead of flour for invisible results.

SMOOTHING BATTER

Thick batters should be smoothed in the pan with an offset spatula to ensure the cake bakes evenly. A flexible spatula, or even the back of a spoon, would also work.

TESTING FOR DONENESS

Insert a cake tester, such as a wooden skewer or toothpick, in the center of a cake. If it comes out clean, or with just a few moist crumbs attached (as some recipes suggest), the cake is done. Other clues that the cake is ready: It feels springy when lightly touched, it's golden on top, and it pulls away from the side of the pan.

INVERTING CAKE

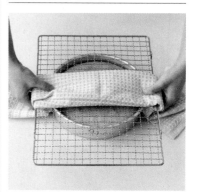

To remove a cake from its pan while the pan is still warm, place a wire rack over the pan, grip pan and rack both with a kitchen towel, then flip over together. Gently lift off the pan, remove parchment, and reinvert cake to another rack.

LEVELING AND SPLITTING

Trimming off the domed tops helps cake layers stack more evenly. Hold the cake steady with one hand, and use a long serrated knife to cut horizontally along the top edge with a gentle sawing motion.

When splitting cakes into multiple layers, measure the height of the cake, then insert toothpicks at the halfway point at intervals around the circumference. Hold the top steady, and cut the cake horizontally just above the toothpicks.

To transfer fragile layers, carefully wedge a cardboard round between the layers, and slide it into place; use the board to support the cake layer as you move it. A cardboard round underneath the bottom of a cake will also make it easier to transfer after it is frosted.

FROSTING A LAYER CAKE

Spread an even layer of frosting on the bottom layer, and top with second layer. (Refrigerate to set frosting if it is soft). Spread a thin layer of frosting on top and side of cake to seal in crumbs (this is called the crumb coat); use a bench scraper or offset spatula to remove any excess. Refrigerate until set, 20 to 30 minutes, or up to overnight.

With an offset spatula, apply a second coat of frosting on top of the crumb coat. To smooth sides, hold an offset spatula or bench scraper at a 45-degree angle while rotating the cake (a turntable helps with this step). For an extra-smooth finish, dip the spatula in hot water and wipe dry as you work.

USING A PASTRY BAG

1

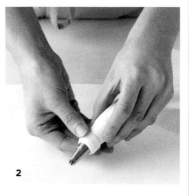

2

Snip the pointed end of the pastry bag just enough to allow the tip or the base of a coupler to fit inside. Insert the coupler base into bag, making sure the screw threads are covered.

Slide the pastry tip over the base of the coupler, then screw on the outer ring to secure the tip in place. Unscrew the ring to change tips.

3

4

Hold the bag with one hand, and fold the top over into a cuff. Fill the bag halfway with frosting (overfilling the bag makes it messy and hard to handle). Unfold the cuff and twist the top of the bag to close; if desired, secure with a rubber band.

To pipe, hold the bag with your writing hand (near the top, so the frosting is squeezed down toward the tip) and use your other hand as a guide. Adjust the pressure on the bag as needed, depending on the piped design and the density of the frosting.

TINTING FROSTING

Reserve a small bowl of plain frosting in case you need to tone down the color. Gel-paste food colorings are your best bet for decorating; they are more concentrated than the liquid variety and will produce truer colors without diluting frostings. Use a toothpick to add food coloring a dab at a time; stir with a flexible spatula to combine. If you over-tint the frosting, add a bit of the reserved frosting to lighten it.

Piping Techniques

Pastry tips are sold individually or in sets, sometimes with a pastry bag and coupler. The tips shown here are the most common. Each "family," such as round, petal, or star, consists of various versions and sizes, each identified with a number. The designs pictured are just a starting point; improvising with different tips is highly encouraged. You may want to practice first: Pipe your design onto a piece of parchment, then scrape off the frosting and try again.

1. SMALL ROUND
Use round (also called plain) tips to write messages or numbers; to draw delicate dots, swags, vines, or teardrops; or to pipe clusters of tiny dots for flower centers.

2. OVERSIZE ROUND
With their wide openings, these are used to pipe large dots, beaded borders, or big swirls of frosting.

3. LEAF

The standard leaf tip has a ridged vein down the center; use it to pipe flat leaves, either singly or in an overlapping border. The V-leaf tip makes a pointier leaf or long petal.

4. PETAL

These tips, which can be straight, slightly curved, or U-shaped, are essential for piping flowers; they also make beautiful ruffles and border designs.

5. BASKET-WEAVE

Named for its most common pattern, this tip also makes lines, swags, and ruffled borders, using either the straight or ridged side.

6. OVERSIZE BASKET-WEAVE

An extra-large basket-weave tip makes wide stripes and can quickly cover the entire surface of a cake.

7. STAR

Open and closed star tips are very versatile for making scalloped borders, starbursts, and decorative swirls. Closed stars have deeper ridges for a more defined result; they can also be used to make rosettes.

8. OVERSIZE STAR

A generously sized star tip makes dramatic large-scale swirls and rosettes as well as tall peaks.

Candied Garnishes

For a bit of shine and sparkle, try one of these easy, make-ahead finishes. Candied citrus begins with a syrup of equal parts sugar and water (enough to completely cover the fruit); boil it until the sugar is dissolved, then simmer the fruit until translucent. If necessary, keep fruit submerged with a parchment round. (Be sure to use organic, unsprayed citrus.) Nuts require only a quick dip in a pan of caramel. Flowers, small berries, and herbs are simply glittered with fine sugar, using diluted egg whites as "glue." All three methods are meant to be versatile; let the flavors of your cake inform your choice.

CANDIED CITRUS SLICES

Bring equal amounts water and sugar (enough to cover the slices) to a boil; cook until sugar dissolves. Add ⅛-inch-thick citrus slices (preferably organic) and cover with a parchment round; simmer gently on low heat, without stirring, until pith is translucent, 30 minutes. Cool slices (off heat) in syrup. Let slices dry in a single layer on a wire rack before using.

CANDIED CITRUS PEEL

Cover ¼-inch strips of citrus peel (pith removed) with cold water in a saucepan, bring to a boil, and then drain. Repeat twice. Bring equal amounts water and sugar (enough

to cover the strips) to a boil; cook until sugar dissolves. Add strips; simmer gently on medium-low until peel is translucent, 1 hour. Let strips cool (off heat) in syrup. Wipe excess syrup from each strip, roll in sugar, and let dry on a wire rack.

CANDIED NUTS
Heat ³⁄₄ cup sugar and 3 table-spoons water over high, swirling, until sugar dissolves. Simmer, swirling occasionally, until medium amber, about 4 minutes. Add 1 cup toasted nuts and ¹⁄₂ teaspoon coarse salt, and stir to coat. Pour mixture onto a baking sheet, and separate nuts using 2 forks. Let cool.

SUGARED GARNISHES
Use this technique for small flowers, rose petals, berries, currants, and herb sprigs. Whisk together 1 egg white and 1 tablespoon water. Hold a rose petal or other garnish with tweezers, and brush with egg-white mixture to coat. Sprinkle superfine sugar over surface. Let dry on a wire rack until crisp, about 8 hours.

CANDIED PINEAPPLE SLICES
Drain 2 cans sliced pineapple, reserving 1¹⁄₂ cups juice. Bring juice, 2¹⁄₂ cups sugar, and ¹⁄₄ cup light corn syrup to a boil; cook on medium heat 4 minutes. Add slices; simmer on low heat, turn-ing frequently, 45 minutes or until

translucent. Transfer slices to a wire rack set over a baking sheet and bake at 200°F until pineapple caramelizes and is less sticky, 60 to 90 minutes. Let cool on rack.

DRIED APPLE OR PEAR SLICES
Squeeze lemon juice over apple or pear slices to coat. Bring equal amounts water and sugar (enough to cover the slices) to a boil; cook until sugar dissolves. Add slices; cook on medium heat 2 minutes. Coat a parchment-lined baking sheet with cooking spray and place drained slices ¹⁄₂ inch apart. Bake at 200°F until dry, 2 hours. Flip; bake until dry and crisp (but not browned), about 20 minutes more.

Chocolate Garnishes

Chocolate's meltable, moldable qualities make it an ideal medium for shaping into shards and curls or coating nuts and fruit. Melt chopped chocolate in a heatproof bowl set over (not in) a pan of simmering water, or microwave in 30-second increments, stirring in between. Store chocolate garnishes (except truffles) at room temperature in an airtight container, layered with parchment if necessary. Store-bought candies (such as malted milk balls and candy-coated chocolates) also make fun and easy embellishments.

CHOCOLATE CURLS
With an offset spatula, spread melted chocolate into a smooth, even layer on the back of a rimmed baking sheet; let stand until just set. Holding a bench scraper at a 45-degree angle, scrape chocolate into curls. Alternatively, use a vegetable peeler to shave curls from a bar of chocolate.

CHOCOLATE-COVERED CITRUS
Dip candied citrus slices or strips of candied peel in melted semisweet or bittersweet chocolate. Place on a parchment-lined baking sheet until set.

CHOCOLATE-COVERED ALMOND PRALINES

Bring 1 cup sugar and $\frac{1}{4}$ cup water to a boil and cook until sugar dissolves. Cook, without stirring, until a candy thermometer reaches 235°F, about 3 minutes. Add $2\frac{1}{2}$ cups toasted almonds. Cook, stirring, until sugar begins to crystallize, 1 minute. Stir in $1\frac{1}{4}$ teaspoons salt. Cook, stirring, until sugar forms a thin, sand-like coating on nuts, 2 to 3 minutes. Pour onto a baking sheet; let cool 30 minutes. Sift nuts in a colander to remove excess sugar; transfer to a bowl. Use immediately or stir in 6 ounces melted semisweet chocolate to coat. Pour onto baking sheet, and separate nuts using 2 forks. Refrigerate 30 minutes. Toss pralines with $\frac{1}{4}$ cup unsweetened cocoa powder.

TRUFFLES

Place 8 ounces finely chopped dark chocolate and a pinch of salt in a heatproof bowl. Bring 1 cup heavy cream just to a boil, then pour over chocolate. Let stand, without stirring, 10 minutes. Stir, scraping sides and bottom of bowl with a flexible spatula, until smooth and shiny. Refrigerate, covered, until firm, at least 4 hours or overnight. Use a small ice cream scoop or tablespoon to scoop truffles, and roll into balls. Roll each ball in unsweetened cocoa powder. Refrigerate truffles 30 minutes, or up to 4 days.

CHOCOLATE MINT LEAVES

Brush a thick coat of melted chocolate onto the textured underside of mint leaves. Place on parchment or, for shape, drape each leaf, chocolate side up, over the handle of a wooden spoon. Refrigerate until set, about 10 minutes. Gently grasp the chocolate layer of each leaf with kitchen tweezers. Holding the stem, peel the leaf away with your fingers.

Glazes

The easiest way to decorate an ordinary cake is with a coat of glaze. The simplest options on these pages barely require a recipe at all: Just mix confectioners' sugar with a liquid, such as milk or lemon juice, adjusting the proportions until you reach the desired thickness; if you like, add a bit of citrus zest, liqueur, vanilla extract, or another flavoring agent. Other glazes feature extra richness from butter, heavy cream, chocolate, or caramel. All of the options should be used immediately after they're made and then given a few minutes to set before serving.

BASIC MILK GLAZE

Whisk together 2 cups confectioners' sugar and $1/4$ cup milk until smooth, adding more milk if needed to reach desired consistency. **Makes about $3/4$ cup**

BROWN-SUGAR GLAZE

Heat 6 tablespoons unsalted butter and $1/2$ cup packed light brown sugar in a saucepan over medium, stirring, until sugar has dissolved. Add 2 tablespoons heavy cream, 1 teaspoon vanilla extract, and $1/2$ teaspoon salt; bring to a boil. Remove from heat; let cool until thickened. **Makes about 1 cup**

LEMON GLAZE

Whisk together 2 cups confectioners' sugar with 2 teaspoons finely grated lemon zest and 1/4 cup fresh lemon juice (from 2 lemons) until smooth. For a poppy seed variation (see recipe on page 272), stir in 2 teaspoons poppy seeds. **Makes about 1 cup**

ESPRESSO GLAZE

Place 3 ounces chopped bittersweet chocolate, 1 1/2 tablespoons unsalted butter, and 2 teaspoons vanilla extract in a heatproof bowl. Bring 1/3 cup heavy cream, 1/3 cup sugar, 1 tablespoon instant espresso powder, and 1/4 teaspoon coarse salt to a boil in a small saucepan, stirring; pour over chocolate mixture. Let stand 2 minutes. Whisk until smooth. **Makes 1 cup**

CHOCOLATE GLAZE

Place 3 ounces chopped bittersweet chocolate in a heatproof bowl. Bring 1/2 cup heavy cream to a simmer in a small saucepan; pour over chocolate. Let stand 2 minutes. Add 2 tablespoons unsalted butter, and mix until smooth. Let stand, stirring occasionally, until slightly thickened. **Makes 1 cup**

CARAMEL GLAZE

Heat 1 cup sugar and 1/4 cup water in a saucepan over medium-high, stirring occasionally, until sugar is dissolved and syrup is clear. Cook, without stirring, until syrup comes to a boil, washing down sides of pan with a wet pastry brush to prevent crystals from forming. Boil, gently swirling, until medium amber. Remove from heat. Pour in 1/4 cup dark rum, if desired, and 2 tablespoons heavy cream. Let cool, stirring, until thickened. **Makes 3/4 cup**

RUM GLAZE

Whisk together 2 cups sugar, 2 tablespoons plus 1 teaspoon rum, and 2 tablespoons plus 1 1/2 teaspoons milk until smooth; add more rum if needed to reach desired consistency. **Makes about 3/4 cup**

Accompaniments

These versatile sauces, compotes, and other accoutrements are meant to be served on the side. They add richness or bold flavors to simple cakes, and allow you to change up your favorites when the mood strikes. As a general rule, stronger flavors pair well with milder ones: Think vibrant lemon curd or seasonal fruit spooned over a slice of pound cake or angel-food cake, or dollops of whipped cream atop a chocolate or fruit-filled cake. Even better, some of these sides can be prepared ahead of time, making them just right for entertaining.

LEMON CURD

Whisk together 2 large eggs and 4 large egg yolks. Combine with 3/4 cup sugar and 1/2 cup fresh lemon juice (from 4 lemons) in a small, heavy-bottomed saucepan. Cook over low heat, stirring constantly, 12 to 14 minutes, or until mixture coats the back of a spoon. Strain into a small bowl. Add 1/2 stick unsalted butter, 1 tablespoon at a time, stirring until smooth. Stir in 1 tablespoon lemon zest (from 2 lemons). Press parchment or plastic wrap directly on surface of curd to prevent a skin from forming. Let cool completely before using; refrigerate up to 2 days.
Makes 2 cups

BLOOD-ORANGE COMPOTE

Peel rind from an orange, leaving pith behind. Cut rind into matchsticks to yield 2 tablespoons. Cut segments of 6 oranges free of membranes. Cut segments in half, and place in bowl with orange-peel matchsticks. Stir in ¼ cup honey. **Makes 1⅓ cups**

WHIPPED CREAM

With an electric mixer (or by hand), whisk 1 cup cold heavy cream in a well-chilled bowl until soft peaks form. Add up to 2 tablespoons confectioners' sugar (or omit, for unsweetened whipped cream), and whisk until medium-stiff peaks form. For a lemon variation, decrease sugar to 1 tablespoon and add 2 teaspoons finely grated lemon zest. For a bourbon variation (see recipe on page 264), add 2 tablespoons bourbon. **Makes about 2 cups**

MACERATED BERRIES

Combine 2¼ cups fresh berries, 2 tablespoons sugar, and 1 teaspoon fresh lemon juice, and let sit 1 hour. **Makes 2¼ cups**

CHOCOLATE-COFFEE LIQUEUR SAUCE

Heat 6 ounces chopped semisweet chocolate, 5 tablespoons Kahlúa, 1 tablespoon vanilla extract, and 1 tablespoon light corn syrup in a heatproof bowl set over (not in) a pan of simmering water. Whisk until chocolate has melted completely. **Makes about ¾ cup**

CARAMEL SAUCE

Bring ½ cup water, 1 cup sugar, and ⅔ cup light corn syrup to a boil in a small saucepan, stirring until sugar is dissolved and washing down side of pan with a wet pastry brush. Cook over medium-high heat until medium amber, about 10 minutes. Remove from heat. Stir in ½ cup plus 3 tablespoons heavy cream and 1 teaspoon vanilla extract. Let cool slightly before serving. **Makes about 1 cup**

Recipes

BASIC BUTTERCREAM FROSTING

MAKES ABOUT 4 CUPS

1½ cups (3 sticks) unsalted butter, room temperature

1 pound (4 cups) confectioners' sugar, sifted

½ teaspoon vanilla extract

1. With an electric mixer on medium-high speed, beat butter until pale and creamy, about 2 minutes. Reduce speed to medium. Add the confectioners' sugar, ½ cup at a time, beating well after each addition and scraping down sides of bowl as needed; after every two additions, raise speed to high and beat 10 seconds to aerate frosting, then return to medium-high. This process should take about 5 minutes. Frosting will be very pale and fluffy.

2. Add vanilla, and beat until frosting is smooth. Frosting can be refrigerated up to 10 days in an airtight container. Bring to room temperature, and beat on low speed before using.

CREAMY VANILLA FROSTING

MAKES 3¾ CUPS

½ cup (1 stick) unsalted butter, room temperature

4 ounces cream cheese, room temperature

5 cups confectioners' sugar

¼ cup milk

½ teaspoon vanilla extract

1. With an electric mixer on medium-high speed, beat butter and cream cheese until pale and creamy, about 1 minute. Reduce speed to medium. Add confectioners' sugar, 1 cup at a time, beating well after each addition.

2. Add milk and vanilla and beat until smooth, about 2 minutes. If not using immediately, press plastic wrap directly onto surface of frosting, and refrigerate in an airtight container up to 1 week. Bring to room temperature, and beat on low speed before using.

CREAM-CHEESE FROSTING

MAKES ABOUT 6 CUPS

1 pound (two 8-ounce bars) cream cheese, room temperature

2 teaspoons vanilla extract

1 cup (2 sticks) unsalted butter, room temperature

2 pounds confectioners' sugar, sifted

1. With an electric mixer on medium speed, beat cream cheese and vanilla until light and creamy, about 2 minutes. Add butter, beating until incorporated.

2. Reduce speed to low. Gradually add confectioners' sugar, 1 cup at a time, and beat until fluffy and smooth. Frosting can be refrigerated in an airtight container up to 3 days. Bring to room temperature, and beat on low speed before using.

CREAM CHEESE–SOUR CREAM FROSTING

We developed this version of cream-cheese frosting to go with the Molasses-Spice Cake (page 148), but it would also pair nicely with chocolate cakes such as One-Bowl Chocolate Cake (page 275), Red Velvet Cake (page 268), and Double-Chocolate Cake (page 296). **MAKES 3 CUPS**

12 ounces cream cheese (one-and-a-half 8-ounce bars), room temperature

1/2 cup (1 stick) unsalted butter, room temperature

1/4 cup sour cream

1/2 cup confectioners' sugar, sifted

1/8 teaspoon salt

With an electric mixer on medium-high speed, beat cream cheese and butter until light and creamy, 3 to 4 minutes. Beat in sour cream, then confectioners' sugar and salt, until smooth. Frosting can be refrigerated in an airtight container up to 1 day. Bring to room temperature, and beat on low speed until smooth before using.

CREAM CHEESE–GOAT CHEESE FROSTING

The unexpected addition of goat cheese makes this frosting uncommonly good—and the perfect partner for our Pumpkin Layer Cake (page 279). Or use it with the Applesauce Cake (page 135) or Maple Cake (page 120). **MAKES 3 1/2 CUPS**

1 1/4 pounds (two-and-a-half 8-ounce bars) cream cheese, room temperature

4 ounces soft goat cheese, room temperature

3/4 cup confectioners' sugar, sifted

With an electric mixer on medium-high speed, beat cream cheese and goat cheese until fluffy, about 4 minutes, scraping down sides of bowl as needed. Add confectioners' sugar, and beat until well combined and creamy, about 4 minutes. Frosting can be refrigerated, in an airtight container, up to 3 days. Bring to room temperature, and beat on low speed until smooth before using.

SEVEN-MINUTE FROSTING

MAKES ABOUT 5 CUPS

1½ cups sugar
 5 large egg whites
 1 tablespoon light corn syrup
 2 teaspoons vanilla extract

1. Whisk together sugar, egg whites, and corn syrup in a heatproof mixer bowl set over (not in) a pan of simmering water. Whisk until warm and sugar is dissolved (mixture should feel completely smooth when rubbed between your fingers), 2 to 3 minutes. Remove from heat.

2. With an electric mixer on high speed, beat until stiff, glossy peaks form, about 7 minutes. Beat in vanilla. Use immediately.

SWISS MERINGUE BUTTERCREAM

Consider this your go-to frosting: It's ultra-rich and delicious, goes on silky smooth, and is well suited to a variety of cake flavors. It also pipes like a dream—see the flowers on both the Rum Rose Cake (page 291) and Almond-Orange Layer Cake (page 304). Swiss Meringue Buttercream keeps beautifully in the refrigerator or freezer, needing only a brief mixing before using. If you are wondering what frosting to pair with a birthday cake, this is the place to start. **MAKES ABOUT 9 CUPS**

2¼ cups sugar
 9 large egg whites
 3 cups (6 sticks) unsalted butter, room temperature, cut into pieces
1½ teaspoons vanilla extract

1. Whisk together sugar and egg whites in a heatproof mixing bowl set over (not in) a pan of simmering water. Whisk until warm and sugar is dissolved (mixture should feel completely smooth when rubbed between your fingers), 2 to 3 minutes. Remove from heat.

2. With an electric mixer on medium speed, whisk egg-white mixture 5 minutes. Increase speed to medium-high, and whisk until stiff, glossy peaks form and meringue has cooled (test by feeling bottom of bowl), about 7 minutes.

3. Reduce speed to medium-low. Add butter, several tablespoons at a time, beating well after each addition. Add vanilla, and continue beating until frosting is smooth and fluffy, 3 to 5 minutes. (If the frosting appears to separate after all the butter has been added, beat on medium-high speed until smooth again.) Buttercream can be refrigerated up to 3 days or frozen up to 3 months in an airtight container. Bring to room temperature, and beat on low speed before using.

MOCHA BUTTERCREAM

We used this frosting to fill, frost, and pipe decorations onto the ever-popular One-Bowl Chocolate Cake (page 275), but it would also work well with other chocolate cakes (look in the index for multiple options) as well as our Vanilla Layer Cake (page 283). **MAKES 4½ CUPS**

1/4 cup plus 2 tablespoons instant espresso powder

1/4 cup plus 2 tablespoons hot water

6 large egg whites

1 3/4 cups sugar

2 1/4 cups (4½ sticks) unsalted butter, cut into pieces, room temperature

12 ounces bittersweet chocolate, chopped, melted, and cooled

1. In a small bowl, combine espresso powder and the hot water; stir until dissolved. In a heatproof bowl set over (not in) a pan of simmering water, whisk together egg whites and sugar until the sugar is dissolved and the mixture is warm to the touch, 2 to 3 minutes.

2. With an electric mixer on high speed, whisk egg-white mixture until cooled and stiff, glossy peaks form, 7 to 10 minutes.

3. Reduce speed to medium-low. Add butter, several tablespoons at a time, beating well after each addition. Continue beating until smooth and fluffy, 3 to 5 minutes. (If the frosting appears to separate after all the butter has been added, beat on medium-high speed until smooth again.) With mixer on low speed, add chocolate, then espresso mixture; beat until smooth, about 1 minute. Beat on the lowest speed to eliminate any air bubbles, about 2 minutes. Frosting can be refrigerated up to 5 days in an airtight container. Bring to room temperature, and beat on low speed before using.

RICH CHOCOLATE FROSTING

The combination of cocoa powder and melted semisweet chocolate gives this frosting a deep, dark, chocolaty flavor. Our food editors love the way it can be beautifully swooped and swirled, as shown on the Chocolate Truffle Cake (page 271). Other great options include One-Bowl Chocolate Cake (page 275) and Vanilla Sheet Cake (page 123). **MAKES 4½ CUPS**

1/2 cup plus 1 tablespoon unsweetened cocoa powder

1/2 cup plus 1 tablespoon warm water

1 1/2 cups (3 sticks) unsalted butter, room temperature

3/4 cup confectioners' sugar

2 1/4 teaspoons coarse salt

1 1/2 pounds semisweet chocolate, chopped, melted, and cooled

Whisk together cocoa and the warm water in a bowl until cocoa dissolves. With an electric mixer on medium speed, beat butter, confectioners' sugar, and salt until pale and fluffy, 3 to 5 minutes. Gradually beat in melted chocolate and then cocoa mixture until combined. Frosting can be refrigerated up to 5 days in an airtight container. Bring to room temperature, and beat on low speed before using.

MILK CHOCOLATE FROSTING

Milk-chocolate lovers will want to use this frosting on all sorts of cakes, and not just the Double-Chocolate Cake (page 296). Think Devil's Food Cake (page 288), Buttermilk Cake (page 259), and Banana Pecan Cake (page 160; you will need only half a batch in this case). **MAKES 5 CUPS**

- 2 cups (4 sticks) unsalted butter, room temperature
- 1 cup confectioners' sugar
- Pinch of coarse salt
- 1 pound milk chocolate, chopped, melted, and cooled
- 1 cup sour cream

With an electric mixer on medium-high speed, beat butter, confectioners' sugar, and salt until pale and fluffy, about 5 minutes. Gradually beat in chocolate, then sour cream, and beat until thoroughly incorporated. Frosting should be spreadable. (If frosting is too soft, refrigerate, stirring occasionally, until thickened.) Frosting can be refrigerated in an airtight container up to 3 days. Bring to room temperature, and beat on low speed until smooth before using.

COCONUT-PECAN FROSTING

MAKES ENOUGH FOR ONE 9-INCH LAYER CAKE

- 3 large egg yolks
- 1 can (12 ounces) evaporated milk
- 1¼ cups packed light brown sugar
- ¾ cup plus 2 tablespoons (1¾ sticks) unsalted butter, cut into small pieces and brought to room temperature
- 1 teaspoon vanilla extract
- ¼ teaspoon salt
- 2 cups (7 ounces) sweetened flaked coconut
- 1¾ cups (7 ounces) pecans, toasted (see page 344) and coarsely chopped

1. Combine egg yolks, evaporated milk, and brown sugar in a saucepan. Add butter; cook over medium heat, stirring constantly, until thickened (mixture should coat the back of a spoon), about 10 minutes. Pour through a fine sieve into a bowl.

2. Stir in vanilla, salt, coconut, and pecans. Let cool completely. Frosting can be refrigerated in an airtight container up to 1 day. Bring to room temperature before using.

MILK CHOCOLATE GANACHE

MAKES ENOUGH FOR ONE 9-INCH CAKE

1½ pounds best-quality milk chocolate, finely chopped

2 cups plus 2 tablespoons heavy cream

1 teaspoon light corn syrup

1. Prepare an ice-water bath. Place chocolate in a medium heatproof bowl. Bring cream to a boil in a small saucepan; pour over chocolate, swirling to cover completely. Let stand until chocolate has melted, about 5 minutes. Add corn syrup; whisk until smooth.

2. Pour 1 cup ganache into a bowl set in ice bath; stir until thick and spreadable. Keep remaining ganache at room temperature, stirring every 15 minutes, until thick enough to coat back of spoon, 12 to 15 minutes. Use immediately.

WHIPPED BITTERSWEET CHOCOLATE GANACHE

Although it was used to fill the layers in the Chocolate Truffle Cake (page 271), this whipped ganache also makes a fine frosting. Try it with One-Bowl Chocolate Cake (page 275) or any time you want a luscious chocolate filling or frosting that's not too sweet. **MAKES ABOUT 4 CUPS**

1 pound bittersweet chocolate, finely chopped

2½ cups heavy cream

1. Place chocolate in a large heatproof bowl. Bring cream to a boil over medium-high heat; pour over chocolate, swirling to cover completely. Let sit 10 minutes. With a flexible spatula or a small whisk, gently stir chocolate and cream until combined.

2. Refrigerate ganache, stirring every 5 minutes until mixture is cool to the touch. Whisk ganache until it just barely begins to hold its shape and is slightly lighter in color. Do not overwhip, or mixture will become grainy (ganache will keep thickening after you stop whisking). Use immediately.

POURED GANACHE VARIATION: Omit step 2. At the end of step 1, let ganache sit at room temperature until just thickened, about 15 minutes. The ganache will get thicker as it sits; it should be pourable but thick enough to fully coat the cake.

PASTRY CREAM

MAKES ABOUT 1½ CUPS

1 large egg plus 1 large
  egg yolk

¼ cup plus 2 tablespoons sugar

3 tablespoons cornstarch

1 cup milk

1½ tablespoons unsalted butter,
  cut into pieces

¾ teaspoon vanilla extract

1. Prepare an ice-water bath. With an electric mixer on medium-high speed, beat egg, yolk, and ¼ cup sugar until pale yellow and thick, 2 to 3 minutes. Sift in cornstarch; beat on medium-low speed until combined.

2. Meanwhile, bring milk and remaining 2 tablespoons sugar to a boil in a saucepan. Whisking constantly, slowly pour half of milk mixture into egg mixture; continue to whisk until smooth. Pour mixture back into saucepan. Whisk over medium heat another 2 to 3 minutes, until mixture is thickened and coats the back of a wooden spoon (it should be the consistency of mayonnaise).

3. Transfer to a large bowl. Add butter, a piece at a time, stirring until melted after each addition. Set over ice-water bath until chilled. Stir in vanilla. Cover with plastic wrap and refrigerate at least 2 hours, or up to overnight, before using.

COCONUT-CREAM FILLING

MAKES 1¾ CUPS

1 large egg plus 1 large
  egg yolk

¼ cup plus 2 tablespoons sugar

2 tablespoons cornstarch
  Pinch of salt

1½ cups milk

2 ounces (¾ cup) sweetened
  flaked coconut

¾ teaspoon vanilla extract
  Unsalted butter, for plastic
  wrap

1. Whisk egg and yolk in a large bowl. Combine sugar, cornstarch, and salt in a medium saucepan. Gradually add milk, whisking constantly. Cook, stirring, over medium-high heat until mixture thickens and just begins to bubble, 2 to 3 minutes. Remove from heat.

2. Whisk ¼ cup hot milk mixture into eggs to temper. Slowly pour warmed eggs into saucepan, stirring constantly. Cook, stirring, over medium-high heat until mixture just begins to bubble, about 1 minute. Remove from heat. Stir in coconut and vanilla.

3. Transfer filling to a medium bowl. Lightly butter a piece of plastic wrap, and press it directly on surface of filling to prevent a skin from forming. Refrigerate until firm and chilled, at least 1 hour and up to 1 day.

APPLE-CIDER APPLESAUCE

MAKES 1½ CUPS

1 pound juicy apples, such as McIntosh, peeled, cored, and quartered

¾ cup apple cider

1 tablespoon sugar, plus more if needed

Pinch of salt

1. Bring apples and cider to a boil in a saucepan over medium-high heat. Cover pan; reduce heat. Simmer until apples are very soft, about 12 minutes. Remove lid; stir in sugar and salt.

2. Cook over medium-low heat until apples are broken up and most of the liquid is evaporated, about 15 minutes. Let cool slightly. Blend in a food processor until smooth. Add more sugar, if desired. Refrigerate in an airtight container up to 2 days.

QUINCE-GINGER COMPOTE

MAKES ABOUT 3½ CUPS

1½ cups off-dry white wine, such as Riesling

¾ cup water, plus more if needed

¾ cup sugar

6 thin slices peeled fresh ginger (from one 1-inch piece)

1½ pounds just ripened quince, peeled, cored, and cut into ½-inch wedges

1½ teaspoons fresh lemon juice

1. Bring wine, the water, sugar, and ginger to a simmer in a medium saucepan over high heat. Cook, stirring, until sugar dissolves, about 5 minutes. Add quince. (Add more water if needed to cover fruit.) Reduce heat, and simmer gently until quinces are tender, 25 to 45 minutes depending on ripeness of fruit.

2. Transfer quince to a bowl using a slotted spoon. Bring liquid in saucepan to a simmer, and cook until slightly syrupy, about 5 minutes. Remove, and discard ginger. Stir in lemon juice. Pour syrup over quince. Let stand until cool.

RUM SYRUP

MAKES 1⅓ CUPS

1 cup sugar

1 cup water

2 tablespoons light rum

Bring sugar and the water to a boil in a saucepan, stirring constantly until sugar has dissolved. Reduce heat; simmer, without stirring, 5 minutes. Remove from heat, and stir in rum. Let cool completely.

MOLASSES-GINGERBREAD COOKIE DOUGH

Use this recipe for the Gingerbread Icebox Cake on page 219 and Gingerbread Cheesecake on page 189. You will only need half the recipe for the cheesecake; use the remaining dough to make cookie cutouts (see variation) or reserve it for another use; it will freeze up to one month. To make a honey gingerbread variation (as pictured on top of the cheesecake), replace ½ cup of the molasses with ½ cup honey, and substitute granulated sugar for the brown sugar.

2¾ cups all-purpose flour

½ teaspoon baking soda

¾ teaspoon salt

2 teaspoons ground ginger

2 teaspoons ground cinnamon

¾ teaspoon ground cloves

½ teaspoon freshly grated nutmeg

½ cup (1 stick) unsalted butter, room temperature

½ cup packed dark brown sugar

1 large egg

¾ cup unsulfured molasses

1. Whisk together flour, baking soda, salt, and spices in a medium bowl.

2. With an electric mixer on medium-high speed, beat butter and brown sugar until fluffy. Add egg, beating well. Beat in molasses. Reduce speed to low. Gradually add flour mixture; beat until just combined. Divide dough into 2 portions; wrap each in plastic. Refrigerate until ready to use, at least 1 hour.

GINGERBREAD-MEN VARIATION: Preheat oven to 350°F. On a generously floured piece of parchment, roll dough to a scant ¼ inch thick. Freeze 15 minutes. Cut out gingerbread men with a 2-inch cookie cutter. Freeze shapes on parchment-lined baking sheets 15 minutes. Bake 6 minutes. Remove sheets from oven; tap firmly on counter. Return to oven; bake until crisp, 6 to 8 minutes. Transfer sheets to wire racks to cool completely. If desired, pipe buttons onto cookies with Royal Icing (recipe follows).

ROYAL ICING

MAKES ABOUT 2½ CUPS

1 pound (4 cups) confectioners' sugar

¼ cup plus 1 tablespoon meringue powder

Scant ½ cup water, plus more as needed

With an electric mixer on low speed, beat all ingredients until smooth, about 7 minutes. If icing is too thick, add more water, a little at a time, beating until icing holds a ribbon on the surface for a few seconds when beater is lifted; if too thin, continue mixing 2 to 3 minutes more. Use immediately, or refrigerate in an airtight container up to 1 week; stir well with a flexible spatula before using.

LEMON-BLACKBERRY SEMIFREDDO

MAKES ABOUT 6 CUPS

2 large whole eggs plus 8 large egg yolks and 3 large egg whites, room temperature

1 cup plus 3 tablespoons plus 1 teaspoon sugar

1 tablespoon plus 1 teaspoon finely grated lemon zest, plus ¾ cup fresh lemon juice (from about 10 lemons)

2 tablespoons unsalted butter

2 tablespoons water

¾ pound mascarpone cheese, room temperature

1 pint fresh blackberries

1. Combine whole eggs, yolks, ¾ cup sugar, and the lemon juice in a heatproof bowl set over (not in) a pan of simmering water. Whisk until mixture is very thick and smooth, and temperature registers 165°F on an instant-read thermometer, about 5 minutes. Remove from heat; whisk in butter until combined. Pour through a fine sieve into another bowl; cover with plastic wrap, pressing it directly on surface of curd to avoid forming a skin. Refrigerate until cool and firm, about 1 hour.

2. With an electric mixer on low speed, whisk egg whites until fluffy. Meanwhile, bring ⅓ cup sugar and the water to a boil in a small saucepan over high heat. Swirl pan to dissolve sugar. Wash down side of pan with a wet pastry brush to prevent crystals from forming. Boil until syrup registers 248°F on an instant-read thermometer. Raise speed to medium-high; beat until whites have formed almost-stiff peaks. With mixer running, slowly pour in syrup; beat until meringue has cooled and stiff, glossy peaks have formed, about 4 minutes.

3. Stir mascarpone in a nonreactive bowl with a flexible spatula until smooth. Fold in lemon curd and lemon zest. Gently but thoroughly fold in meringue. Pulse berries and remaining 2 tablespoons sugar in a food processor until berries are broken up. Fold into lemon mixture, leaving it swirled. Freeze until slightly firm, about 20 minutes. Use immediately.

Recipe Tips & Techniques

MEASURING DRY INGREDIENTS Measure dry ingredients (such as flour and sugar) and semisolid ingredients (such as peanut butter and sour cream) in graduated dry measuring cups. For flour, spoon flour into the cup and fill to overflowing, then level with a straightedge such as a knife. (Don't shake the cup or tap it on the counter to level; both will lead to inaccurate measurements.) If a recipe calls for "sifted flour," sift the flour first, then measure it; if it calls for "flour, sifted," measure first, then sift. When measuring brown sugar, pack firmly into a dry cup.

MEASURING WET INGREDIENTS Measure liquid ingredients such as milk in a liquid measuring cup; to read, set the cup on a flat surface and view the measurement at eye level.

SOFTENING BUTTER Room-temperature butter creams more readily, resulting in a fluffier cake. Butter is the right temperature when the stick is soft enough that you can make an indentation easily when you press it with your finger but not so soft that it loses its shape. Never microwave butter to speed things up; cut the cold butter into slices so it softens more quickly.

SOFTENING BROWN SUGAR To soften brown sugar that has hardened, place a wedge of apple in the bag, and reseal; leave a day or two, until sugar is sufficiently soft, then remove apple.

TOASTING AND CHOPPING NUTS To toast nuts such as pecans, walnuts, and almonds, spread them in a single layer on a rimmed baking sheet and bake in a 350°F oven until fragrant, about 10 minutes. (Start checking after 6 minutes if toasting sliced or chopped nuts.) Toast hazelnuts in a 375°F oven until skins split, 10 to 12 minutes; when cool enough to handle, rub warm nuts in a clean kitchen towel to remove skins. Chop cooled nuts coarsely or finely with a chef's knife, or pulse them in a food processor to grind. Do not overprocess, or nuts will turn into a paste.

TOASTING COCONUT Spread coconut in a single layer on a rimmed baking sheet, and bake in a 350°F oven until starting to brown, tossing occasionally, 5 to 10 minutes.

STORING SPICES Keep spices in a cool, dark place for up to a year; labeling jars with the date when you buy them will remind you when it's time to replace them.

GRATING NUTMEG Nutmeg has a nutty, spicy flavor that beautifully complements aromatic spices such as cinnamon and ginger. Grating fresh nutmeg results in a more complex, nuanced flavor; whole nutmeg also has a longer shelf life than ground. Use a specialty nutmeg grater or a rasp grater. If you would like to substitute ground nutmeg for freshly grated, use half the amount.

MELTING CHOCOLATE Melt chocolate in a metal bowl set over (not in) a pan of simmering water, or in a double boiler. Alternatively, you can melt chocolate in the microwave: In a microwave-safe bowl, heat chocolate in 30-second intervals, stirring after each, until almost melted. Remove from microwave, and stir to melt completely.

ZESTING CITRUS Use a rasp grater such as a Microplane to remove citrus fruits' flavorful zest while leaving the bitter white pith behind. A citrus zester (a small tool with a row of small, sharp holes at one end) makes decorative curls for garnishes.

Sources

The following is a list of the trusted vendors our food editors turn to most often for supplies, as well as specific source information for the recipes and photographs on the pages indicated. All addresses, phone numbers, and websites were verified at the time of publication, but please keep in mind that this information is subject to change.

BAKING TOOLS AND EQUIPMENT

ABLEKITCHEN.COM
877-268-1264
Mini nonstick savarin molds and other baking equipment

BRIDGE KITCHENWARE
973-884-9000
bridgekitchenware.com
General baking equipment

BROADWAY PANHANDLER
866-266-5927
broadwaypanhandler.com
General baking equipment

CANDYLAND CRAFTS
877-487-4289
candylandcrafts.com
Baking pans, pastry bags, and tips

JOANN
888-739-4120
joann.com
Martha Stewart Crafts cupcake and cake stencils

MACY'S
800-289-6229
macys.com
Martha Stewart Collection cake pans, cake stands, spatulas, and general baking equipment

NORDIC WARE
877-466-7342
nordicware.com
Bundt and other specialty pans

WILLIAMS-SONOMA
877-812-6235
williams-sonoma.com
Rolling pins, pastry bags and tips, spatulas, whisks, small kitchen torches

SPECIALTY INGREDIENTS

BEECHWOOD WINE AND LIQUORS
908-277-0202
budgetbottle.com
Specialty liqueurs, including Nocello

ECONOMY CANDY
212-254-1531
economycandy.com
Assorted candies, including chocolates, gumdrops, and licorice

KALUSTYAN'S
800-352-3451
kalustyans.com
Dried fruit, nuts, spices, coconut flakes, candied orange peels, marrons glaces

MY M&M'S
888-696-6788
mymms.com
Personalized and specialty-colored candies

PENZEYS SPICES
800-741-7787
penzeys.com
Spices, extracts, vanilla beans

SUGARCRAFT
513-896-7089
sugarcraft.com
Candy sprinkles, nonpareils

THE SWEET LIFE
800-692-6887
sweetlifeny.com
Assorted candies, including chocolates and malt balls

Photo Credits

SANG AN: pages 35, 118, 138, 172, 186–88, 214–15, 218, 262, 320 (top right), 321 (top right)

IAIN BAGWELL: page 210

JAMES BAIGRIE: page 242

CHRISTOPHER BAKER: page 230

STEVE BAXTER: page 204

EARL CARTER: page 141

CHRIS COURT: pages 74, 150, 217

BEATRIZ DA COSTA: pages 153, 170

KATIE QUINN DAVIES: pages 43, 247

JOSEPH DE LEO: page 47

TARA DONNE: pages 244, 281

DANA GALLAGHER: pages 27, 82, 105, 179

BRYAN GARDNER: pages 208, 312, 314, 317–18, 320 (top left and top middle), 321 (all except top right), 322–25

GENTL + HYERS: pages 28, 238

RAYMOND HOM: page 195

LISA HUBBARD: pages 132, 158

DITTE ISAGER: pages 192, 194

RICHARD GERHARD JUNG: page 97

JOHN KERNICK: pages 66, 196–97

YUNHEE KIM: pages 31, 39, 80–81, 249

DAVID LOFTUS: pages 32, 113, 162

JONATHAN LOVEKIN: front cover, pages 2, 5–10, 12, 36, 44–45, 77, 85, 89, 90, 94, 122, 125, 137, 145–46, 154, 161, 164, 173, 176, 222, 229, 234, 241, 252, 256, 258, 266, 270, 274, 278, 285–86, 289–91, 294, 297, 305, 326–33, back cover

KATE MATHIS: page 226

DAVID MEREDITH: page 23

JAMES MERRELL: page 114

JOHNNY MILLER: pages 48, 101, 157, 182, 224, 243, 255, 265, 282

MINH + WASS: page 24

AMY NEUNSINGER: page 251

NGOC MINH NGO: page 309

MARCUS NILSSON: pages 61, 261

CON POULOS: pages 14, 16, 18–19, 50, 56, 59–60, 62–63, 70, 92, 98, 102, 106, 110, 116, 121, 126, 129, 134, 149, 169, 174–75, 180, 183–84, 198, 201, 205–06, 209, 213, 220, 225, 248, 269, 277, 293, 301–2

DAVID PRINCE: page 202

JOSÉ MANUEL PICAYO RIVERA: page 69

MARIA ROBLEDO: pages 142, 191, 273, 298, 306

CHARLES SCHILLER: pages 124, 130, 166

BRETT STEVENS: page 52

KIRSTEN STRECKER: page 78

CLIVE STREETER: pages 20, 40, 65, 233

SIMON WATSON: page 310

ANNA WILLIAMS: pages 55, 73, 109, 133, 237

ROMULO YANES: pages 86, 320 (bottom left, middle, and right)

Index

Note: Page references in *italics* indicate photographs.

A

accompaniments. *See also* compotes
  Caramel Sauce, 333, *333*
  Chocolate–Coffee Liqueur Sauce, 333, *333*
  Lemon Curd, 332, *332*
  Macerated Berries, 333, *333*
  Whipped Cream, *332*, 333
Allspice Angel-Food Cakes, 66, 67
almond:
  –Berry Coffee Cake, *114*, 115
  Coffee Cakes, Mini, *98*, 99
  –Orange Layer Cake, 304, *305*
  Pralines, Chocolate-Covered, 329, *329*
  Semolina Cake, 152, *153*
  Torte with Pears, 156, *157*
Angel-Food Cake, *60*, 61
  Allspice, 66, 67
  Brown Sugar, 63, *63*
  Chocolate, *62*, 63
  Lemon, 63, *63*
  Mocha-Chip, 62, *62*
  Raspberry-Swirl, 62, *62*
Anise–Olive Oil Mini Bundt Cakes, 84, *85*
apple(s):
  Apple-Cider Applesauce, 341
  Applesauce Coffee Cake, *102*, 103
  Compote, 128, *129*
  –Ginger Stack Cake, 284, *285*
  Pie Upside-Down Cake, *234*, 235
  Slices, Dried, 327, *327*
  Sticky Buckwheat Cake, 112, *113*
applesauce:
  Apple-Cider, 341
  Cake, *134*, 135
  Coffee Cake, *102*, 103
apricot(s):
  Fruitcake, 36, 37
  Poached, Cheesecake with, 168, *169*
  Stone Fruit Upside-Down Cake, *226*, 227

B

Baked Alaskas, Chocolate, *206*, 206–7
Baking soda and baking powder, 315
banana(s):
  Chiffon Cake, *74*, 75
  Chocolate, and Graham Cracker Icebox Cake, *202*, 203
  Hummingbird Cake, *286*, 287
  Pecan Cake, 160, *161*
Basil-Strawberry Shortcake, 246, *247*
berry(ies). *See also specific berries*
  –Almond Coffee Cake, *114*, 115
  –Coconut-Lime Cake, 228, *229*
  Macerated, 333, *333*
  1-2-3-4 Lemon Cake, *298*, 299
blackberry(ies):
  Chocolate-Berry Ice-Cream Cake, 212, *213*
  Cornmeal Cake, 250, *251*
  –Lemon Semifreddo, 343
  –Lemon Semifreddo Roll, 204, *205*
Black Forest Cake, *310*, 311
blood orange(s):
  Compote, *332*, 333
  Gingerbread Icebox Cake, *218*, 219
  No-Bake Cheesecake, *176*, 177
  –Olive Oil Pound Cake, 22, *23*
blueberry:
  –Lemon Bundt Cake, 64, *65*
  –Sour Cream Pound Cake, 19, *19*
  Wild-, Buckle, *106*, 107
brandy:
  Glazed Pecan-Raisin Cake, *82*, 83
  Sticky Buckwheat Cake, 112, *113*
Breton Butter Cake, 124, *125*
brown sugar:
  about, 315
  Angel-Food Cake, 63, *63*
  Glaze, 330, *330*
  softening, 344
Buckwheat Cake, Sticky, 112, *113*
Bundt cakes:
  Blueberry-Lemon, 64, *65*

Cannelés, 72, *73*
Chocolate, 58, *59*
Coconut-Rum Raisin, 76, 77
Fresh Ginger–Molasses, 78, 79
Lemon-Ginger, *52*, 53
Olive Oil–Anise Mini, 84, *85*
Peaches-and-Cream, 54, *55*
Pecan-Raisin, Glazed, *82*, 83
Prune, Spiced, 68, *69*
Rum, Mini, 56, 57
Sour Cherry Savarins, 80, *81*
Tangerine, *86*, 87
Zucchini, 88, *89*
butter:
  for recipes, 315
  softening, 344
buttermilk:
  Cake with Chocolate Frosting, *258*, 259
  making your own, 315

C

Cannelés, 72, *73*
caramel:
  Glaze, 331, *331*
  Sauce, 333, *333*
  –Swirl Cheesecake, 174, *174*
carrot:
  Cake, 300, *301*
  Tea Cake, 48, 49
cheese. *See also* cream cheese; Mascarpone
  Blood-Orange No-Bake Cheesecake, *176*, 177
  Goat, –Cream Cheese Frosting, 335
  Ricotta Cheesecake, 178, *179*
cheesecakes:
  Blood-Orange No-Bake, *176*, 177
  Caramel-Swirl, 174, *174*
  Chocolate, 186, *187*
  Chocolate–Peanut Butter Bull's-Eye, 174, *174*-75
  Frozen Espresso, *214*, 215
  Gingerbread, *188*, 189

cheesecakes (*continued*):
  Lemon-Swirl, 172, *173*
  Maple, with Roasted Pears, 184,
    185
  Margarita, *180*, 181
  New York–Style, *166*, 167
  No-Bake, with Pomegranate, 190,
    191
  No-Bake Spiderweb, 182, *183*
  with Poached Apricots, 168, *169*
  Pumpkin-Swirl, 175, *175*
  Raspberry-Swirl, 175, *175*
  Ricotta, 178, *179*
  Strawberries-and-Cream, *170*, 171
cherry(ies):
  Black Forest Cake, *310*, 311
  -Chocolate-Stout Cake, *154*, 155
  -Chocolate Upside-Down Cake,
    254, *255*
  -Pecan Streusel Loaves, Mini, *110*,
    111
  Sour, Savarins, 80, *81*
chestnut:
  -Chocolate Layer Cake, *302*, 303
  Mousse–Chocolate Cake, 200, *201*
chocolate:
  Angel-Food Cake, *62*, 63
  Baked Alaskas, *206*, 206–7
  Banana, and Graham Cracker
    Icebox Cake, *202*, 203
  -Berry Ice-Cream Cake, 212, *213*
  Bittersweet, Ganache, Whipped,
    339
  Black Forest Cake, *310*, 311
  Blood Orange–Olive Oil Pound
    Cake, 22, *23*
  Bundt Cake, 58, *59*
  buying, for recipes, 316
  Cake, Lighter, *126*, 127
  Cake, One-Bowl, with Mocha
    Buttercream, *274*, 275
  Cake, Rich, *118*, 119
  Cakes, Molten, *146*, 147
  Cheesecake, 186, *187*
  Cheesecake Crust, 182, 186
  -Cherry-Stout Cake, *154*, 155
  -Cherry Upside-Down Cake, 254,
    255
  -Chestnut Layer Cake, *302*, 303
  -Chestnut Mousse Cake, 200, *201*
  -Chip-Cookie Icebox Cake, *210*, 211
  -Chip Pound Cake, 18, *18*
  -Coconut Sheet Cake, *150*, 151
  -Coffee Liqueur Sauce, *333*, 333

  -Covered Almond Pralines, 329,
    329
  -Covered Citrus, 328, *328*
  Curls, 328, *328*
  Devil's Food Cake, 288, *289*
  Double- , Cake, 296, *297*
  -Espresso Cake, Flourless, 136, *137*
  Frosting, Buttermilk Cake with,
    258, 259
  Frosting, Rich, 337
  Frozen Espresso Cheesecake, *214*,
    215
  German, Cake, 292, *293*
  -Ginger Marble Cakes, *44*, 45
  Glaze, 331, *331*
  -Hazelnut Ice-Cream Cake, 216,
    217
  and Hazelnut Meringue Cake, 132,
    133
  Layer Cake, Gluten-Free, 308, *309*
  Malted- , Frosting, *122*, 123
  Marble Pound Cake, 19, *19*
  melting, 344
  Milk, Frosting, 338
  Milk, Ganache, 339
  Milk, Ganache, Coconut-Pecan
    Cake with, *262*, 263
  -Mint Chip Cake, *198*, 199
  Mint Leaves, 329, *329*
  Mocha Buttercream, 337
  Mocha-Chip Angel-Food Cake,
    62, *62*
  No-Bake Spiderweb Cheesecake,
    182, *183*
  -Peanut Butter Bull's-Eye
    Cheesecake, *174*, 174–75
  -Peanut Butter Icebox Cake, 196,
    197
  Red Velvet Cake, 268, *269*
  Truffle Cake, 270, *271*
  Truffles, 329, *329*
Cinnamon Streusel Coffee Cake,
  100, *101*
citrus. *See also specific citrus fruits*
  Cake, *158*, 159
  Chocolate-Covered, 328, *328*
  flavoring cakes with, 316
  Peel, Candied, 326, 326–27
  -Poppy Seed Cake, 272, *273*
  Slices, Candied, 326, *326*
  -Vanilla Compote, 178, *179*
  zesting, 344
Clementine–Vanilla Bean Loaf Cake,
  30, *31*

cocoa powder, 316
coconut:
  buying, for recipes, 316
  Cake with Tropical Fruit, 144, *145*
  -Chocolate Sheet Cake, *150*, 151
  -Cream Filling, 340
  Fruitcake, *36*, 37
  German Chocolate Cake, 292, *293*
  Hummingbird Cake, *286*, 287
  Layer Cake, *306*, 307
  -Lime-Berry Cake, 228, *229*
  -Pecan Cake with Milk Chocolate
    Ganache, *262*, 263
  -Pecan Frosting, 338
  Raspberry White Cake, *294*, 295
  -Rum Raisin Cake, 76, *77*
  Toasted, Pound Cake, 19, *19*
coffee cakes:
  Almond, Mini, *98*, 99
  Almond-Berry, *114*, 115
  Applesauce, *102*, 103
  Cherry-Pecan Streusel Loaves,
    Mini, *110*, 111
  Cinnamon Streusel, 100, *101*
  Crumb, New York–Style, *94*, 95
  Meyer-Lemon, 108, *109*
  Plum-Nectarine Buckle, 104, *105*
  Sticky Buckwheat, 112, *113*
  Ultimate Streusel, 96, *97*
  Wild-Blueberry Buckle, *106*, 107
Coffee Liqueur–Chocolate Sauce,
  333, *333*
compotes:
  Apple, 128, *129*
  Blood-Orange, *332*, 333
  Citrus-Vanilla, 178, *179*
  Quince-Ginger, 341
  Strawberry, 124, *125*
Cookie Dough, Molasses-
  Gingerbread, 342
cornmeal:
  Blackberry Cake, 250, *251*
  -Buttermilk Loaf Cake, *40*, 41
  Olive-Oil Cake with Red Grapes,
    243, *243*
  and Peach Upside-Down Cake,
    248, 249
  for recipes, 316
cranberry:
  -Orange-Walnut Tea Cakes, 46, *47*
  Upside-Down Cake, *222*, 223
cream cheese:
  Blood-Orange No-Bake
    Cheesecake, *176*, 177

Caramel-Swirl Cheesecake, 174, *174*
Cheesecake with Poached Apricot, 168, *169*
Chocolate Cheesecake, 186, *187*
Chocolate-Peanut Butter Bull's-Eye Cheesecake, *174*, 174–75
Citrus-Poppy Seed Cake, 272, *273*
Frosting, 335
Frosting for Carrot Tea Cake, *48*, 49
Frosting for Pumpkin Spice Cake, *162*, 163
Gingerbread Cheesecake, *188*, 189
-Goat Cheese Frosting, 335
Lemon-Swirl Cheesecake, 172, *173*
Maple Cheesecake with Roasted Pears, *184*, 185
Margarita Cheesecake, *180*, 181
New York–Style Cheesecake, *166*, 167
No-Bake Cheesecakes with Pomegranate, 190, *191*
No-Bake Spiderweb Cheesecake, 182, *183*
Pound Cake, *24*, 25
Pumpkin-Swirl Cheesecake, 175, *175*
Raspberry-Swirl Cheesecake, 175, *175*
-Sour Cream Frosting, 335
Strawberries-and-Cream Cheesecake, *170*, 171
Curd, Lemon, 332, *332*

D
dairy products, 315
Devil's Food Cake, 288, *289*

E
eggs, 315
equipment, 319
espresso:
    Cheesecake, Frozen, *214*, 215
    -Chocolate Cake, Flourless, 136, *137*
    Glaze, 331, *331*
    Mocha Buttercream, 337
    Mocha-Chip Angel-Food Cake, *62*, 62

F
fig(s):
    Fruitcake, *36*, 37
    -Lemon Cake, 232, *233*

Flour, 315
Flourless Chocolate-Espresso Cake, 136, *137*
Flourless Pecan Torte, 140, *141*
frostings. *See also specific cake recipes*
    applying to layer cakes, 322
    Buttercream, Basic, 334
    Chocolate, Rich, 337
    Coconut-Pecan, 338
    Cream-Cheese, 335
    Cream Cheese–Goat Cheese, 335
    Cream Cheese–Sour Cream, 335
    Malted-Chocolate, *122*, 123
    Milk Chocolate, 338
    Mocha Buttercream, 337
    piping techniques, 324–25
    Seven-Minute, 336
    Swiss Meringue Buttercream, 336
    tinting, 323
    using pastry bag with, 323
    Vanilla, Creamy, 334
fruit. *See also* berry(ies); citrus; *specific fruits*
    Fruitcake, *36*, 37
    Ginger-Poached, Golden Cakes with, *90*, 91
    Tropical, Coconut Cake with, 144, *145*
fruit-based cakes:
    Apple Pie Upside-Down, *234*, 235
    Blackberry Cornmeal, 250, *251*
    Chocolate-Cherry Upside-Down, 254, *255*
    Coconut-Lime-Berry, 228, *229*
    Cranberry Upside-Down, 222, 223
    Gingerbread-Pear Upside-Down, *252*, 253
    Lemon-Fig, 232, *233*
    Mandarin Orange and Vanilla Upside-Down, *230*, 231
    Olive-Oil, with Red Grapes, 243, *243*
    Peach and Cornmeal Upside-Down, *248*, 249
    Pear Pavlova, 240–42, *241*
    Pineapple Upside-Down, 224, *225*
    Plum Skillet, *244*, 245
    Rhubarb Upside-Down, 236, *237*
    Stone Fruit Upside-Down, *226*, 227
    Strawberry, *238*, 239
    Strawberry-Basil Shortcake, 246, *247*

G
ganache:
    Milk Chocolate, 339
    Whipped Bittersweet Chocolate, 339
garnishes:
    Candied Citrus Peel, *326*, 326–27
    Candied Citrus Slices, 326, *326*
    Candied Nuts, 327, *327*
    Candied Pineapple Slices, 327, *327*
    Chocolate-Covered Almond Pralines, 329, *329*
    Chocolate-Covered Citrus, 328, *328*
    Chocolate Curls, 328, *328*
    Chocolate Mint Leaves, 329, *329*
    Dried Apple or Pear Slices, 327, *327*
    Sugared, 327, *327*
    Truffles, 329, *329*
German Chocolate Cake, 292, *293*
ginger. *See also* gingerbread
    -Apple Stack Cake, 284, *285*
    -Chocolate Marble Cakes, *44*, 45
    Fresh, -Molasses Cake, 78, *79*
    Fruitcake, *36*, 37
    -Lemon Bundt Cake, *52*, 53
    Molasses-Spice Cake, 148, *149*
    -Poached Fruit, Golden Cakes with, *90*, 91
    -Quince Compote, 341
    Sticky Buckwheat Cake, 112, *113*
    -Vanilla Bean Pound Cake, 18, *18*
Gingerbread, 26, *27*
    Cheesecake, *188*, 189
    Icebox Cake, *218*, 219
    Molasses-, Cookie Dough, 342
    -Pear Upside-Down Cake, *252*, 253
glazes:
    Brown-Sugar, 330, *330*
    Caramel, 331, *331*
    Chocolate, 331, *331*
    Espresso, 331, *331*
    Lemon, *330*, 331
    Milk, Basic, 330, *330*
    Rum, 331, *331*
Gluten-Free Chocolate Layer Cake, 308, *309*
Goat Cheese–Cream Cheese Frosting, 335
graham cracker(s):
    for cake recipes, 316
    Chocolate, and Banana Icebox Cake, *202*, 203

graham cracker(s) (*continued*):
 Crust, recipes using, 171, 172, 177, 190
 Grapes, Red, Olive-Oil Cake with, 243, *243*

H
hazelnut:
 -Chocolate Ice-Cream Cake, 216, *217*
 Meringue and Chocolate Cake, 132, *133*
honey:
 Cake with Pears, *130*, 131
 for recipes, 316
 Rosemary, 42, *43*
Hummingbird Cake, *286*, 287

I
icebox cakes:
 Chocolate, Banana, and Graham Cracker, *202*, 203
 Chocolate Baked Alaskas, *206*, 206–7
 Chocolate-Berry Ice-Cream, 212, *213*
 Chocolate-Chestnut Mousse, 200, *201*
 Chocolate-Chip-Cookie, *210*, 211
 Chocolate-Hazelnut Ice-Cream, 216, *217*
 Chocolate-Peanut Butter, 196, *197*
 Frozen Espresso Cheesecake, *214*, 215
 Gingerbread, *218*, 219
 Lemon-Blackberry Semifreddo Roll, 204, *205*
 Mint Chocolate-Chip, *198*, 199
 Raspberry Ice-Cream, 209, *209*
 Striped Ice-Cream, *194*, 195
ice cream:
 Cake, Chocolate-Berry, 212, *213*
 Cake, Chocolate-Hazelnut, 216, *217*
 Cake, Raspberry, 209, *209*
 Chocolate Baked Alaskas, *206*, 206–7
 Mint Chocolate-Chip Cake, *198*, 199
Icing, Royal, 342
ingredients:
 essential, 315
 measuring, 344
 specialty, 316

L
layer cakes:
 Almond-Orange, 304, *305*
 Apple-Ginger Stack, 284, *285*
 Black Forest, *310*, 311
 Buttermilk, with Chocolate Frosting, *258*, 259
 Candied-Pecan, with Browned-Butter Pears, 264, *265*
 Carrot, 300, *301*
 Chestnut-Chocolate, *302*, 303
 Chiffon, with Strawberries and Cream, 260, *261*
 Chocolate, Double-, 296, *297*
 Chocolate, Gluten-Free, 308, *309*
 Chocolate, One-Bowl, with Mocha Buttercream, *274*, 275
 Chocolate Truffle, *270*, 271
 Citrus-Poppy Seed, *272*, 273
 Coconut, *306*, 307
 Coconut-Pecan, with Milk Chocolate Ganache, *262*, 263
 Devil's Food, 288, *289*
 frosting, techniques for, 322
 German Chocolate, 292, *293*
 Hummingbird, *286*, 287
 Lemon, 1-2-3-4, *298*, 299
 Lemon, Tender, *266*, 267
 Lemon Meringue, 276, *277*
 leveling and splitting layers, 322
 Pumpkin, *278*, 279
 Raspberry White, *294*, 295
 Red Velvet, 268, *269*
 Rum Rose, *290*, 291
 Sugar-and-Spice, 280, *281*
 Vanilla, *282*, 283
layer cakes (single layer):
 Almond Semolina, 152, *153*
 Almond Torte with Pears, 156, *157*
 Applesauce, *134*, 135
 Banana Pecan, 160, *161*
 Breton Butter, 124, *125*
 Chocolate, Lighter, *126*, 127
 Chocolate, Molten, *146*, 147
 Chocolate, Rich, *118*, 119
 Chocolate and Hazelnut Meringue, 132, *133*
 Chocolate-Cherry-Stout, *154*, 155
 Chocolate-Coconut Sheet, *150*, 151
 Chocolate-Espresso, Flourless, 136, *137*
 Citrus, *158*, 159

 Coconut, with Tropical Fruit, 144, *145*
 Flourless Pecan Torte, 140, *141*
 Honey, with Pears, *130*, 131
 Maple, 120, *121*
 Molasses-Spice, 148, *149*
 Orange-Yogurt, *138*, 139
 Poppy-Seed Torte, *142*, 143
 Pumpkin Spice, *162*, 163
 Vanilla Sheet, with Malted-Chocolate Frosting, *122*, 123
 Walnut-Olive Oil, 128, *129*
lemon:
 Angel-Food Cake, 63, *63*
 -Blackberry Semifreddo Roll, 204, *205*
 -Blueberry Bundt Cake, 64, *65*
 Cake, 1-2-3-4, *298*, 299
 Cake, Tender, *266*, 267
 Chiffon Cake, *70*, 71
 Citrus Cake, *158*, 159
 Citrus-Poppy Seed Cake, *272*, 273
 Curd, 332, *332*
 -Fig Cake, 232, *233*
 -Ginger Bundt Cake, *52*, 53
 Glaze, *330*, 331
 Meringue Cake, 276, *277*
 Meyer- , Coffee Cake, 108, *109*
 Pound Cakes, *20*, 21
 -Swirl Cheesecake, *172*, 173
lime:
 Citrus-Poppy Seed Cake, *272*, 273
 -Coconut-Berry Cake, 228, *229*
 -Mango Sauce, 19, *19*
 Margarita Cheesecake, *180*, 181
loaf cakes. *See also* pound cakes
 Blood Orange-Olive Oil, 22, *23*
 Carrot Tea, 48, 49
 Chocolate-Ginger Marble, *44*, 45
 Clementine-Vanilla Bean, 30, *31*
 Cornmeal-Buttermilk, *40*, 41
 Cranberry-Orange-Walnut Tea, 46, *47*
 Fruitcake, *36*, 37
 Gingerbread, 26, *27*
 Pumpkin, Sage, and Browned-Butter, 38, *39*
 Rhubarb Tea, *32*, 33
 Two-Colored-Squash, *28*, 29

M
Malted-Chocolate Frosting, *122*, 123
Mandarin Orange and Vanilla Upside-Down Cake, *230*, 231